Journal of Prisoners on Prisons

... allowing our experiences and analysis to be added to the forum that will constitute public opinion could help halt the disastrous trend toward building more fortresses of fear which will become in the 21st century this generation's monuments to failure.

Jo-Ann Mayhew (1988)

Volume 33
Number 1
2024

JOURNAL OF PRISONERS ON PRISONS

EDITORIAL STAFF:

Editors:	Justin Piché	Dialogue Editor:	Olivia Gemma
	Kevin Walby	Prisoners' Struggles Editor:	Vicki Chartrand
Editorial Assistants:	Victoria Hunter	Book Review Editor:	Melissa Munn
	Zimo Meng	Online Production Editor:	Victoria Morris
	Nicole Necsefor	Issue Editors:	Grant Tietjen, Alison Cox
	Tammy Simpson		and J. Renee Trombley

The *Journal of Prisoners on Prisons* publishes two issues a year. Its purpose is to encourage research on a wide range of issues related to crime, justice, and punishment by current and former prisoners. Donations to the *JPP* are welcomed.

SUBMISSIONS: Current and former prisoners are encouraged to submit original papers, collaborative essays, discussions transcribed from tape, book reviews, and photo or graphic essays that have not been published elsewhere. The *Journal* does not usually publish fiction or poetry. The *Journal* will publish articles in either French or English. Articles should be no longer than 20 pages typed and double-spaced or legibly handwritten. Electronic submissions are gratefully received. Writers may elect to write anonymously or under a pseudonym. For references cited in an article, the writer should attempt to provide the necessary bibliographic information. Refer to the references cited in this issue for examples. Submissions are reviewed by members of the Editorial Board. Selected articles are corrected for composition and returned to the authors for their approval before publication. Papers not selected are returned with editorial comments. Revised papers may be resubmitted. Please submit bibliographical and contact information, to be published alongside articles unless otherwise indicated.

SUBSCRIPTIONS, SUBMISSIONS AND ALL OTHER CORRESPONDENCE:
Journal of Prisoners on Prisons
c/o Justin Piché, PhD
Department of Criminology, University of Ottawa
Ottawa, Ontario, Canada K1N 6N5

e-mail: jpp@uottawa.ca
website: www.jpp.org

SUBSCRIPTIONS:	**One Year**	**Two Years**	**Three Years**
Incarcerated Subscribers	$30.00	$50.00	$60.00
Non-incarcerated Subscribers	$40.00	$70.00	$90.00
Prison Libraries & Schools, Libraries & Institutions	$60.00	$110.00	$150.00

Subscriptions by mail are payable in Canadian or American dollars. In Canada, 5% HST must be added to all orders. We encourage subscription purchases online at https://press.uottawa.ca/en/journal-of-prisoners-on-prisons/

BACK ISSUES:
Each back issue is $20 and each back double-issue is $35 (Canadian dollars) + shipping costs. In Canada, 5% HST must be added to all orders. Back issues can be purchased from the University of Ottawa Press at https://press.uottawa.ca/en/search-results/?keyword=Journal+of+Prisoners+on+Prisons. If interested in obtaining issues that are out of print, please contact the *JPP* directly. Further information regarding course orders and distribution can be obtained from the University of Ottawa Press at:

University of Ottawa Press
99 Bank, Suite G006
Ottawa, Ontario, Canada K1P 6B9

phone: 1-613-562-5246

email: puo-uop@uottawa.ca
website: www.press.uottawa.ca

Co-published by the University of Ottawa Press and the Journal of Prisoners on Prisons.

ISSN 0838-164X (print) | 2816-7570 (online)
ISBN 978-0-7766-4031-0 (print) | 978-0-7766-4032-7 (online)

In This Issue

BOOK REVIEWS

UPCOMING SPECIAL ISSUE – CALL FOR PAPERS

COVER ART

INTRODUCTION FROM THE ISSUE EDITORS

Marking 25 Years of Convict Criminology by Building a New Table: Transformative Social Justice, Inclusion and Activism as Part of a Larger Social Movement
Grant Tietjen, Alison Cox and J. Renee Trombley

In the last 25 years, the social climate within the United States and globally has shifted and changed in many different ways. While some progress has been made within the world of system-affected people, such as the establishment of numerous resourced organizations that support academics that have experienced criminalization (e.g. Underground Scholars in the University of California system, California State University's Project Rebound, the Formerly Incarcerated College Graduates Network, the Huskies Post Prison Pathways at the University of Washington – Tacoma, etc.), we still face oppression. For example, in recent years, formerly incarcerated (FI) students have challenged exclusion from graduate programs from major universities that have claimed that they support FI students and perspectives. In the last 10 years, FI students have filed complaints with universities to challenge their exclusion from research projects on the basis of their race and legal backgrounds. Many of our conversations have evolved, however many issues remain the same. Amongst many ongoing actions to amplify our voices, create awareness for our cause, and fight stigmatization, some of us now spend more time working on prison abolitionism, racism, and classism in higher education and the criminal legal system, while actively building equal rights initiatives.

Yet, a social movement has begun, a movement of System Affected Academics (Tietjen, forthcoming), and Convict Criminology (CC) is part of this movement. The system affected academic (SAA) movement is comprised of the cumulative actions of multiple organized groups of justice-involved individuals in academic roles, working towards justice and equality focused societal change for fellow system affected people. The adjective *affected,* meaning acted upon or influenced, was not chosen out of convenience, but out of a sense of the breadth of variation in experiences and interpretations that carcerally-impacted individuals describe in regards to how the criminal justice system interacts with their lives. The advocacy, activism, and activist-scholarship of system affected groups affiliated with higher education are impacting change, and we are taking seats at the tables of justice policy organizations. More importantly, system affected

1

academics are building their own table, by creating their own structures and networks of systemic change. By engaging in transformative social justice, purposive efforts of inclusion and activism, we are building a *new table* as part of a larger social movement.

CC at twenty-five years is a story of stepping up to cultural, social, and policy shifts within both the criminal legal system and society. In the tough-on-crime harshness of the 1990s, founding members and supporters of CC began having conversations. Amongst these system-contacted scholars and aspiring scholars, they shared that their research and academic voices were being ignored and/or not taken seriously by the academy. Since the term "convict" was a pejorative term being used to stigmatize them, they decided to take this term back as an act of language reclamation, thus calling themselves Convict Criminology. Yet, the social and cultural climate of the United States has shifted in the last few decades, allowing for a more rehabilitative perspective within the criminal legal system. This has perhaps allowed CC scholars to engage with further transformative work more successfully. New CC scholars see the carceral system from both similar and different perspectives (more social acceptance and resources for system-contacted people) compared to the first generation CC scholars of a quarter century ago. Some CC scholars are also discussing discontinuing the use of the term convict to bring our discipline more in alignment with current cultural norms that value person first language usage as a means to overcome the impacts of labeling and stigmatization. As mentioned above, pervasive systemic discrimination and bias that system-contacted people face is still here. However, decades of working for change within these oppressive systems has provided our movement a knowledge collective from which we can draw upon.

This special issue highlights the advocacy for the strong and growing presence of women within CC, with women comprising approximately 50% of membership within the American Society of Criminology (ASC) Division of Convict Criminology that was formed in 2020. For example, Dr. Alison Cox and Dr. Michelle Malkin, longstanding CC members who are both contributing authors to this issue, address the "struggle for inclusion" that persists in CC in their new *Critical Criminology* article (2023), "Feminist Convict Criminology for the Future". As women's incarceration has outgrown the pace of men's incarceration in recent decades (Carson,

2021; Kajstura & Sawyer, 2023), their experiences in correctional settings are also unique from that of their male counterparts (DeHart & Lynch, 2021). Cox and Malkin (2023) note the importance of incorporating feminist epistemology and theory into the discipline to help shape a more diverse and inclusive CC. Feminist criminology has provided insight into the lived experience of women who are criminalized, as well as individuals with multiple oppressed/stigmatized statuses. Feminist *convict* criminology is one method to boost scholarship documenting the unique, intersectional, and shared experiences of formerly incarcerated and system-affected people in terms of age, race, gender and gender identity, sexuality, and nationality.

Malkin and Cox open this issue through their ethnographic analysis, which provides a first-hand account of how one woman experienced her incarceration at a women's federal medical center. Their research provides insight into both women's and LGBTQ advocacy efforts from a CC perspective. In "Here She Comes: Women of Convict Criminology", Dr. Denise Woodall provides a powerful exploration of CC women's struggle to be heard within "malestream" criminology. Finally, Dr. J. Renee Trombley engages in the feminist methodological tool of reflexivity to provide an auto-ethnographic analysis of identity and intersectionality within the CC perspective.

This issue also demonstrates the strength that is fostered through activism. After twenty-five years, it is important to recognize that activism within CC is rooted in a scholarly history of empowerment and overcoming adversity. Dr. Jennifer Ortiz suggests, rightfully so, that our activism needs to move outside academia and beyond the "ivory tower" to truly make both a difference and an impact. This is imperative in regard to the current social climate we find ourselves in, as well as the larger social movement as a whole. In her piece, she calls for the need for collective activism among CC scholars and those involved with the discipline. Relatedly, Dr. Jeffrey Ian Ross and Dr. Grant Tietjen provide both a framing and understanding of activism within CC to date. Dr. Daniel Kavish uses quantitative analysis to answer questions about who becomes labeled and what effects this has on the development of criminality, through an interactionist lens. The discussion on the future of CC is again taken up in the *Responses* to this issue of the *JPP* with pieces by Dr. Jeffrey Ian Ross, one of the founders of CC, along with Dr. Jennifer Ortiz, who is the current Chair of the Division of Convict Criminology for the American Society of Criminology.

REFERENCES

Carson, E. Ann (2021) *Prisoners in 2020 – Statistical Tables* (NCJ 302776), Washington (DC): US Department of Justice/Bureau of Justice Statistics.

Cox, Alison & Michelle L. Malkin (2023) "Feminist Convict Criminology for the Future", *Critical Criminology*, 1-21.

DeHart, Dana & Shannon Lynch (2021) *Women's and Girls' Pathways through the Criminal Legal System: Addressing Trauma, Mental Health, and Marginalization*, South Beach (CA): Cognella.

Kajstura, Aleks & Wendy Sawyer (20203) *Women's Mass Incarceration: The Whole Pie 2023*, New York: Prison Policy Initiative. Retrieved from https://www.prisonpolicy.org/reports/pie2023women.html.

Tietjen, Grant (forthcoming) *Teaching the Criminal Justice System a Lesson: The Rise of Carcerally-Impacted Scholar Groups*, book under contract with the University of California Press.

ABOUT THE SPECIAL ISSUE EDITORS

Grant E. Tietjen, PhD is an Associate Professor in the Criminal Justice Program at the School of Social Work and Criminal Justice at the University of Washington – Tacoma (UWT). He earned his PhD from the Department of Sociology at the University of Nebraska – Lincoln (UNL) in 2013. Dr. Tietjen has written, researched, and lectured on convict criminology, mass incarceration, class inequality, criminological theory, and pathways to correctional/postcorrectional education. He has published multiple peer reviewed papers in journals and edited volumes, including most recently in *Humanity and Society, Social Justice: A Journal of Crime, Conflict & World Order*, and *Criminal Justice Studies*. He is the author of *Justice Lessons: The Rise of the System Affect Academic Movement,* with the University of California Press, slated for publication in 2024. Dr. Tietjen works closely with multiple System Affected Academic organizations, including Huskies Post Prison Pathways (HP3) at UWT and the Division Convict Criminology (DCC) in the American Society of Criminology (ASC). HP3 is a support program for formerly-incarcerated students. As part of UWT HP3, he is a member of the Steering Committee for this growing initiative. He has also been involved with the CC discipline since 2005, mentoring new CC members, and serving as the group's Co-Chair from 2017-2019. During this time, Dr. Tietjen has worked with many other dedicated CC members to strengthen the CC organization. In 2020, he was appointed as the inaugural

Chair of the newly formed American Society of Criminology Division of Convict Criminology, and currently serves as DCC Vice-Chair. Dr. Tietjen can be reached for questions at grantt5@uw.edu.

Alison Cox, PhD is an Assistant Professor at East Carolina University in the Department of Criminal Justice and Criminology. Her research interests include prison visitation, the impact of incarceration on families, critical criminology (e.g. convict, feminist, queer, and rural), and qualitative methods. Her scholarship has been published in *Criminal Justice Studies* and *Critical Criminology*. She is also a contributing author to *Convict Criminology for the Future*, edited by Dr. Jeffrey Ian Ross (University of Baltimore) and Dr. Francesca Vianello (University of Padua).

Dr. J. Renee Trombley is an Assistant Professor in Criminal Justice and Criminology at Metropolitan State University – Denver, where she also serves as a Faculty Fellow and is currently developing the Justice Impacted Scholars Alliance. Dr. Trombley is dedicated to building opportunities in higher education for justice impacted folks, both in the community and in prisons and jails. Her research interests include restorative justice, peacemaking criminology, convict criminology, violence and victimization among youth, and juvenile justice and delinquency, as well as the use of qualitative methods in academic research. Dr. Trombley has spent time writing, publishing, and presenting on issues related to trauma among youth, juvenile justice and schools, restorative justice and reentry, restorative justice in higher education, and convict criminology and identity.

ARTICLES

Self-Efficacy Toward Release and Transfer in a Women's Federal Medical Center: An Ethnographic Analysis of a Prisoner's Blog

Michelle L. Malkin and Alison Cox

INTRODUCTION

Self-efficacy is an individual's confidence that they personally have the capacity to accomplish their goals (Bandura, 1978). The basic premise of the theory is that people can recognize their accomplishments through their own actions and behavioral decisions. Levels of recognition are based on the person's ability to cope, put in the effort, self-advocate, and sustain adverse obstacles without defensive behavior. Self-efficacy also connects a person's thoughts to their behavior. This concept has been explored among various populations, including incarcerated people (Allred et al., 2013; Friestad & Hansen, 2005; Jonesa et al., 2013; Loeb et al., 2010; Pelissier & Jones, 2006), which has aided understanding some of the individual impacts of incarceration, as well as how some are able to achieve life-positive goals during their confinement while others cannot. Examinations of self-efficacy are especially important in relation to women's prison experiences, as much of the research conducted thus far has focused on the experiences of male prisoners (Friestad & Hansen, 2005; Loeb et al., 2010). Additionally, self-efficacy among incarcerated women requires further exploration as the concept can differ between male and female prisoners (Pelissier & Jones, 2006).

Over the past two decades, there has been an increase in the amount of research conducted on the experiences of women in prison, yet a vast range of topics remain to be explored (Drake et al., 2015; Lahm, 2015, 2016; Pelissier & Jones, 2006; Rowe, 2015; Terry, 2016; Willingham, 2011). It is crucial to continue to focus on the experiences of incarcerated women as there has been a profound change in their involvement within the criminal justice system (Monazzam & Budd, 2022). Although comprising approximately 10% of the total incarcerated population, women still represent a larger portion of people in prisons and jails than in previous decades (Kajstura, 2019). Between 1980 and 2020, the number of incarcerated women increased by more than 475 percent, rising from 26,362 in 1980 to 152,854 in 2020 (Monazzam & Budd, 2022). When expanded to include immigration detention centers and youth confinement, others have reported more than 231,000 women and girls locked up in the United States at the end of 2018 (Kajstura, 2019). Given the drastic increase in female incarcerated populations, there is great value in understanding the lived experience of imprisonment from the perspectives of women. Moreover, few studies have been able to examine the lives of women incarcerated in federal prisons from inside prison walls (Bosworth et al., 2005; Pelissier & Jones, 2006; Wooldredge & Steiner, 2014). In addition, there is a lack of research conducted in federal prisons, especially federal medical centers, due to increased ethical and legal standards that must be met (Cislo & Trestman, 2013; Kalmback & Lyons, 2003). For instance, it is nearly impossible to access federal prisoners until they are under parole supervision or released.

The current study uses an ethnographic analysis of a female prisoner's blog during her incarceration in a women's federal medical center to examine self-efficacy toward release and transfer. To date, little is known about the process women in the federal system go through to obtain a transfer from a medical facility and/or toward securing release. The current study is also situated within the Convict Criminology (CC) perspective. As the convict voice has traditionally been ignored in the fields of criminology, criminal justice, and corrections scholarly research, policy, and practices (Ross & Richards, 2003), this ethnographic analysis provides a first-hand account of how one woman experienced her incarceration at a women's federal medical center. CC includes people who are currently incarcerated, those who are formerly incarcerated, and justice-impacted (or system) individuals. Formerly incarcerated individuals that have earned their doctorate degree offer a unique perspective to criminal justice research that combines subjectivity with reflexivity to better inform methodological approaches (Jones et al., 2009; Newbold et al., 2014; Richards, 2013; Ross & Vianello, 2021).

One methodological approach that seems to be central for CC is prison ethnography or autoethnography for first-hand individual experiences, which "involves communicating personal experience and investing in its particulars in order to locate our biographies and our lives as we have lived them, in the abstract ideas, social structures and historical contexts we analyse [sic] as criminologists" (Earle, 2021, pp. 38-39). Most autoethnographic accounts of incarceration (including prison ethnography), however, have been written by men or conducted within male correctional facilities (for review see Drake et al., 2015, p. 252-270). Few accounts focus on women's experiences or within female facilities. While early CC scholars published several prison ethnographies, there is a lack of prison ethnography conducted within *women's* facilities, especially within women's federal prisons. Thus, utilizing data from a personal blog written by a woman sentenced to serve one year and one day in a federal women's prison is an appropriate methodological choice to examine self-efficacy. Furthermore, using CC as the theoretical framework vastly extends ethnographic research on the incarceration experiences of women as only a handful of studies have been conducted since the development of this approach in the mid-1990s (Bozkurt & Aresti, 2018; Jones, 1993; Kuhlmann, 2005). It also sheds light on how and when incarcerated women are able to demonstrate self-efficacy despite their confinement, as well as recognizing some of the barriers to those efforts.

LITERATURE REVIEW

Prisoner Self-Efficacy

Displays of self-efficacy are unique in the prison environment (Allred et al., 2013; Friestad & Hansen, 2005; Loeb et al., 2010; Pelissier & Jones, 2006). According to Allred and colleagues (2013) "in the context of a prison culture, normal life challenges that may thwart self-efficacy among incarcerated individuals are of a different form and may assume a different meaning" (p. 215). Pelissier and Jones (2006) simplified the definition of self-efficacy in the prison context to a "person's sense of successful determination in relationship to reaching his or her general goals" (p. 116). Difficult prison experiences must be taken into context in determining whether the prisoner is self-advocating and making healthy choices (Loeb et al., 2010). For instance, Loeb and colleagues (2010) found that while prisoners have reduced "decision-making opportunity or control over day-to-day life" (p. 817), they are able to engage in positive forms of self-efficacy by making healthy decisions.

Most of these studies utilized standardized survey instruments to measure prisoner self-efficacy (Allred et al., 2013; Loeb et al., 2010; Jonesa et al., 2013). Although likely to have increased generalizability across incarcerated populations, survey questionnaires may not always capture conceptualizations of self-efficacy accurately for individual respondents. Therefore, it is important to expand and sensitize conceptualizations of self-efficacy through qualitative methodological approaches. Surveys often rely on the judgment of what a prisoner would do in a specific context (vignettes). However, in an ethnographic research design, measures of self-efficacy can go beyond individual perception by recognizing actions and behavior. Friestad and Hansen (2005) support broadening this definition in that self-efficacy is more than just individual perception in that it should also relate to real-life circumstances.

Some studies have already demonstrated how self-efficacy is put into action among sample populations of incarcerated women (Pelissier & Jones, 2006; Rowe, 2015; Willingham, 2011). In looking at how women are able to utilize power and agency to solve problems within the prison system, Rowe (2015) discovered that female prisoners were strategic based on the complexity of the issue and constraints of the prison system. Such "tactics" would often lead to positive outcomes such as having their basic material needs met and resolving complex problems of impression management. However, none of these studies focused on an ethnographic approach to understanding self-efficacy, nor on the focus of transfer and release.

When examining the differences between male and female prisoners in the areas of motivation, self-efficacy, and coping styles, results demonstrated that women reported a greater recognition of having a substance use problem and accepting responsibility as compared with men (Pelissier & Jones, 2006). Additionally, women that were successful in completing legally mandated drug and alcohol treatment programs showed higher levels of self-efficacy (Pelissier & Jones, 2006). Related to substance use programming, Willingham (2011) found that for some women, prison can be a place of positive self-efficacy toward addiction recovery. However, results also gleaned that women who actively practiced higher levels of self-efficacy were more likely to be seen as targets for violence from other female prisoners (Willingham, 2011). Thus, it is crucial that this topic is explored further and expanded to include the variety of ways in which women utilize self-efficacy within prison settings, as well as what sort of results their actions and behavior may have on their incarceration experience.

Ethnography and Convict Criminology
Recent inquiries have challenged the automatic distrust of "self" in ethnographic methodological studies and instead have embraced the ability

to obtain enhanced knowledge, context, and insider status that comes through them (Anderson, 2006; Jewkes, 2012; Richie, 2004; Wakeman, 2014). Ethnographic studies provide a unique window into understanding the complexity of prisoner lives, whereas mainstream research is often "confined by official data sets and crime reports" (Leyva & Bickel, 2010, p. 58), which can limit full understanding of the experiences.

In the context of prisons, emotional responsiveness is a natural experience that should not be ignored in the ethnographic experience. According to Jewkes (2012), criminology should not conceal the "anger, frustration, fear, and outrage" (p. 72) that prisoners feel at times during their imprisonment and these emotions should be revealed by the researcher as well. Confessing these feelings as part of one's epistemological and theoretical orientation should not diminish its worthiness as research, but rather make it more disclosing toward the process of understanding the ethnographic insider status of the researcher (Jewkes, 2012; Newbold et al., 2014). When the ethnographer is an ex-prisoner, Jewkes' (2012) inclusion of emotional experience in prison research becomes even more important (Newbold et al., 2014). For many who experience time in prison, their desire to produce academic scholarship in criminal justice is often out of frustration in finding that scholarly literature lacks many prison realities (Jones et al., 2009; Richards, 2013; Richards et al., 2008; Ross et al., 2014). According to Richards (2013), this frustration became the impetus for developing the theoretical perspective of Convict Criminology.

CC is practiced by academic scholars, as it "represents the works of convicts or ex-convicts who are in possession of a PhD or on their way to completing one ... led by former prisoners who are now among the ranks of academic faculty" (Jones et al., 2009, p. 152). CC is not merely giving a prisoner perspective like narratives often provide in research (Richards et al., 2008). While a "convict perspective is that of a person in prison, in contrast the convict criminology perspective is that of a former prisoner who uses his or her experience to better inform the study of prisons" (Richards et al., 2008, p. 122).

The use of direct observation and personal experience is an integral part of the process of understanding the criminal justice system (Jones et al., 2009). Data collection within CC can include personal correspondence, interviews, retrospective interpretation of experiences, and current observations and writings (Jones et al., 2009; Richards, 2013). CC also encourages the use of empowering terms (Jewkes, 2012; Jones et al., 2009; Richards, 2013).[1]

Authors within CC also admit to their subjectivity and use their experience with a critical eye to better inform meaning (Jones et al., 2009). As stated by Terry (2003), "like other ethnographies, what is expressed here may be viewed as anecdotal and not generalizable. However, it does demonstrate natural and recurring situations I am privy to because of who I am, where I've been, who I know, and what I do" (p. 44). Specifically, personal writing may form important meaning for the incarcerated individual (Willingham, 2011). Writing can help some prisoners better cope with the emotional realities of prison. Prisoner writing is important to analyze as it may better help understand concepts of "captivity, racism, classism and oppression" (Willingham, 2011, p. 57) among other prison experiences. The value of this reality cannot be discounted when it comes to understanding the lives of prisoners through their own experiences.

There are several examples of prison ethnography within CC (see Earle, 2013; Earle & Phillips, 2015; Newbold et al., 2014). Most of these focus on how to perform autoethnography or why this methodological practice is important, rather than detailing the lived experience of the incarcerated first-hand (Bolden, 2020; Carceral & Bernard, 2004). Furthermore, there is limited evidence based on women's experiences with incarceration, especially within federal settings. The current research addresses this deficiency by exploring prisoner self-efficacy from a CC perspective. Recognizing the value in prisoner writing (Willingham, 2011), this study involved the analysis of blog entries written by a woman incarcerated in a federal medical center to explore how she and other women utilize self-efficacy to secure their right to transfer and release within the Federal Bureau of Prisons (BOP).

We expect that if incarcerated women are able to garner self-efficacy despite their confinement, various "tactics" towards securing release and transfer will be present. These tactics may be rooted in performance accomplishments, vicarious experiences, verbal persuasion, and emotional arousal. Similar to Rowe's (2015) findings, we also expect women will experience both positive and negative outcomes, which may result in moments where self-efficacy is obtained and other times not. This points to the complexity of prisoner self-efficacy and the constraints put on them by the BOP, prison administration, and correctional staff.

METHOD

This study provides an ethnographic analysis of the self-efficacy of incarcerated women detained in a federal medical center. The data collected were drawn from the "One Year and One Day" blog maintained by one of this article's authors under the pseudonym "Dragonfly Hazel" during her incarceration at FMC Carswell in Fort Worth, Texas. Both authors then later analyzed the blog entries. Examining blog posts and personal letters, this study explores individual and group identities as they relate to the complexities surrounding prisoner self-efficacy, as well as how interactions with the prison administration and correctional staff may directly or indirectly affect efficacy decisions and efforts in relation to having their basic needs met, or attempts in securing their release and transfer.

Self-efficacy is defined to include instances where a prisoner takes appropriate steps toward accomplishing a goal through their own actions and self-advocacy, making decisions that appear healthy given the obstacles that lay before them in the context of imprisonment. As emphasized in Badura's (1978) theory, self-efficacy is about a person's ability to cope while facing such adverse obstacles – and without exhibiting defensive or unhealthy behavior.

FMC Carswell

The research setting for this study is in a southern state due to FMC Carswell being the only federal security administrative prison for women in the United States (Federal Bureau of Prisons, n.d. a, b, c). FMC Carswell also serves as a maximum-security prison, medium-security general population prison, residential drug and alcohol program, dual-diagnosis drug abuse treatment program, sex offender management program, administrative prison, psychiatric referral center, faith-based residential program, and medical center for all security level prisoners. Finally, it also has a 250-bed separate minimum-security satellite camp adjacent to its property and can house up to a total of 1,870 prisoners (Federal Bureau of Prisons, n.d. b; FMC Carswell, 2015). About half of the prisoners at FMC Carswell were there for healthcare purposes and the others were there for local designation (live within a specific distance), programming, or administrative purposes (such as death row, mental health, and escape risks).

While this facility does not appear to release statistics based on care level or security level, some demographic information is available. See *Table 1* for a demographic breakdown of the incarcerated population at the time of Dragonfly Hazel's incarceration (2013-2014).

Table 1: Demographic Breakdown of Female Prisoners at FMC Carswell

Race/Ethnicity*	White (Non-Hispanic)	37.5%*
	Hispanic/Latino	36.0%
	African-American	22.5%
	Native American, Asian, etc. (Other)	3.6%
Age	Average Age	41 years
	Age Range	19 - 88 years
Citizenship	U.S. Citizen	78.0%
	Non-U.S. Citizen**	22.0%
Crime Type*	Drug offenses	54.3%
	Extortion, bribery, fraud	12.9%
	Immigration	10.5%
	Weapons, explosives, arson	2.3%
	Banking, counterfeit, extortion	1.9%
Sentence Length	Mean Sentence	91.3 months
	Median Sentence	64.0 months
	Sentences of 20 years	5.2% (n=96)
	Life sentences	1.3% (n=24)

*Source did not appear to consider multi-racial identity.
**Likely to be deported at end of incarceration.
***Non-exclusive – does not equal 100% (FMC Carswell, 2015).

One Year and One Day Blog

Blog entries were primarily written using the Trust Fund Limited Inmate Computer System (TRULINCS) application offered throughout the federal prison system (Federal Bureau of Prisons, n.d. b). Access to TRULINCS was controlled and cost prisoners five cents per minute. As part of the service, prisoners consented to have all incoming and outgoing messages monitored. All blog entries were written and sent to an email address as prisoners were not allowed direct access to the Internet. An academic colleague volunteered to check the email regularly and post all messages to the blog upon receipt. Included in the blog are also seven personal letters and two personal notes written during the same period that were added post-incarceration and posted to the dates they were written.

Initial writing on the blog began on 25 June 2013, four days after Dragonfly Hazel (hereafter "DF Hazel") was sentenced to federal prison for one count of wire fraud. The initial intention of the blog was to create a place to help other women who may also need to learn about preparing for federal prison: "I looked all over online and found very little real information about preparing to go inside for women" (DF Hazel, 6/25/2013). The blog became a place for DF Hazel to share her experiences, observations, reflections, hopes, and goals as she prepared for prison, did her time, and settled into life after incarceration on supervision. Over the course of her incarceration, DF Hazel wrote a total of 278 blog posts, averaging nearly one post per day. Descriptive statistics for the entirety of all blog posts demonstrated that a majority of entries focused on life in prison (75%), with some containing personal reflections written by DF Hazel (10%), or a combination of both (15%).

The blog posts primarily include the personal observations and experiences of DF Hazel and a group of other prisoners with whom she interacted daily. However, all posts for the current analysis were written by DF Hazel, except for one written by Freckles, which was given to DF Hazel to post. DF Hazel spent between ten minutes to one hour a day on the TRULINCS application and wrote one or more messages for the blog. She frequently carried a notebook and wrote notes throughout the day to help prepare for her next post. On several occasions, DF Hazel would spend time with other women and pose a question to have everyone discuss the topic together. Next, she would prepare a blog post from their responses. During meals, she would engage in conversations or spend time observing the behavior of prisoners and write about those experiences.

Blog posts also included a combination of daily experiences, focused topics, humorous anecdotes, prison metaphors, emotional realism, and advice for those facing similar situations or those who are supporting someone who happens to be in prison. DF Hazel is also in recovery from Gambling Disorder and many posts include her hope, strength, and challenges as she sought serenity inside a medium-security prison as a minimum-security prisoner. Reviewing the general content of blog posts, half (50%) focused on primary experiences of prison life, while approximately the other half (43%) focused on DF Hazel describing her life. A small amount of blog posts focused on the lives of incarcerated women other than DF Hazel (7%). Individuals referred to by name in the blog were given pseudonyms. DF Hazel allowed acquaintances to select their own pseudonyms when they voluntarily agreed to be an active part of the blog. Assigned pseudonyms were based on an observational characteristic or trait. No personal information of any participant was revealed other than her own.

When it came to her own identity, DF Hazel understood that this would be difficult to hide as she shared personal traits of her background on the blog. She chose to be as honest on the blog as possible to meet the goals and objectives of providing an accurate account of what life is like where she was incarcerated. Given that FMC Carswell was the only federal prison that could house DF Hazel based on her medical status, she chose not to make the location anonymous within the blog. Therefore, she was aware that she could be identified at any time should others read the blog. She was made aware early in her imprisonment that prison staff members were reading the blog. She also experienced threats from several inmates due to its existence, which resulted in a short break from writing. After about a week, DF Hazel started writing again after realizing how important her observational writing and blog became: "It's my reflection on the world and the world's reflection on me. It keeps me sane and lets me share the insane. It is how I think, learn, reflect, share, find substance, care, and pay everything forward. I need to keep writing" (DF Hazel, 1/30/14).

These experiences inevitably affected how and what she was able to write. There were many observations and experiences that DF Hazel was unable to write, threatened that she would face terrible consequences if she shared or was simply too scared to write. Although what she wrote was honest, she sometimes had to leave out certain details or did not document an important incident out of fear or the prospect of retaliation from others. Had she done so, it is possible that the data for this study could be richer and with a thicker description. This is a major limitation of the data the authors recognize.

Data Analysis

Analyses of blog posts were facilitated by Dedoose software and proceeded in several stages. First, the transcripts were read for familiarization with the data, as well as to refine any mistakes. Second, the data were openly coded (Charmaz, 2014) for the month written, any specific location, author, and type of post (i.e., blog post, letter, or note). This resulted in the generation of a range of initial codes and categories of the data. Third, each post was selectively coded for whether it contained evidence of self-efficacy, along with how interaction with staff may influence levels of efficacy, personal identity, and group identity. Finally, blog posts were coded a third time (axial coding) for whether it was primarily about prison life, a personal reflection written by DF Hazel, or a combination of the two.

After the coding process was complete, the authors reviewed all themes and sub-themes several times until a preliminary set of themes was identified and conceptualized based on prior research on prisoner self-efficacy. Any duplicate codes were combined in Microsoft Excel to allow each post to be analyzed individually for the codes of self-efficacy and/or collective efficacy. Overall, 217 posts (78%) included examples of self-efficacy.

Positionality of the Researchers

The data were originally collected and analyzed by one of the authors when she was a graduate student. Although the methodology of this study was originally autoethnographic in nature, we refer to the author of the blog posts in the third-person as "Dragonfly Hazel" (or DF Hazel) to stay consistent with the data and avoid additional details or context not provided directly within the original blog posts. While this seems to be an uncommon practice, some autobiographical ethnographers make the methodological decision to write in the third-person to avoid the risk of attachment and adding more to memories (Caulley, 2008; Denshire, 2014). Additionally, using a third-person point of view helps avoid reader confusion of first-person accounts from multiple writers of blog posts provided as examples. Finally, bringing a second author to this project made it no longer entirely autoethnographic.

Findings were revisited by both authors who currently work in tenure-track faculty positions. Additional representation of the authors includes both being White women who also identify as LGBTQ+ (Lesbian, Gay, Bisexual, Trans,

Queer). Both authors have earned their master's degrees (MS) and doctorate degrees (PhD). One author of the study has also earned a juris doctorate (JD). These positions contrast with the demographics of many of the incarcerated women discussed in blog posts regarding race, criminal history, and level of education. Notably, however, both authors have had direct or indirect experiences related to incarceration. One author was formerly incarcerated, while the other experienced parental incarceration at two separate times, which likely shaped the interpretation of the results and findings.

RESULTS

As a reminder, for this study self-efficacy is defined to include instances where a prisoner takes appropriate steps toward accomplishing a goal through their own actions and self-advocacy, making decisions that appear healthy given the obstacles that lay before them in the context of imprisonment. The authors specifically looked at the themes of women utilizing self-efficacy in order to seek transfer to another facility and/or toward securing their release. Three themes were coded to be related to self-efficacy of transfer/release: "reducing medical care level", "transfer to another prison", and "securing release." However, two other themes were discovered to be a hindrance to self-efficacy and presented barriers or complications to securing transfer and release: "staff treatment of prisoners" and "sex and relationships". Each theme is discussed and illustrated with representative blog post quotes below, which include observations.

Reducing Medical Care Level
It is not possible to focus on transfer or release from FMC Carswell without consideration of medical designations and care levels, which serve as barriers to release, but also provide much evidence of prisoner self-efficacy. People with serious medical conditions or who need specialized care and/ or medications in the federal carceral system often were initially designated (or transferred) to a medical facility (BOP, 2015, 2022). In the male system, there are many medical centers at all security levels, but in the female system there is only one named FMC Carswell. This resulted in women being housed at all security levels, including minimum-security prisoners who were eligible for prison camp, but who were ultimately required to

complete their sentence in a higher security prison due to it being the only one. FMC Carswell was not just a medical center but housed non-medical in-custody security (low, medium, high, and max) prisoners as well. Medical care levels were decided initially by the central placement offices based on the reading of pre-sentence and sentencing reports, not a medical exam. The prison population at FMC Carswell included women at all care levels, from one to four. A prisoner at Level 1 or Level 2 could be in any prison, as all prisons were set up to handle general medical needs.

Medical centers were the only places where Level 3 and Level 4 prisoners could be housed. To obtain transfer (and often release for "good time") out of FMC Carswell, prisoners had to work with the medical department to lower their care level, which oftentimes took substantial self-efficacy. These issues became evident often in DF Hazel's blog, which included 66 posts that referred to designated care levels.

Interacting with care levels at FMC Carswell was the designated security level. Security levels at FMC Carswell were minimum-out, minimum-in, low, medium, high, and max (including death row prisoners). The difference between minimum in and minimum out was described in the data:

> It's easy, first, to explain "out". "Out" is that we are camp status, can be in a non-secured environment, and can see medical providers and others off the prison grounds without being handcuffed and shackled when we go. "In", is the opposite of that. "In" means that we are designated to a secured environment, it's a higher level of security, and if we have an appointment off the facilities [sic] grounds, we are shackled and handcuffed.
>
> – DF Hazel, 12/22/13

At each security level, prisoners would demonstrate self-efficacy to seek opportunities that could lower their security level allowing for possible transfer to lower security carceral settings. One example was that DF Hazel's friend, Freckles, went off important medication to lower her Care Level from 3 to 2. Therefore, within the themes of seeking transfer to another prison and securing release, the data showed that women not only sought to lower their care level, but also used self-efficacy to lower their security level.

Transfer to Another Prison

While many people outside of the carceral system may assume that prison transfers occur automatically and without prisoner influence, in fact many transfers occur through self-efficacy requests by the prisoner. This process usually starts by standing in long lines to speak with the women's assigned case manager:

> Every day, as I sit outside my case manager's office, I see the women enter and leave her office. We all just want to get out of here – some to transfer to a different facility, some to halfway house, some just across the street, and some to home confinement or home at the end of their sentence. No matter what, we stand there, waiting, for her attention to tell us our next steps and hear news. Often, many of us leave with frowns. No new news. No known next steps. Just wait.
>
> – DF Hazel, 5/2/22

For example, very early in her imprisonment DF Hazel sought a transfer from her caseworker to the minimum-security prison camp across the street (which housed among its minimum-out security prisoners many individuals who required some access to the medical department). DF Hazel was initially placed in the medical facility with a minimum-in security level due to requiring an injection twice a week (a medication she administered herself before prison), which resulted in her being designated a Care Level 3. DF Hazel was then informed by her case manager within the first two months of her incarceration that she was being transferred across the street to the camp:

> I started here as "minimum in" = the "in" was due to my needing to be inside a medical facility. Well, she [case worker] forgot that last week she was supposed to tell me that my status was changed to "minimum out" – the status I should have started with to be sent to a camp. And, in fact, they are sending me to a camp... across the street (not closer to home). She was supposed to tell me last week, all she said yesterday was, "Oops". She says my transfer to the camp will occur, "before Christmas". Had I not gone to her office yesterday, I would have only had a day's notice (the day I have to pack out my locker). Now, I get to prepare.
>
> – DF Hazel, 11/29/13

DF Hazel did start to prepare: "For the last several days, I have been informing friends and those that 'should' know (such as coworkers) about my pending transfer across the street" (DF Hazel, 12/1/13). She waited for the transfer, waiting at least weekly in long lines to inquire, and was consistently being told that it would occur. Months passed and she was not transferred, although her caseworker repeatedly indicated that it would occur at any moment. She tried to self-advocate for the move to the camp. However, she was continuously told that there was nothing she could personally do as the process was already in the works. She then learned that she was not medically cleared to go to camp, which led DF Hazel to send in requests to see her doctor:

> As it turns out, when I went to medical in December to inquire whether this transfer was occurring, I was told that I was not medically cleared to go. My doctor was not signing off on it until she has a chance to see me. I had no choice but to accept that reality and start sending in "cop-outs" to try to get my doctor to make an appointment with me. If you are not medically cleared, there's very little you can do.
>
> – DF Hazel, 2/1/14

Later, however, she saw on her medical records that she was medically cleared to go to the camp five months earlier. Being told several times that it would occur, despite any change or resolution, led DF Hazel to continue to demonstrate self-efficacy toward securing her transfer:

> Last week I went right up to the prison warden and told him about my "camp" transfer approval from October and that I was repeatedly told that clearance had never occurred. Well, I guess that got things moving, because I just received an email from the Warden's email letting me know that my "exit" paperwork (i.e. transfer to the camp) is being processed. Looks like I will actually be going there to finish out my sentence.
>
> – DF Hazel, 2/8/14

However, soon after her email from the Warden, DF Hazel was officially informed that she was unable to transfer due to a medical hold for an appointment with an outside rheumatologist that would occur at some point.

About halfway through her imprisonment, an outside appointment with a rheumatologist occurred. This led to another act of self-efficacy, this time in terms of refusing treatment:

> [The rheumatologist] was starting to say that she wants to see me in two months, when I told her, "No, you don't". I explained that nothing happens in two months... it would be more like 5 (again) and I would not be allowed to be released from my medical hold at Carswell. I explained that I will follow up with my rheumatologist back home. The officer with me verified what I was saying.
>
> – DF Hazel, 1/30/14

By asking the medical provider not to require another appointment, DF Hazel sought to have the medical hold lifted to be able to obtain her transfer (or possible release). DF Hazel self-advocated for her potential transfer over her healthcare needs to avoid further medical holds in the prison. After that appointment, the medical hold on DF Hazel's paperwork was lifted and she was again told that she would be transferred across the street until she officially learned for herself through another meeting with a prison official that she was denied camp transfer even though her caseworker kept insisting it was to occur:

> I have officially been DENIED for the camp. I will not be going to the camp. Not even my caseworker (the one who swears I'll be at the camp any day...) knows. The reason is due to my medication regimen. So, no matter what, I am in the medical facility's high security environment for the rest of my incarceration.
>
> – DF Hazel, 3/22/14

As shown through DF Hazel's experience, even with practicing self-efficacy, many prisoners were unsuccessful at obtaining a transfer. After her friend Lola successfully self-advocated for a transfer across the street to the camp, DF Hazel learned that many women there were on similar injections. The denial based on her medications for transfer appeared arbitrary: "The medical team refused my transfer without ever meeting me. I guess I was just someone who's [sic] paperwork found the wrong person on the wrong day – result 'transfer to camp denied'" (DF Hazel, 7/19/14).

If a woman was looking to transfer and they require medical clearance (called a "413") there was just one person at the prison who decided if a prisoner was cleared for transfer. The 413 meetings were only available one day per month, and people lined up early and waited up to seven hours to be seen. If they were too low on the list, they had to line up again the following month, as there was no guarantee to be seen and when the one employee who completed 413 paperwork was done for the day, everyone remaining was sent back to their units. Sometimes, the prisoners would be notified that there would be no 413 meetings that month and the women would wait yet again. Women with Care Level 3 or 4 designations often waited in the long line, only to be told that they could not transfer, even to the Carswell camp across the street for minimum-security prisoners (that housed women with Level 1 through 3 care levels), due to the need for a doctor to approve the transfer or a medical hold. DF Hazel chose to wait in that line twice, only to be told both times that she did not have medical clearance for the transfer. Other women went monthly seeking a transfer. The fact that the meetings were only one day per month in a prison that housed thousands of women is an example of how bureaucratic policies often barred self-efficacy toward transfer.

Some women, like Lola, were successful in getting a "413" and obtaining a medical release and transfer out of FMC Carswell. In the blog, DF Hazel discussed how another woman went monthly to obtain a "413" and after about five monthly appointments, was transferred to a minimum-security camp in Florida: "My friend that recently lost her husband left yesterday morning to go to a camp, much closer to her home. She'd worked hard to get medically released and waited months before finally getting a date that she was to be transferred" (DF Hazel, 4/19/14). Due to a seat shortage on the bus, the woman had to wait another week and a half to transfer to the prison camp. Similarly, Nurse sought a transfer from the time of her incarceration to be closer to her family in California. She was in FMC Carswell due to having gastric bypass surgery and had no medical needs other than a special diet. It took approximately a year for her medical release to be successful and for Nurse to be transferred to a camp in California. After so many dead ends regarding DF Hazel's transfer, she started to concentrate her self-efficacy efforts on getting out of prison by her halfway house date, rather than focus on transferring to the camp.

Securing Release

Self-efficacy was evident in prisoners' consistent work toward their own releases and/or increased halfway house time close to home. Programming was one way individuals utilized self-efficacy to seek earlier release. Prisoners worked hard toward obtaining timely releases by earning Century points by choosing to participate in educational opportunities and other prison programming. Century points could help lower a prisoner's security level and help them earn good time.

Another way prisoners self-advocated toward release was by participating in the Residential Drug and Alcohol Program (RDAP). Prisoners with a history of drugs and/or alcohol (especially those with drug-related charges) sought entry into RDAP to earn earlier release and increased halfway house time:

> People who qualify for the program can receive up to 9 months off their time in prison (they receive extra halfway house time). Their "out date" is changed as soon as they start the program. If they finish it, and don't quit or get into trouble, they are guaranteed that new out date. For those who come into prison with a history of drug or alcohol abuse, it's a great way to change your thinking, yourself, and hope for a different future.
>
> – DF Hazel, 2/16/14

For some prisoners, however, they had to show resilience and self-efficacy to get into RDAP, stay in RDAP, and advocate for the maximum time off their sentence:

> Freckles is now trying desperately to jump through those same hoops I did, as she was denied halfway house for no reason and doing RDAP, she is guaranteed halfway house. Even staff look at her record and do not understand why she's been denied the halfway house, but it's the team that does our exit summaries that needs to make the change...
>
> – DF Hazel, 4/5/14

As demonstrated in the quote above, Freckles consistently fought staff on every level for her halfway house time and successfully gained the maximum amount of time offered to RDAP graduates. Later, Freckles shared on the blog the necessity to practice self-efficacy to max out potential halfway house time:

No one in prison is going to give you anything unless you ask for it. You yourself are your best – and most likely only – advocate. So, start early, know the trends, what's been done at your institution in the past, what's done at other institutions – knowledge is power and sometimes will work to your advantage. Keep your head up and don't get discouraged – nothing comes easy in the "system" – but we all will get through it.

– Freckles, 3/15/15

Some prison programming that would assist toward early release was entirely voluntary. For example, Life Connections was an 18-month religious program that women would participate in to build self-esteem and make healthier decisions. Women with prison sentences long enough for participation would move into a special programming housing unit and agree to live under stricter rules. As a result, the women would earn Century points and the potential for increased halfway house time (earlier release from prison). Self-efficacy was not just necessary to get released earlier, but was often needed to be released by the date posted according to the BOP. Anyone with a sentence of a year and a day or longer was eligible for both halfway house time and good time off their sentence. Additionally, some of the halfway house time could include home confinement.

Individuals at FMC Carswell ultimately learned that the idea that release would just occur based on dates on paperwork was a fallacy. According to the data, self-efficacy was necessary for many individuals, especially those with medical issues, to be released to go to a halfway house based on good time. While "[m]any inmates believe the prison will just do the paperwork" (DF Hazel, 2/8/14), the experiences of other prisoners showed that failure to act on behalf of oneself meant not getting out of prison on time and prisoners having to max-out to the date of release. For example, South did not obtain the earlier release to the halfway house promised to her on her paperwork:

South learned, officially, that she will not be going home on her home confinement date, but rather she will have to max out. That makes her out date exactly one month from today. I'm frustrated that we are given all these dates, but in reality, so many people are forced to max out their time. I don't know why no one made the arrangements for her to be able to go home, but she still has to see someone about her travel arrangements, even though they are currently doing travel for people not leaving until March.

Somehow, since her case worker left late last year, someone seems to have dropped the ball on her paperwork. The one good thing, though, is that they cannot keep her a day after February 10th.

– DF Hazel, 1/10/14

To ensure that they did not max out their time, the data showed that many prisoners advocated for themselves toward halfway house and home confinement time on a regular basis. Failure to practice such self-efficacy would result in failure to obtain these benefits due to the opacity of the prison procedures. Prisoners would spend hours each day trying to get the system to work in their favor:

It is truly a full-time job to try to get yourself OUT of prison. As you know, I've been struggling with getting them to complete my exit paperwork. Yesterday, I went to my case worker and my unit manager, during their office hours, in order to get assistance. My case worker's hands are tied now, she's done everything on her part. My unit manager was busy and didn't come to his office hours, so I filled out a cop-out and brought it directly to him this morning.

– DF Hazel, 3/22/14

As the above quote shows, prisoners often had to seek out assistance from staff in various positions to obtain the proper paperwork.

A barrier to obtaining these rights is the designated care level for those prisoners with medical conditions. It was not impossible for prisoners over a Care Level 2 to receive home confinement or halfway house, but it was up to them and self-efficacy to push the medical department to allow them that right and submit "exit summary paperwork" that would allow for the process to be completed. Exit summaries generally listed prisoners' current and past health problems, medications, and tuberculosis (TB) status. The process of obtaining an exit summary was often self-defeating. According to the woman who completed them, they took less than ten minutes to complete, yet were so difficult to obtain:

I fret all the time that I am so powerless to get myself out of here. How is it possible that one piece of paperwork can hold up someone from gaining the access to their right for consideration for halfway house and/or home confinement? How is it possible that the responsibility for doing that paperwork for the number of inmates here all falls on one person?

– DF Hazel, 3/12/14

The medical hold discussed in the above section on transfer also halted DF Hazel from obtaining the halfway house paperwork:

> I have a "medical hold". If my medical hold is not lifted, I will be ineligible for halfway house or home confinement and will have to stay through the end of my sentence in July. If the hold does get lifted, I could be heading out of here to a halfway house anytime between March and May.
>
> – DF Hazel, 1/6/14

Eventually, DF Hazel learned that she was denied halfway house due to her designated care level:

> It's been about 7 months since I've seen any doctor here, and more than 6 since my new doctor was assigned. For being chronic care, and her making decisions about what I'm "eligible" for upon release in terms of community programs, it really bugs me that she's never met me and just makes a decision based on notes in a medical file.
>
> – DF Hazel, 5/22/14

It was later that DF Hazel learned that her doctor would recommend that she not be eligible for a halfway house due to medical concerns. This did not stop DF Hazel from continuing to try to get out of the prison earlier than her max out date. She noted: "I will keep going, every day, to my case manager's office for an update. It's the only thing I have the ability to do" (DF Hazel, 5/2/14).

One unexpected barrier DF Hazel came across, which usually stopped Care Level 3 and 4 prisoners from further pursuing release, was the requirement to find their own source of health insurance prior to release. It was the responsibility of the Care Level 3 or 4 prisoner to prove health insurance before the possibility of release could occur. The data showed many "hoops" prisoners had to jump through and people they had to persuade to help them figure out the medical insurance requirement; it was like a "full-time job" (DF Hazel, 3/22/14). After waiting four and a half hours to see the only person in the medical facility that could upload the exit summary papers to be approved for home confinement, DF Hazel faced this unknown barrier:

> "Well, do you have proof of health insurance?" Ummm, I'm a prisoner and have no job... Answer: "NO". She said that I have to prove I'll have some health insurance, or they can't recommend me for home confinement. Really??? I can't apply for Obamacare until I am home and I am not on disability or anything like that. ... She said I had to go to Social Work and have them send her an email saying that I have the medical coverage to go to home confinement.
>
> – DF Hazel, 3/22/14

DF Hazel then sought out a social worker, which required more waiting. While the social worker looked up the new *Affordable Care Act* (also known as "Obamacare"), she refused to look any further on the website to see if it would cover DF Hazel when she was released. She told DF Hazel that she "had to get printed proof of the state being under the ACA and what it covers", yet, as DF Hazel wrote, "It's not like I have access to the internet to do this search..." (DF Hazel, 3/22/14). This was one of many examples of how correctional staff could become a barrier to self-efficacy. Often, self-efficacy depended on having staff do their job – and in a timely manner – to which prison bureaucracy did not always lend itself.

DF Hazel turned to another staff member, her unit caseworker, whom she sought out nearly every day for updates on how to get herself out of the prison. Her caseworker had never been asked to do that search before, but due to knowing DF Hazel from her frequent visits of self-efficacy seeking advice on the next steps for release, she printed out the proof DF Hazel needed to show she would be eligible for Obamacare upon release. This was an example of how a correctional staff member could help with self-efficacy. DF Hazel then had to wait for another day during open office hours to seek out the social worker to show the documents she was able to obtain. All this work and self-advocacy was necessary to try and obtain her exit summary:

> After spending hours in the clinic, nearly stalking the woman who hadn't uploaded my exit summary yet, I caught her in the hall, plead my case, and she said somewhat regretfully, "I'll get it done by the end of the day". Later, I headed to my case manager's office and she checked, no

> exit summary at 2pm. I said I'd check again at 3. Amazingly, she said, "Okay", even though she doesn't offer open house hours today. She would be leaving by 4pm... After months, starting in December, asking for this document, it is there, in my file, saying that I am approved and medically appropriate for home confinement. My knees hurt from jumping through so many hoops, but there it is.
>
> – DF Hazel, 3/22/14

Once the exit summary was completed, the caseworker was able to process DF Hazel's home confinement. She had to wait in long lines to see her caseworker, the exit summary medical employee, and the social worker multiple times, be prepared for the meetings, negotiate for them to do the work she needed them to perform on her behalf, and then see them again to ask them to complete the next step. Simple emails or phone calls between the staff might have been more effective, yet only prisoner self-efficacy would achieve the goals of getting the paperwork uploaded into the system.[2]

Based on her experiences, every time DF Hazel encountered someone who started complaining that they were being denied home confinement or halfway house due to their care level, she began suggesting how to advocate for themselves and who to see. To help others, DF Hazel drafted up eight steps to getting out of prison if a woman was a Care Level 3 based on the lessons she learned, "I decided to sit down and write the full process of trying to be eligible for community programs for people who are a Care Level 3 at Carswell. I wrote, and wrote, and wrote – 6 pages worth of steps and information for everyone to consider" (DF Hazel, 3/22/14). They passed it around the prison and it was shared on the blog so families and loved ones could advocate for people they knew. Soon, women were able to familiarize themselves with the steps of self-efficacy for release:

> Due to my experience, I watched one woman jump about three of the initial hoops just today – she went to social work, she talked with the person responsible for the paperwork and she went to team to get the official paperwork request. All these things could take weeks/months if you don't know the process.
>
> – DF Hazel, 3/22/14

DF Hazel eventually was successful at her self-efficacy toward release. She left the medical center on 28 May 2014 (approximately 10 months into her year and a day sentence), served five days in a halfway house, and then did a month of home confinement until her official out date on 2 July 2014. She also completed her three-year probation early, being fully released ("off paper") after approximately two years.

Staff Treatment of Prisoners as a Barrier to Self-Efficacy
While some staff were able to see that not all prisoners are the same – that they have different backgrounds, different crimes, different security levels, and different needs – several staff members simply saw women in "greys" or "khakis" and decided to treat the prisoners all the same no matter who they were. For example, one staff member told his students, "You are all inmates. Inmates lie. I am not going to believe your stories, even if you say you are not lying, because you are manipulative and criminals" (DF Hazel, 12/13/13). Statements such as these made some prisoners feel disempowered from acts of self-efficacy:

> ...I realized that I don't have a "voice" in prison. As long as I wear the prison uniform, I am just the same as anyone else. If some inmates lie, we all lie. If some inmates are bad, we are all bad. If some inmates steal, we all steal. It is not the truth, but that's the way we are treated. When something bad happens, all the inmates are punished – either as a compound or as a unit. One inmate will cause trouble over a television and the televisions are cut off from the entire unit for days. One inmate leaves food in a microwave, and the microwave is taken away from everyone. One inmate doesn't go to the lieutenant's office on time and the entire compound is closed and all inmates have to stay in their units. That is how a large place like Carswell controls 1800 inmates. They just see us all as the same.
>
> – DF Hazel, 11/24/13

Such disempowerment affected the attitude and ability at times for imprisoned people to work toward their own goals.

Staff constantly establish prison hierarchy, with prisoners frequently being reminded of their place. One of the teachers that DF Hazel worked for refused to call her by name and instead would scream "'Hey!' and/ or snap her finger" (DF Hazel, 9/24/13) when she wanted her. DF

Hazel wrote that she felt a bit like a dog and when she tried to have a conversation with the teacher, the latter walked away from her. Another staff member walked around the compound consistently screaming at different prisoners, "'Tuck in your shirt!' 'Button your shirt!' or 'Where is your uniform?'" (DF Hazel, 12/13/13).

Sex and Relationships Complicated Self-Efficacy
toward Transfer and Release
Differences between sexual orientation, prisoner gender identity, and intimate relationships between prisoners were also discovered in the data, which complicated efforts of self-efficacy toward transfer and release. Sexual orientation referred to the prisoner's general pattern of attraction toward males, females, or both, most often prior to imprisonment. Gender included the internal gender identity of prisoners and their outward appearance. Sexual behavior was separate from both sexual orientation and gender (although some gender play overlapped with sexual behavior) and focused on those prisoners who selected to be in same-sex intimate relationships while imprisoned. Based on the data, the majority of issues around self-efficacy were impacted by sexual behavior and not sexual orientation or gender.

DF Hazel's account of in-prison intimate relationships displayed a mostly adverse effect on self-efficacy toward transfer and/or release. FMC Carswell had a policy with "a strict 'zero tolerance' policy concerning sexual relations within the institution" between prisoners (Federal Bureau of Prisons, 2011, p. 5). According to disciplinary policy at the prison, a sexual act with another prisoner received a 200-level "high severity" shot, which often led to time in the Special Housing Unit (SHU) and the loss of other valuable prison privileges. Yet, according to the data, many women engaged in relationships and sexual acts that "will get you put in the SHU... take away your 'good time', so you have to be here longer..." if caught (DF Hazel, 10/15/13).

Relationships could negatively impact self-efficacy to the point where an individual chose to extend their prison time to remain in prison with their girlfriend. The woman with more time in the prison sometimes chose to get their girlfriend in trouble in hopes that it would result in lost good time. Similarly, when one girlfriend would be sent to the SHU, it was commonplace for the other girlfriend to attempt to be sent to the SHU in solidarity with their girlfriend even though they would not necessarily share the same cell. Getting in trouble could result in being denied a transfer and/ or losing a potential halfway house or good time.

DISCUSSION

The analysis above provides evidence that there are many ways female prisoners exhibit self-efficacy in the federal medical center regarding transfer and release. The findings support much of the literature that currently exists centering incarcerated women and offers insight into directions for future research. This section will explore these areas.

Potentially unique to current understandings of self-efficacy was the ability to examine self-efficacy issues within the context of a medical center operated by the Federal Bureau of Prisons. There was strong evidence of self-efficacy among prisoners who tried to lower their designated care and security levels. At times this was not necessarily in the prisoner's long-term self-interest, such as Freckles giving up all medication to qualify as a Care Level 2. Another similar finding was how prisoners used self-efficacy to get medical holds removed from their paperwork. Prisoners often had to work around the bureaucracy and the restricted access to use the medical facilities to obtain proper care. For example, DF Hazel refused to accept an outside appointment with a rheumatologist due to the medical hold it would place on her file. Yet, prisoners still went through the rituals of sending cop-outs, waiting in long lines, and attending "413" medical meetings knowing that limitations to what would be done for them existed.

Barriers toward self-efficacy were also evident. The current research also offered a glimpse into the fear that many lower security prisoners may feel being locked up with higher security level inmates. Although the study shows that violent propensity is based much more on prior violent acts (that may or may not equal security levels), minimum-security prisoners with no violent tendencies can be thwarted from potential self-efficacy for fear of how a higher security prisoner may respond. The data also provided examples of how staff treatment of prisoners created barriers to self-efficacy, resulting in feelings of disempowerment. Intimate relationships between prisoners also could serve as a barrier, as both punishment for sexual activities and unhealthy relationship expectations sometimes circumvented self-efficacy toward transfer and release.

Considered as a whole, there was frequent evidence of collective and self-efficacy among the data. The primary blog post author, DF Hazel exemplified a prisoner doing whatever she could to leave the high-security environment. Even when her self-efficacy to be transferred across the street failed, she turned her efforts toward the paperwork for release. Some gave up, such as South who stopped trying to get out early due to exhaustion and dead ends. She ended up maxing out her time. Yet others pursued every avenue for success, such as Freckles choosing the intensive and restrictive RDAP program to reduce her prison time and increase her halfway house and home confinement time. The current data were rich with examples of self-efficacy.

As part of the new wave of Convict Criminology, this research provides insight into the daily lives of women in a federal women's medical center. The voices and perspectives of the prisoners provide insight into the realities they faced daily. Self-efficacy toward transfer and release was one way to look at the data, and in turn, showed a unique perspective of how women did time.

Limitations and Future Research
As is a limit in most CC work, these data could be questioned for potential bias. While the writings were primarily from the point of view of one individual, they were not originally written with the goal of academic research. The writings contained only what was important for the DF Hazel to share with readers at the time and did not contain any additional content to try and come to preconceived desires of what this research could show.

Generalizability is also another limitation of the current research study. Using a single prison raises questions about whether or to what extent findings apply to other correctional facilities that house women. However, as noted by Lahm (2016), many women's prisons in the U.S. house women from all security levels and with all types of medical issues. Another generalizability issue is that the primary author and most of the writing were done by first-timer, minimum-security, educated prisoners with healthcare needs. Perspective can mean a lot in prison, and the perspective of DF Hazel and her colleagues may not apply across all prisoner backgrounds.

CONCLUSION

Self-efficacy among incarcerated women is a topic that needs further exploration. The carceral system's dehumanizing nature has resulted in many women having to show strong self-efficacy to secure transfer or release from incarceration, especially those who are among the most vulnerable within the system – women with medical issues. This study provided insight into the barriers women face within the U.S. federal system trying to reduce security and care levels, as well as unique documented experiences of unfair expectations for women to force those working within the system to follow through with the bureaucratic systems that may keep women in more secure prisons longer than necessary. While within this study some were successful at securing transfer and/or release due to self-efficacy, others were unsuccessful or simply gave up due to the energy it took for an individual to fight the system. The findings further confirm the various ways incarcerated women attempt to advocate for themselves to make their incarcerated lives more livable.

While documenting examples of women's self-efficacy in the context of the federal women's medical center is important, it is also important that the systems that resulted in the deprivation of rights to do time in a safe space and get released when appropriate be changed to allow more women such opportunities. As existing research has established prisoner self-efficacy, it is imperative for future research to continue exploring this issue (Fayter, 2022), especially from a feminist convict criminologist perspective (Cox & Malkin, 2023). Ultimately, there is much more that needs to be addressed regarding this issue and its implications for how incarcerated women navigate their time in confinement.

ENDNOTES

[1] There is an ongoing debate over the use of "convict" and some of the language used within Convict Criminology research. Although there are arguments for and against using the term formerly incarcerated versus ex-con, Convict Criminology also recognizes the importance of self-disclosure, and it is the individual choice of the authors to choose the term that they believe is most appropriate to refer to the population they want to describe (Ross & Vianello, 2021). For a recent discussion on this topic, see Ortiz and colleagues (2022).

[2] What was unknown to DF Hazel at the time was that she was the first prisoner at FMC Carswell to have been successful in that exact process, as most prisoners failed at proving insurance if they did not already have it. The new *Affordable Care Act* became a way for ex-prisoners to qualify for home confinement who otherwise were denied it in the past. She notes: "If it were not for this affordable health insurance, I, along with countless others, would be forced to remain in prison due to our medical and/or medication needs" (DF Hazel, 3/22/14). The prison Social Worker asked

DF Hazel to write in and let her know if she was successful in obtaining health insurance, which DF Hazel did do.

REFERENCES

Allred, Sarah L., Lana D. Harrison & Daniel J. O'Connell (2013) "Self-efficacy: An Important Aspect of Prison-based Learning", *Prison Journal,* 93(2): 211-233.

Anderson, Leon (2006) "Analytical Autoethnography", *Journal of Contemporary Ethnography,* 35(4): 373-395.

Bandura, Albert (1977) "Self-efficacy: Toward a Unifying Theory of Behavioral Change", *Psychological Review*, 84(2): 191.

Bolden, Christian L. (2020) *Out of the Red,* New Brunswick (NJ): Rutgers University Press.

Bosworth, Mary, Debi Campbell, Bonita Demby, Seth M. Ferranti & Michael (2005) "Doing Prison Research: Views from Inside", *Qualitative Inquiry*, 11(2): 249-264.

Bozkurt, Sinem Safak, & Andreas Aresti (2018) "Absent Voices: Experiencing Prison Life from Both Sides of the Fence: A Turkish Female's Perspective", *Journal of Prisoners on Prisons,* 27(2): 17-36.

Caulley, Darrel N. (2008) "Making Qualitative Research Reports Less Boring: The Techniques of Writing Creative Nonfiction", *Qualitative Inquiry,* 14(3): 424-449.

Carceral, K.C. & Thomas J. Bernard (2004) *Behind a Convict's Eyes: Doing Time in a Modern Prison*, Belmont: Wadsworth Publishing Company.

Charmaz, Kathy (2014) "Grounded Theory in Global Perspective: Reviews by International Researchers", *Qualitative Inquiry,* 20(9): 1074–1084.

Cislo, Andrew M. & Robert Trestman (2013) "Challenges and Solutions for Conducting Research in Correctional Settings: The U.S. Experience", *International Journal of Law and Psychiatry,* 36(3-4): 304-310.

Denshire, Sally (2014) "On Auto-ethnography", *Current Sociology,* 62(6): 831-850.

Drake, Deborah H., Rod Earle & Jennifer Sloan (eds.) (2015) *The Palgrave Handbook of Prison Ethnography*, London: Palgrave Macmillan.

Earle, Rod (2021) "Exploring Narrative, Convictions, and Autoethnography as a Convict Criminologist", *Journal of Culture and Crime,* 2020(3): 80-96.

Earle, Rod & Coretta Phillips (2015) "Prison Ethnography at the Threshold of Race, Reflexivity, and Difference", in Deborah H. Drake, Rod Earl & Jennifer Sloan (eds.), *The Palgrave Handbook of Prison Ethnography*, London: Palgrave Macmillan, pp. 230-251.

Fayter, Rachel (2022) "Shifting Societal Perceptions of Criminalized Women: From Frameworks of Risks and Deficits Towards Narratives of Strength and Wellness", *Journal of Prisoners on Prisons*, 31(1): 133-148.

Federal Bureau of Prison (n.d. a) *Designations*. Retrieved from https://www.bop.gov/ inmates/ custody_and_care/designations.jsp

Federal Bureau of Prison (n.d. b) *FMC Carswell*. Retrieved from http://www.bop.gov/ locations/ institutions/crw/

Federal Bureau of Prison (n.d. c). *Medical Designations and Referral Services for Federal Prisoners*. Retrieved from https://www.bop.gov/policy/progstat/6270_001.pdf

Friestad, Christine & Inger Lise Skog Hansen (2005) "Mental Health Problems Among Prison Inmates: The Effect of Welfare Deficiencies, Drug Use and Self-efficacy", *Journal of Scandinavian Studies in Criminology & Crime Prevention,* 6(2): 183-196.

Hazel, Dragonfly (2013) "One Year and One Day", *Blogger – June 25.* Retrieved from http://dragonflyhazel.blogspot.com/2013/06/my-name-is-dragonfly-hazel.html

Jewkes, Yvonne (2012) "Autoethnography and Emotion as Intellectual Resources: Doing Prison Research Differently", *Qualitative Inquiry,* 18(1): 63-75.

Jones, Richard S. (1993) "Coping with Separation: Adaptive Responses of Women Prisoners", *Women & Criminal Justice,* 5(1): 71-97.

Jones, Richard S., Jeffrey Ian Ross, Stephen C. Richards & Daniel S. Murphy (2009) "The First Dime: A Decade of Convict Criminology", *The Prison Journal,* 89(2): 151-171.

Jonesa, Lise Øen, Terje Mangerb, Ole-Johan Eikeland & Arve Asbjørnsen (2013) "Participation in Prison Education: Is It a Question of Reading and Writing Self-efficacy Rather than Actual Skills?", *Journal of Correctional Education,* 64(2): 41-62.

Kajstura, Aleks (2019) "Women's Mass Incarceration: The Whole Pie 2019", *Prison Policy Initiative* – October 29. Retrieved from https://www.prisonpolicy.org/reports/pie2019women.html

Kalmbach, Karen C. & Phillip M. Lyons (2003) "Ethical and Legal Standards for Research in Prisons", *Behavioral Sciences & the Law,* 21(5): 671-686.

Kuhlmann, Annette (2005) "The View from the Other Side of the Fence: Incarcerated Women Talk About Themselves", *Justice Policy Journal,* 2(1): 5-8.

Lahm, Karen (2016) "Official Incidents of Inmate-on-Inmate Misconduct at a Women's Prison: Using Importation and Deprivation Theories to Compare Perpetrators to Victims", *Criminal Justice Studies,* 29(3): 214-231.

Lahm, Karen F. (2015) "Predictors of Violent and Nonviolent Victimization Behind Bars: An Exploration of Women Inmates", *Women & Criminal Justice,* 25(4): 273-291.

Leyva, Martin & Christopher Bickel (2010) "From Corrections to College: The Value of a Convict's Voice", *Western Criminology Review,* 11(1): 50-60.

Loeb, Susan J., Darrell Steffensmeier & Cathy Kassab (2011) "Predictors of Self-efficacy and Self-rated Health for Older Male Inmates", *Journal of Advanced Nursing,* 67(4): 811-820.

Monazzam, Niki & Kristen M. Budd (2022) *Incarcerated Women and Girls,* New York: The Sentencing Project. Retrieved from https://www.sentencingproject.org/publications/incarcerated-women-and-girls/

Newbold, Greg, Jeffrey Ian Ross, Richard S. Jones, Stephen C. Richards & Michael Lenza (2014) "Prison Research from the Inside: The Role of Convict Autoethnography", *Qualitative Inquiry,* 20(4): 439-448.

Pelissier, Bernadette & Nicole Jones (2006) "Differences in Motivation, Coping Style, and Self-Efficacy Among Incarcerated Male and Female Drug Users", *Journal of Substance Abuse Treatment,* 30(2): 113-120.

Richards, Stephen C. (2013) "The New School of Convict Criminology Thrives and Matures", *Critical Criminology,* 21(3): 375-387.

Richards, Stephen C., Donald Faggiani, Jed Roffers, Richard Hendricksen, & Jerrick Krueger (2008) "Convict Criminology: Voices from Prison", *Race/Ethnicity: Multidisciplinary Global Contexts,* 2(1): 121-136.

Richie, Beth E. (2004) "Feminist Ethnographies of Women in Prison", *Feminist Studies,* 30(2): 438.

Ross, Jeffrey Ian, Sacha Darke, Andreas Aresti, Greg Newbold & Rod Earle (2014) "Developing Convict Criminology Beyond North America", *International Criminal Justice Review,* 24(2): 121-133.

Ross, Jeffrey Ian & Stephen C. Richards (2003) *Convict Criminology*, Belmont (CA): Wadsworth/Thomson Learning.

Ross, Jeffrey Ian & Francesca Vianello (eds.) (2021) *Convict Criminology for the Future*, New York: Routledge.

Rowe, Abigail (2016) "'Tactics', Agency and Power in Women's Prisons", *British Journal of Criminology*, 56(2): 332-349.

Terry, April (2016) "Surveying Issues That Arise in Women's Prisons: A Content Critique of Orange Is the New Black", *Sociology Compass*, 10(7): 553-566.

Terry, Charles M. (2004) "Managing Prisoners as Problem Populations and the Evolving Nature of Imprisonment: A Convict Perspective", *Critical Criminology*, 12(1): 43-66.

Wakeman, Stephen (2014) "Fieldwork, Biography and Emotion: Doing Criminological Autoethnography", *British Journal of Criminology*, 54(5): 705-721.

Willingham, Breea C. (2011) "Black Women's Prison Narratives and the Intersections of Race, Gender, and Sexuality in U.S. Prisons", *Critical Survey,* 23(3): 55-66.

Wooldredge, John & Benjamin Steiner (2016) "Assessing the Need for Gender-specific Explanations of Prisoner Victimization", *Justice Quarterly*, 33(2): 209-238.

ABOUT THE AUTHORS

Michelle L. Malkin, JD, PhD is an Assistant Professor of Criminal Justice and Criminology at East Carolina University. Dr. Malkin's research interests include a focus on gambling-related harms, gambling-motivated crime, LGBTQ+ and Gambling Disorder, and the experiences of LGBTQ+ people in the carceral system. In 2018, she received a research fellowship for her scholarship on women and gambling-motivated crime from the Center for Gaming Studies at University of Nevada, Las Vegas. Her research on the Problem Gambling, General Strain Theory and Gender received the 2022 Dr. Durand Jacobs Dissertation Award from the National Council on Problem Gambling. She is currently conducting several research studies relevant to further understanding of gambling and gambling-related harms, including projects on college-student gambling risk and behavior, gambling behavior and risk among LGBTQ+ individuals, the national landscape of self-exclusion based on jurisdictional legality, and an evaluation of the Clark County Gambling Treatment Diversion Court.

Alison Cox, PhD is an Assistant Professor at East Carolina University in the Department of Criminal Justice and Criminology. Her research interests include prison visitation, the impact of incarceration on families, critical criminology (e.g. convict, feminist, queer, and rural), and qualitative methods. Her scholarship has been published in *Criminal Justice Studies* and *Critical Criminology*. She is also a contributing author to *Convict Criminology for the Future*, edited by Dr. Jeffrey Ian Ross (University of Baltimore) and Dr. Francesca Vianello (University of Padua).

Here She Comes:
Women of Convict Criminology
Denise Woodall

ABSTRACT

In response to Joanne Belknap's 2014 presidential address in which she critiqued the white male dominance of Convict Criminology, formerly incarcerated women formed the group's first thematic panel on "Women of Convict Criminology" at the American Society of Criminology annual conference in 2016. This article reports the results of an analysis presented in the first session that illustrates the invisibility of directly impacted women contributors to our knowledgebase and recaps the inspiration, courage, and empiricism that sparked the presence of a new, more diverse group of directly impacted people fighting for recognition and inclusion in knowledge construction within 'malestream' criminology. Ways of conceptualizing carceral status as one axis of oppressions and directions for the future of Convict Criminology are discussed.

Keywords:
Feminism, Convict Criminology, Higher Education, Intersectionality, Carceral Status

INTRODUCTION

Convict Criminology (CC) had a primarily long-standing strong white male membership until a 2014 American Society of Criminology presidential address by feminist criminologist Joanne Belknap, which shook its patriarchal structure to its core. She publicly named and criticized the CC group for its failure to bring forth voices of women and people of color. Although the published formal response to her was white and male, quietly women, queer, people of color organized and began discussing these very relevant problems in our ranks that Belknap said out loud. Directly impacted white, Black, brown, and/or queer women began to speak up to establish a presence in the previously male-dominated space of standpoint criminological knowledge production.

This paper traces some of the important moments that led myself and other women to come forward in our professional space to redirect a very white and male CC that, although it had provided us with 25 years of important trailblazing, needed a different face to forge an inclusive path into the future. CC has encountered recent rifts in its membership. With some seeking diversification, re-definitions, and new language, others sought to maintain the status quo with mere tokenistic inclusion, while others still clung to an imagined diversity that had not yet been present – until recently. As members squabbled over how to broaden, deepen, widen, and diversify its ranks, I argue that the transformations must go far deeper than tokenism, performances to gain big-name sponsorship, and "adding women and stirring" style inclusion. Members will need to acknowledge and demand that multiple marginalized identities are squarely seated at the table shoulder-to-shoulder designing and directing our future, even if that means Black and brown people, women, trans, or queer identified people lead the way. Considering the legacy of slavery and colonial rule, it is possible that Black, brown, trans women will not trust a group with such a white male dominated patriarchal lineage. They may seek to create something uniquely their own, or more people from diverse backgrounds and experiences may opt to join us. It is hard to know what will happen, but it is certain that in order to engage in meaningful explorations of ways to honor, create safety, and lift those voices most marginalized, Convict Criminology needs to continue to take hard looks at its white male character, and know that it still has work to do.

I will first recap the genealogy of the Women of CC group from my perspective. Then, I will report on data illustrating the lack of presence of women, particularly women of color, trans, and queer carceral citizens in our knowledgebase, that I presented in 2016 at our first thematic panel on "Women of Convict Criminology". I will also touch on what little has changed on the publication front of CC. Following that, I set forth a guide for allies who, as I argue, will be imperative for opening doors of academia to the most marginalized carceral citizens, less we have to kick them down.

Before doing so, however, a brief note on language is needed. All humans act in ways that transgress laws (Baxter, 2017; Coyle, 2018; Woodall, 2016, 2019). Yet those captured by the carceral state are marked and subjugated, while others are privileged to evade such categorization. The criminal label translates individuals into *carceral citizens* available for legal and social exclusions that *conventional citizens* are not subject to (Miller & Stuart, 2017). Therefore, I use the term carceral citizens as a replacement to Convict Criminology's use of the term "con".

A BRIEF GENEALOGY OF THE WOMEN
OF THE CC GROUP

As a woman member of the new school of CC, I would first like to credit them for being a powerful defender of the rights of carceral citizens and an incredible resource for helping those in various stages of incarceration navigate the pressures of graduate applications and studies, research, and faculty life. However, I have joined in the chorus of rising voices signaling the dangers of presenting a largely white male-dominated group, like CC, as the authority on insider experiential knowledge within the criminal justice system. I do so, in efforts to improve the chances that women, trans, and queer people of color will be acknowledged and heard so that we can build a safer and more dignified future for everyone harmed by the criminal justice system.

Women carceral citizens may have gotten used to being alone since the relevance of our experiences in criminological thought is so often sidelined to the idea that "there are so few of us" or that "we don't have it as bad as men". As we enact our inside-voice eye-roll at those familiar statements, we do so – alone. Indeed, us women may have likely grown accustomed to being the only woman she knows who has had direct carceral experience in our academic circles. So, when Joanne Belknap delivered her 2014 Presidential Address encompassing a scathing critique of the invisibility of directly impacted women, particularly women of color in our professional circles or in our knowledgebase, setting her critique squarely on the white male dominated "voice" of the incarcerated in criminological thought of CC, our spirits were re-kindled.

Many women at the time who "ran" in our CC circles were early-stage faculty, graduate, or even undergraduate students. The men swiftly set out to construct a response to Belknap's critiques with the few women I knew respectfully declining to get involved or being downright rejected from the 2016 *Critical Criminology* special edition response to Belknap that was colonialishly dominated by white men. Titling a response to Belknap mansplaining why women or people of color are not invisibilized, called "The struggle for inclusion", with four white men at the authorial helm was quite frankly, publicly embarrassing. I found myself making excuses for the men arguing, "They just don't know better" or self-blaming excuses like "well, none of us, white, brown, Black or queer women were around, available, or stepping up to write a response to Belknap". However, looking back, it would not have been that difficult for someone, anyone, to interview women and people of color in the group to get our take on Belknap's address, and keep our identities confidential. Perhaps asking a queer woman of color to author a paper that interviewed directly impacted Black, brown, women, trans, and queer people of color who have knowledge of the Convict Criminology group would have at least been something to show the professional community that there was an acknowledgement of the severe historical imbalance of white male voices in the group and an illustrated attempt, by the members, to right that wrong. Instead, the professional community received howls of defense and excuses from male members of the group while it was clear for anyone to see, Convict Criminology had been, and looked as if it was going to continue to be, a white men's club.

By late-2015, the year after Belknap gave her critique, every woman with direct experience that had set foot in a CC session at the ASC in Washington, DC really started talking. We had dinner, lunches, and coffee, and we decided that it was time for a "Women of Convict Criminology" session at our next annual meeting. We knew also that women of color, trans, and queer people were under-represented at our tables, so we decided to add an additional session on strategizing for inclusion.

In 2016, the very first "Women of Convict Criminology" session took place. The room was packed, but with depressingly very few male members in attendance. The most fully glorious, intelligent, articulate, powerful, upstanding, fighters for justice stood at the podium, and continued to do so year after year. Their direct accounts of gendered and racialized carceral violence revealed the myriads of ways that the criminal justice system symbolically and physically kicks, brutalizes, beats, batters, humiliates, shames, bars, and blocks – compoundingly. Each bright shining participant boldly stepped forward to highlight how multiple layers of oppression lay upon her compounding harms and indignities with narrative-busting purpose and visions for change. I thought, "I can't believe it took this long for us to do this!" Even quite established women scholars exuberantly cheered from the audience, "It's about time!" Indeed, it was about time. The people who presented in the feminist CC sessions year after year thoughtfully centered the experience of the carceral system around their multiply marginalized identities of being women, queer, non-binary, non-white or otherwise, feminist.

Even the roundtables were exciting as attendees expressed feverish longing for a diverse CC group. But like many well-meaning and needed initiatives, few of us had time to build an empire as we were saddled with living life as multiply marginalized people in the world. What we are learning is that – shocker – women, trans, and queer people of color have a lot going on! Women, particularly women of color, already struggle to gain recognition for their achievements in academic settings (Croom, 2017; Griffin, 2019). Men and women of color are also coping with racial battle fatigue (Smith et al., 2011; Corbin et al., 2018), while trans people are just trying to gain access at all to these spaces (Holley, 2011).

The stratification of criminalized people mirrors the broader society, therefore, more white male carceral citizens are heard. Fewer individuals with multiple characteristics of identity that intersect with carceral citizen status to amplify oppression, ever make it through the doors. Critics agree, the male dominated voice permeates crime studies (Belknap, 2014; Chesney-Lind & Pasko, 2012) and I have to agree that this has bled into CC (Belknap, 2014). Based on my own directly impacted status, my work with re-entering women for 17 years in service, activism, and research, as well as my collegial work with CC group since 2012, I know that our discipline would benefit greatly from a convict feminist standpoint that privileges marginalized perspectives (MacKinnon, 2004; Bartlett, 1990; Perkins, 2000). For application in the discipline of crime, law, or deviance, this process would require greater involvement of women carceral citizens in knowledge production.

Making this happen is fraught with difficulties that seemed to be overlooked in the Belknap's presidential address. The patriarchial framework of the broader society also structures academia and the carceral citizen population, making the raising of directly impacted women's voices exceedingly difficult. Women are discriminated against and struggle more than men do in academia (Miller & Miller, 2002). It is essentially a "double whammy" to also be formerly incarcerated. We know little about how these identities intersect and compound the likelihood of stigmatization and discrimination in academia. I read much "critical" work with authorial claims of support for women carceral citizens. They declare our "voices should be lifted" and that "we should be heard". However, I see few of them writing about how they are actually facilitating those contributions.

It seems that Belknap has tasted the Convict Criminology frustration in her own attempts to bring a convicted woman into a graduate program as her strong recommendation was rejected by a graduate committee in her own department. In my experience, I see that CC group members share this pain with her. I have witnessed and experienced CC group recommendations go unheeded. The CC group's hands have been tied in a similar fashion to the way Belknap's have been in efforts to get women carceral citizens accepted into graduate programs. It appears that CC group diversity question is less about mentorship quality, although much more could have been done, and more about the limits of their power. I argue that solving the problem of CC group diversity cannot fall completely on the shoulders of the CC ranks as change is needed in the ranks of academia as well. This requires a commitment to recruiting, mentoring, and defending convicted women and minority group members in ways that lift them up into positions of power. There are few, if any, hiring committees or graduate committees completely comprised of Convict Criminologists. Thus, it is up to the intelligentsia to help us up! Those of us who are intersectionally marginalized need chances to be given to us by those who have the power and privilege to do so.

Before I engage in a deeper discussion of allyship, I would like to turn to the data as evidence of the ongoing difficulty of women carceral citizen's scholarship to be located in our knowledge base. It will be difficult to make use of women's voices to disrupt problematic unaffected ivory tower truth claims if we cannot find them. I confirm through the data described below, although I think we already knew it, that there is an ongoing invisibility of directly impacted women informing, rather not informing, our scientific understanding of crime and justice. If she is there, it is hard to know it. If her experience is shooting through the academic empire authority on criminal justice, it too often does so in disguise.

LOCATING DIRECTLY IMPACTED WOMEN IN OUR KNOWLEDGEBASE

In search of directly impacted women scholarship, I pursued three sources, Convict Criminology publications listed on their website, the *Journal of Prisoners on Prisons* (now CC group's official journal), and a Sociological Index search for particular phrases that I thought would guide me to women carceral citizen scholarship. I engaged in this work to mimic what any scholar might do in attempts to find women scholars writing on issues of criminal justice from a directly impacted and experienced perspective. I conducted this research in preparation for the 2017 "Women of Convict Criminology" session that I had organized, and it had remained unpublished until now.

The Sociological Index search was conducted by entering the phrases "incarcerated autoethnography", "as a formerly incarcerated woman", "I was incarcerated" and "convict criminology", then analyzing the publications published since 2006. The *Journal of Prisoners on Prisons* site was searched in its entirety since 2006 and the Convict Criminology site was analyzed in its entirety.

Table 1: The Difficulty of Locating Women
Carceral Citizen Scholarship in the Knowledgebase

Source searched	# of WOMEN authors who were possibly directly Impacted.	# of total Articles WITH WOMEN as authors	# Articles NO WOMEN authors	Total Articles	Notes
SOCINDEX SEARCHES [1][2]	5 (14% of total)	6 (16%)	30 (83%)	36	Not-centred poc, trans, or queer
CONVICT CRIMINOLOGY SITE (2016)	12 (15% of total)	23 (30%)	56 (71%)	79	Non-centred poc, trans, or queer
JOURNAL OF PRISONERS ON PRISONS [1]	57 (28% of total)	60 (30%)	142 (70%)	202	Some centred poc, non-centred queer and trans

[1] Since 2006
[2] "incarcerated autoethnography" / "as a formerly incarcerated woman" / "I was incarcerated" / convict criminology"

Figure 1: The Difficulty of Locating Women Carceral Citizen Scholarship 2016 Chart

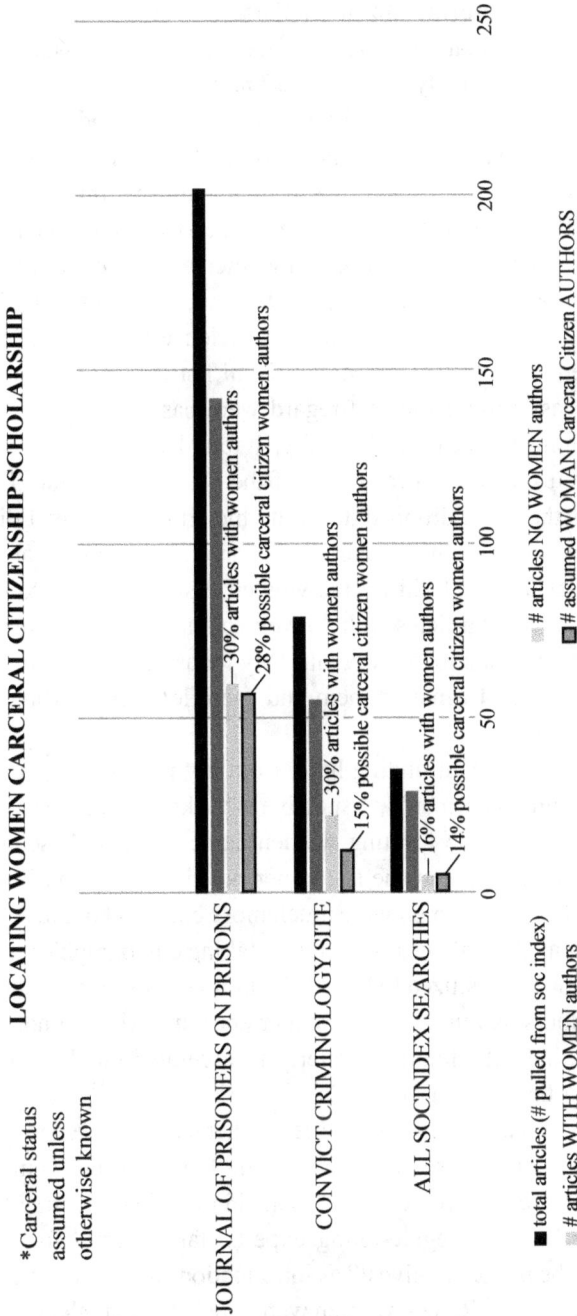

LOCATING WOMEN CARCERAL CITIZENSHIP SCHOLARSHIP

*Carceral status assumed unless otherwise known

JOURNAL OF PRISONERS ON PRISONS
— 30% articles with women authors
— 28% possible carceral citizen women authors

CONVICT CRIMINOLOGY SITE
— 30% articles with women authors
— 15% possible carceral citizen women authors

ALL SOCINDEX SEARCHES
— 16% articles with women authors
— 14% possible carceral citizen women authors

- total articles (# pulled from soc index)
- # articles WITH WOMEN authors
- # articles NO WOMEN authors
- # assumed WOMAN Carceral Citizen AUTHORS

0   50   100   150   200   250

Clearly, women carceral citizen scholarship is difficult to find. Before I go into a deeper explanation, there are three major sorting issues with the data that I would like to justify as I describe *Table 1* and *Figure 1*. First, I have raw number and percentage of total articles by women, and a raw number and percentage of women authors who I assumed to be directly impacted. I did this to prevent counts of the same woman authoring multiple manuscripts. Women with incarceration experience can be tokenized and I did not want to list a percentage of directly impacted women authors out of my results total that was basically the same woman. Second, I had difficulty determining whether a woman author had direct experience with the carceral system, but I tallied her into the 'carceral citizen' list if I even got a hint of that status. My assumptions in that regard were based on reading the abstract and skimming the article. Generally, I found no mention of a woman's carceral status stated in nearly any of the abstracts. Instead, I had to hunt down hints that were dropped deep into the articles. Lastly, I did not spend time sorting out the same breakdown of carceral citizen men authors to men authored articles like I did for the women. I simply aimed to illustrate the general numbers of articles with no women authorship compared to articles with women authorship in my results. My focus here was on finding women representation, so I centered them and spent less time sorting through the specifics about men.

The most important finding here, from my perspective, is that locating formerly incarcerated men's perspective in the knowledgebase was relatively straightforward, while locating women carceral citizen's scholarship was nearly impossible. When she stated her position as author, it was done so with vagueness, while men were much more blatant about it. As I sifted and sorted my way through the three sources taking ethnographic notes along the way, I remained sensitized to how difficult it was for me to determine which women authors had incarceration experience and who did not. The bottom line is, qualitatively, finding formerly incarcerated men's scholarship was much easier than finding women's.

When a woman has direct experience, her status is often revealed deeper in the article than those written by men. There are no women members proclaiming she is a "voice from prison" in the title or quoting "to hell with the classroom bred, degree-toting experts, far removed from the grubby realities of the prisoner's lives!" as introductions to their chapters as I found with men's writing. Rather, women were much more subtle, with statements like "one of the authors has this [sentencing] experience" and "experienced carceral harm first-hand..." found buried in the middle of a paragraph often several pages into an article. Men, on the other hand, boldly proclaimed their carceral status and proudly asserted how their experience has the power to challenge what decades of white masculine criminological ivory tower empiricism has set forth as legitimate in the abstracts and even titles of their papers. Reading how women interjected their experience into knowledge production more subtly, quietly, and in ways that took up less critical space disturbed me terribly. Why could we not jump onto our soapbox and tell all masculine science and the intelligentsia "how it is"? Why were we not purporting that our ways of knowing were superior? Well, at this point I would like to do what all good scholars do – draw from what we already know, infer them to my data, and tell some stories about the "why" question.

Quite simply, I think that finding formerly incarcerated women (much less queer, trans, or women of color) was incredibly difficult because we are already marginalized in the broader society and have tended to not be granted historical access to take on patriarchal power anywhere, including the academy. It is not a far-reaching to expect to see the same phenomena mirrored in our knowledgebase, which was built by, and for, white men. Furthermore, being incarcerated is a masculine act. If it is something to do with getting arrested for violence, drugs, or some other ways that boys are just being boys, then, there is much less harm in coming forward about that if you are a white male, than it is if you are a woman, black, queer, or trans person. To admit to criminal acts and past arrest experiences for us would be admitting to double and triple norm violations! Her positionality in the matrix of domination, exacerbates the harm for her to do this. Women carceral citizens struggle with the contentious forces of deviance and femininity. On the other hand, white men can achieve an almost heightened status by sharing stories of their time in prison. They win masculine brownie points for being tough and enduring carceral violence, whereas women, particularly mothers, gender non-conforming women, or racially diverse women, are constructed as hysterical, crazy, or at the very least, not a real woman. Our social identities take a harder hit with the carceral citizen label attached to our gender and racial identity than white men do.

Although there have been times when writing opportunities have come available for women in the CC group circles, I would argue that we are often juggling the feminine pressures of home, family, social relations, and heavy clerical and emotion-work duties tasked to us in graduate school and our early faculty years to be able to take part in these endeavors on intensely crunched deadlines. In my case, I care for my grandson and my father, act as mediator to family troubles, provision, and taxi family members in need around. I cook, clean, shop, give emotional support to friends, family, and community, all while working harder than many of my male counterparts for a fraction of the pay. These are experiences that many women, including women carceral citizens, are all too familiar with. The double shifts we work make publishing on a man's timeline challenging to say the least.

To see how much or how little CC groups have accomplished in showcasing women and other gender identities has changed in these few years, I took another look at the CC site alone as I prepared this article. As *Table 2* illustrates, it is clear that not much progress has been made. However, to be fair, the wheels of academic knowledge-building churn slowly in its attempt to build inclusivity. This is certainly in the works, but the proof has still not quite yet seeped into the pudding.

Table 2 illustrates that not much has changed in the way of women representation, but it is becoming clear that we are here. The site underwent an overhaul and many papers in the resource section were traded out. Some of the women and people with experience are currently present and active members of the group. That should bring us hope.

As *Figure 2* depicts, carceral status must be understood as a subject position in the social strata that is deeply shaped by one's placement in other hierarchies. Intersectionality is not only the sum of added oppressions. Rather, it represents the acknowledgement and analysis of positionalities produced by systems of oppression that are interwoven, overlapping, and multiplicative (Collins, 1986; Crenshaw, 1990). There is no one 'convict' experience, and the best way to illustrate this is to be representative of more people situated in different social positions with different life experiences. If Convict Criminology wants to be that voice, they will have to be much more colorful and diverse than they have been and currently are.

Regardless of its problems, many of our members would surely agree with the fact that CC has been a powerful catalyst for empowering carceral citizens and giving them voices. The CC group remains a largely safe haven for the white woman carceral citizen who is rationally fearful to step out and lay her head upon the proverbial chopping block of administrative policy and departmental prejudices. It is yet to be seen if it is safe for the queer, trans,

Table 2: Women Representation Still Waning on the Convict Criminology Site

Source searched	# of WOMEN authors who were possibly directly Impacted.	# of total Articles WITH WOMEN as authors	# Articles NO WOMEN authors	Total Articles	Notes
CONVICT CRIMINOLOGY SITE 2017	12 (15%)	23 (30%)	56 (71%)	79	Not-centred poc, trans, or queer
CONVICT CRIMINOLOGY SITE 2021	12 (21%)	14 (24%)	44 (76%)	58	Non-centred poc, trans, or queer
	# of directly impacted Women authors change	# of total articles with women change	# articles with NO women authors change	total	Notes
CONVICT CRIMINOLOGY SITE CHANGE	No raw increase, but increase in percentage due to fewer total articles	Decrease in articles with women authors	Higher percentage of articles with no women authors	Fewer authors all together	More articles featuring women of color and queer (counted 4)

woman of color. The CC group cannot liberate women or women of color because this requires change in the broader social political system and allies are needed to make opportunities for women to apply their knowledge. We can, however, support one another and forge a direction that is dignifying to us. Beware that expecting a directly impacted woman to climb out onto the

Figure 2: Denise Woodall's Conceptualization
How Carceral Status Interlocks With Other Aspects of Identity
to Compoundingly Privilege and Oppress Individuals*

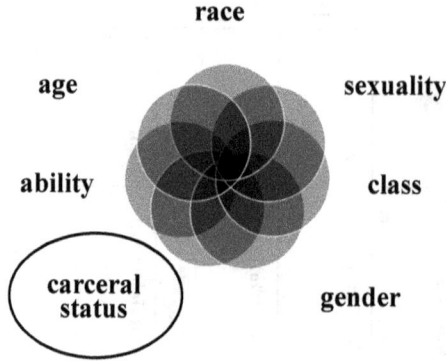

*Note: reproduced from Denise Woodall's dissertation and manuscript in progress on carceral status.

cross to be crucified for the sake of making a stand for convicted women's rights in academia, so that she can lose her job, while non-carceral citizens sit and write about how awful that is, adding more lines to their CV at her expense, is not justice.

What I have personally gained from the mentorship, partnership, and allyship in CC group is that I have come to personally know scholars around the world, I have been provided opportunities for service in the way of organizing conference sessions, designing research, and managing the group's membership list. I have been offered opportunities for collaborative research and writing in an environment that welcomes and entertains my ideas, as well as understands the preciousness of my unique experience with discrimination. Action behind their support is measurable in the way that I have been ushered into a leadership position, and the way I feel safe and secure in a hostile academic environment, and even to write this paper. However, I am in many ways retained in precarious work situations, struggle with melding my direct experience and my scholarly writing, found dodging questions about my past, yet still feeling strong desires to change the narrative. Know that men's experience of incarceration cannot explain women's because white men's identities are invisible while our carceral status is transformed by the nature of our differing gendered experiences. Where women, and particularly women of color's, identities are on display and in constant active operation in her daily life, white men carceral citizens enjoy invisibility along race and gender axes of oppression making only their carceral status stand out. Advantaging men more is that a "con" status is a perfectly acceptable masculine characteristic. Male authors in my knowledgebase searches found proclamations galore of their prison experience, while women's positionality are communicated in much more vague terms. Indeed, men experience discrimination based on their carceral status, but women in academia, must already endure the fight for legitimacy that all other women in academia vie for as well, then the criminal history further hinders our progress. If you add together all of the struggles being a person of color, queer, a mother, disabled, and/or poor entail, well, as one white man member of the group declared in rejection of a woman's paper – that is just "too much."

Asking felons to create a more inclusive academia for ourselves is unfair. It is the people who hold power in our respective fields who must also be charged with fighting for us and creating spaces that make it safe to come out. An ally does that. An ally fights, an ally gets results, and you will know you are an ally when a convict publishes an article, gets a job, or gets accepted to a graduate program and thanks you for it. If no one is thanking you, then you might want to assess what you have actually done for a directly impacted person. We need policies to change and actual acceptance letters to graduate programs. We need publishing opportunities with flexible deadlines, writing assistance, collaborators, contracts, book deals, tenure-track positions, career security, and equal pay because this oppression is often sanctioned by university policies, making it even easier to bar a woman of color from opportunities when they have the official excuse of her criminal record.

If the lack of diversity among our convict ranks worries you and you see a necessity for standpoint perspectives of minority carceral citizens across our discipline, then hire a Black carceral citizen, co-author with a transgendered prisoner, nominate a queer formerly incarcerated person's work for an award, accept a directly impacted woman to a PhD program – and engage in the fight. Do not give up until the job is done. When you do so, then you are an ally! Carceral citizens need you, as my very good friends in CC group can do only so much. If they could change the world, I believe they would.

As I reflect on the history of Convict Criminology and where I hope it goes, I would like to leave you with this final statement to help you understand where we are. I wrote this when I was deep in the throes of my dissertation writing where I was seeped in the interviews of dozens of directly impacted people trying to change the world. As I found myself citing non-carceral citizens who kept saying how important our voices were, but who failed to actually help a single one of us, I wrote the following in a cathartic fit of frustration that is nonetheless, as I have shared these paragraphs with directly impacted colleagues, extremely timely and relevant.

Formerly incarcerated scholar-activism is a personal journey in, and as, a daily negotiation for survival. I understand this struggle personally as a formerly incarcerated scholar-activist myself. Our trials and our triumphs are not only social goods for change that others get to benefit from – they are also uniquely our own. There are those who merely refer to us from a distance and have placed no investment in our personal life. We are not sharing our experience solely for the purpose of an academic's tenure or the politician's photo opportunity. Although we "take one for the team" when we are exploited, have our needs disregarded, or are left behind, so long as, ultimately, our work, investment or unauthorized sharing of our story will push positive social change, we grind forward without public protestation.

There is a private reality that directly impacted people experience in their fights for justice that go unspoken. It is money in our bank account, it is our chance to fly in an airplane, it is our personal victory to stand at the podium, and it is our intimate bravery that we draw from to step onto the political platform. Those who celebrate our wins as new possibilities for social change, we appreciate. We deeply regard our guides, our sages, and our allies – those who opened up doors of possibility for us, and who are crucial to providing us with immense opportunities to give a voice to ourselves and those like us. They ensure we are cared for. Even the best of allies, at the end of the day, are not experiencing supervised visitation with their own children, their own pocketbooks do not shrink when we are rejected from an economic opportunity, they are not emotionally feeling our internal self-doubt and our fear that comes with wondering each day how our criminal history will come back to re-victimize us, they are not personally denied acceptance to graduate programs and jobs because of a carceral status, nor are they intimately struggling to master a new professional language or feeling the personal embarrassment of violating an academic social norm and having that attributed to a criminal past. Our allies allow us to share those struggles and together we challenge devastating social problems, shoulder-to-shoulder, while others simply theorize about us from a distance under the banner of social justice. In the end, the intimate experiences of formerly incarcerated activists, our joys and our personal pains, academically and politically, have often been treated as insignificant or unimportant, but to us, they are imperative.

Although the visual spectacle of formerly incarcerated activists' work powerfully to re-shape social conditions for directly impacted subjects and everyone harmed by the carceral state, the daily struggle is also happening in every inhale and exhale of life lived as a formerly incarcerated person, and that matters as well. May the new face of Convict Criminology be a thousand kaleidoscope variations of queer, trans, disabled, adult parent, working-class women of color with endlessly riveting and necessary stories of triumph to inform our future.

REFERENCES

Bartlett, Katherine (1990) "Feminist Legal Methods", *Harvard Law Review*, 103(4): 829-888.

Baxter, Emily (2017) *We Are All Criminals: One in Four People has a Criminal Record; Four in Four have a Criminal History,* St. Paul: (self-published).

Belknap, Joanne (2015) "Activist Criminology: Criminologists' Responsibility to Advocate for Social and Legal Justice", *Criminology*, 53(1): 1-22.

Belknap, Joanne (2014) *The Invisible Woman: Gender, Crime, and Justice*, Stanford: Cengage Learning.

Chesney-Lind, Meda & Lisa Pasko (2012) *The Female Offender: Girls, Women, and Crime*, Thousand Oaks: Sage Publications.

Collins, Patricia Hill (1986) "Learning from the Outsider Within: The Sociological Significance of Black Feminist Thought", *Social Problems*, 33(6):14-32.

Corbin, Nicola A., William A. Smith & J. Roberto Garcia (2018) "Trapped Between Justified Anger and Being the Strong Black Woman: Black College Women Coping with Racial Battle Fatigue at Historically and Predominantly White Institutions", *International Journal of Qualitative Studies in Education*, 31(7): 626-643.

Coyle, Michael J. (2018) "Transgression and Standard Theories: Contributions Toward Penal Abolition", *Critical Criminology*, 26: 325-339.

Crenshaw, Kimberle (1990) "Mapping the Margins: Intersectionality, Identity Politics, and Violence Against Women of Color", *Stanford Law Review*, 43(6): 1241-1299.

Croom, Natasha N. (2017) "Promotion Beyond Tenure: Unpacking Racism and Sexism in the Experiences of Black Womyn Professors", *The Review of Higher Education*, 40(4): 557-583.

Griffin, Kimberly A. (2019) "Institutional Barriers, Strategies, and Benefits to Increasing the Representation of Women and Men of Color in the Professoriate: Looking Beyond the Pipeline", *Higher Education: Handbook of Theory and Research*, 35: 1-73.

Holley, Matthew (2011) "Gay and Lesbian Faculty Issues", *Journal of the Student Personnel Association at Indiana University*, 39: 5-13.

MacKinnon, Catherine A. (2004) "Feminism, Marxism, Method and the State: Toward Feminist Jurisprudence", in Sandra Harding (ed.), *The Feminist Standpoint Theory Reader: Intellectual and Political Controversies*, East Sussex: Psychology Press, pp. 169-180.

Miller, Kenneth L. & Susan M. Miller (2002) "A Model for Evaluating Gender Equity in Academe", in JoAnn DiGeorgio-Lutz (ed.), *Women in Higher Education: Empowering Change*, Westport: Praeger, pp. 103-114.

Miller, Reuben J. & Forrest Stuart (2017) "Carceral Citizenship: Race, Rights and Responsibility in the Age of Mass Supervision", *Theoretical Criminology*, 21(4): 532-548.

Perkins, Margo V. (2000) *Autobiography as Activism: Three Black Women of the Sixties*, Jackson: University Press of Mississippi.

Smith, William A., Man Hung & Jeremy D. Franklin (2011) "Racial Battle Fatigue and the Miseducation of Black Men: Racial Microaggressions, Societal Problems, and Environmental Stress", *The Journal of Negro Education*, 80(1): 63-82.

Woodall, Denise (2019) "We Are All Criminals: The Abolitionist Potential of Remembering", *Social Justice,* 45(4):117-140.

Woodall, Denise (2016) "Interrupting Constructions of a Criminalized Other through a Revised Criminal Activities Checklist Classroom Exercise", *Teaching Sociology*, 45(2): 161-167.

ABOUT THE AUTHOR

Denise Ruth Woodall, PhD is a directly impacted feminist criminologist and critical sociologist serving as Senior Lecturer of Sociology at the University of North Georgia and Instructor for Life University's Chillon Project inside of Lee Arrendale State Prison. Her research focuses on identities, inequalities, drug use, carceral status, and social change.

Standing at the Intersection of Identity and Convict Criminology: A Brief Exercise in Reflexivity
J. Renee Trombley

INTRODUCTION:
THE PROMISE OF CONVICT CRIMINOLOGY

The first Convict Criminology (CC) session took place in 1997 at the American Society of Criminology's (ASC) annual meeting. The session was organized by members with personal experiences with the correctional system as formerly incarcerated (FI), as well as their allies. There was consensus among the group that many of the teachers in corrections had little, if any, experience in jails or prisons and lacked knowledge of what really took place behind their walls. In 2001, Richards and Ross defined the purpose and practice of CC, suggesting that those with first-hand knowledge can provide an informed perspective on the functions and effects of prisons and jails. Merging insider knowledge, personal experience, and academic research related to criminal justice provides a paradigmatic approach that offers distinct and relevant perspectives (Richards and Ross, 2001; Ross and Richards, 2003). In 2020, the Division of Convict Criminology (DCC) officially became part of the ASC. The original CC group was not particularly diverse, but over the last decade, the membership of CC has become more diverse in gender, sexuality, race and ethnicity, and FI background. The intersection of these identities among the members further increases the perspective and diversity of this group.

As a CC member and the first vice-chair of the DCC, supporting the mission and goals of the organization – including building diversity – are particularly important to me. Diverse experiences and voices support CC's mission to support justice-impacted scholars in providing rigorous research that examines all aspects of the criminal justice system, including policing, courts, and corrections, from those who have lived experiences within the field (Tietjen, 2019).

The DCC has explicitly addressed this issue, arguing that those in academia have largely ignored research from those who are formerly incarcerated or have had direct contact with the system. Acknowledging that the relevance of research conducted by incarcerated or FI individuals is often overlooked is significant to the DCC's (2021) purpose:

> ...to provide an intellectual home for all scholars/scientists who are interested in the study of Convict Criminology. The members of the

DCC are students, researchers, and faculty members from diverse backgrounds—both with and without criminal records—that mentor formerly-incarcerated students and junior faculty, conduct relevant research, and advocate for progressive justice reform for formerly incarcerated individuals and all of society.

Appreciating what it means for me to be here, as a professor and a scholar, is humbling. Understanding that I made it despite many obstacles, as a justice system-impacted youth who transitioned from foster care to the juvenile justice system and then to the adult system, yet somehow made a way into higher education, earned a PhD in juvenile justice, and developed a passion for academic life along the way. I credit this to my faith, and grace and mercy from my Creator. Finding CC, in many ways, saved me. I was not sure I would be able to do anything with a PhD, and I was not quite convinced that I would not just end up back in the hood, sitting on the front porch, selling dime bags of weed and talking about the injustice that I saw everywhere I looked. I credit mentorship by Stephen Richards, one of CC's founding members, with giving me the courage and confidence to believe that I could find my way in the academy.

There were many barriers that I had to overcome to reach this place, and so many things that could have stopped me along the way. Though I have found space in academia, I have also continued to struggle with aspects of my identity and the stigma I faced along the way. Being labelled as a "convict" is not seen as a good thing, whether in the academy or elsewhere. Stigma poses a significant barrier for CC scholars to overcome, and discussions regarding the stigma often faced by FI individuals in the academy are plentiful (Copenhaver et al., 2007; Frana et al., 2012; Ross & Richards 2003; Tietjen, 2013). Maruna (2001) argues that the idea that folx who have done "bad" things can overcome and become "good" people "seems to contradict a fundamental belief of contemporary society" (p. 5).

In 1997, when the first CC section was officially organized at the ASC annual meeting, I was twenty-five years old, a mother of three small children, and enrolling in college classes for the second time. When I finally made it to higher education, I felt as many of CC's original members did. I sat in criminal justice classes listening to professors describe a system that they seemed to know little about (Ross et al., 2016). However, it was not until

2002 when I started graduate school that I found out about CC. I had just read Austin and Irwin's (2002) *It's About Time: America's Imprisonment Binge* and was excited to talk about how much I enjoyed it. One of my professors told me about Irwin's role in starting the CC group at ASC and suggested I might find a place there. When I read Irwin's (1985) book on jails, his work spoke to me on a personal level. Despite our differences, his work was inspiring and filled my heart with hope.

I had spent a lot of time in jails. I learned a great deal from the way different jails operated and the folx who ended up there. At one point, I was in and out of a city jail so frequently that when I arrived the guards would often laugh and referring to the women's cellblock in the back of the jail, would tell me to show the other women who had been arrested the way to my house, simply because I had been there so often. Some swear that prison life is harder than being in jail. I disagree with this statement based on my own experiences. Jails are very chaotic and depressing, with more restrictions and less access to services. I believe that most people who have experienced both, if given a choice, would rather go to prison than a city or county jail, and a federal prison would be even better. I am not alone in these conclusions (Irwin, 1985; Tietjen, 2013).

I was excited when I was able to read research that reflected this reality, and I cannot explain how earth-shattering it was for me to find research, books, and articles by Convict Criminologists. Writing and conducting research was something I had dreamed about, and the thought that I could use my own experiences to inform my research and help others in the process warmed my heart in a special fuzzy kind of way. Finding Convict Criminologists, reading their research, presenting alongside the group at conferences, and having the mentorship and support of the group encouraged me and gave me hope to believe in possibilities for myself.

Convict Criminology helped me find space to be me and it gave me courage to believe that one day I could make a difference in the way we understand justice. Coming from where I had come from, I was used to surviving in the streets and personally dealing with the justice system, but I had little knowledge of higher education and what it would take to survive in this space. It can be tough and for some it may seem impossible. I was struggling as a single mother, carrying the label of ex-offender and system-involved youth, and I was just trying to find a place in academia where I might fit. I realized that my struggles with identity influenced my own perspective and academic research. Individual and social identity is influential in so many ways. I have found it interesting that, even as a group, CC has also struggled with identity issues. Identity and the language we use to describe it can be powerful. Even within CC, issues of identity are debated and represent different perspectives on labels and personal and social identification, as well as discussions of the implications for those who involve themselves with the group. I recently found out, while talking with the daughter of one of the movement's founders, that this conversation has been going on for the last twenty-five years.

Overall, I am left thinking about how diverse and different our members are, each of us in our own right. As a group, I see persistent determination to take things to a new level, as we bring with us different experiences, yet offer inclusion for all those who come to the table. As a group, we are always striving to build a bigger table for more folx to be able to sit. We have travelled different pathways to CC while carrying different layers of stigma attached to our own personal and social identities.

In her paper "Experience as Evidence", Joan Scott (1991) points out that for historical perspectives seeing is the origin of knowing and becomes evidence for the fact of difference. Central to the proposition of this current work is precisely the differences among our group. We are not all the same. Scott (1991, p. 778) notes:

> ...but the project of making experience visible precludes critical examination of the workings of the ideological system itself, its categories of representation (homosexual/heterosexual, man/woman, black/white as fixed immutable identities), its premises about what these categories mean and how they operate, and of its notions of subjects, origin, and cause.

This paper argues that the idea of intersectionality can help us center these discussions to facilitate critical examination of the criminal justice system. Utilizing a framework of intersectionality, this paper extends the discussion on personal and social identity, and its implications for the group of Convict Criminology. Engaging the reader in an exploration of a personal narrative provides the foundation for this paper, which weaves traditional research with reflections on my own personal experiences.

STANDING AT THE INTERSECTION

Criminal justice research is often rooted in discussions of differences across race, class, and gender. Kimberlé Crenshaw (1989) introduced the concept of intersectionality after finding applications of a single-axis framework for understanding race and gender discrimination contributed to increases in the marginalization of Black women. A single-axis framework, she argued, negated the importance of experiences – not just being Black and not just being a woman, but in being Black *and* being a woman. Examining the implications for intersectional research suggests that moving away from an additive approach can overcome research limitations that exist through dichotomous and either/or classifications (Cho et al., 2013; Collins, 1993; Hancock, 2007). This is particularly useful when examining issues of identity and access to higher education, including potential barriers and obstacles. As it is anti-essentialist, intersectionality recognizes that there is no one definition of what it means to be a woman or a man, to be Black or white, rich or poor, young or old. Within each of us, these identities represent variations that fall along various continuums (Witt, 1995).

Race, ethnicity, nationality, culture, ability, class, gender, sexuality, carceral status, and age all significantly, and differentially, impact social identification (Miller & Corbone-Lopez, 2015; Woodall, 2019). How individuals experience themselves and are responded to by others based on their categories of identity have both specific and cumulative effects. These characteristics all intertwine into narratives that impact people in different ways and across different experiences. Some people are impacted more by certain identities at different points in their life, while others experience stigmatized and marginalized identities quite differently at different times (Carbado, 2013; Wesely & Miller, 2018). It is imperative that the practical implications of policies and practices that either prevent or promote systematic harm be examined from an intersectional perspective to specify cumulative consequences and effects, within higher education generally and CC specifically.

Moreover, intersectionality extends the conversation to conceptualizations about how these characteristics impact people individually and collectively, both within groups and between groups. This lends significantly to answering questions about the impact of multiple marginalized identities (Crenshaw, 1991). Potter (2013) brought these discussions to the study of criminology, highlighting the significance of intersectional research.

Utilizing critical race theory and Black feminist thought, Potter argues that current explorations in the discipline that ignore intersectional theory can only provide limited utility for accurate research and effective policy (Potter, 2015). Warren-Gordon (2020) extended this conversation in her presidential address at the Midwestern Criminal Justice Association by urging us to consider the vitality of utilizing intersectional research in criminal justice and criminology to provide more opportunities for the inclusion of voices from marginalized populations. Over the past several years, scholars have used intersection to examine race, gender, and class issues in criminal justice and criminology, as well as rural criminology, juvenile justice, critical criminology theory, feminist drug research, and the potential impact for research in higher education, just to name a few (Carrington et al., 2014; Miller & Corbone-Lopez, 2015; Moore et al., 2018; Museus & Griffin, 2011; Paik, 2016; Veenstra, 2012).

While each of these identities are important, by themselves they can only provide an incomplete picture. It is through an intersectional lens that we begin to see the totality of individual identities, marginalized or not, and the resulting implications of a person's social location (Barak et al., 2018). In studying criminology, those who insist on dismissing the personal narratives of those with lived experiences and who choose to stay distant and detached in places of "neutrality", only further exacerbate the problem. Kathryn Henne and Emily Troshynski (2013) note that "the neutrality of criminological truth claims operates as another formation of violence that obscures marginalized and subaltern subjects. Its violence is cyclical and continually engrained through its disengaged disposition" (p. 466). The value of personal narratives, explored through an intersectional lens, bears witness to the experiences of those who represent multiple marginalized identities and their struggle to survive in academic settings, while supporting the validity of the impact of their experiences on the research they conduct.

METHOD

Offering personal narratives in the path to reflexivity is a common strategy in CC's approach to examining the influence of carceral experiences in guiding and analyzing criminal justice and criminology research. As Williams and colleagues (2014) note, "CC draws on real-life experiences of ex-cons working as professors, this form of critical criminology directly addresses othering and dehumanization that appears to be rampant, yet often unseen by those studying the U.S. criminal justice system" (p. 392). When examining research in general, we find that this is often a critically missing element from the field.

Autoethnography, involving both collaborative and reflexive research, can give voice to the researcher's lived experiences, the impact they have on research, and how these experiences shape the researcher's analysis (Reed-Danahay, 2017). Since it is focused specifically on identity, using an intersectional lens as part of this autoethnographic narrative on identity makes sense. As Esposito and Evans-Winters (2022, p. 4) note:

> …a singular analytical focus on one identity ignored and erased the multiple identities and lived realities of women of color and others who were impacted in multifarious ways by systematic inequality and thus were more vulnerable to structural violence. Intersectionality concerns itself with the multiple ways in which one's identity makes one simultaneously invisible and hypervisible.

I started by examining the intersection of my social and personal identities. I knew that based on race, gender, and class, my social identity impacted my experiences in meaningful ways, both inside and outside of academia. While my personal identity had been shaped by my social identity, my view from the intersection of these identities made me realize how influential this was in my experiences with both the justice system and higher education. While this exercise in reflexivity may have sought answers for myself, I also believe this analysis demonstrates the importance of intersectionality to support folx coming into the academy from marginalized populations, to bear witness to the barriers they face and to give hope to others as they gather strength to tell their own stories. I know from experience that this is no easy task.

As researchers, it is important to realize how our own personal and social identities affect the ways we engage in academia, the questions we ask, and the ones we do not (Esposito & Evans-Winters, 2022; Potter, 2015). I share my own story to illustrate how race, class, gender, education, and carceral status shaped my lived experience, including my access to and encounters with higher education. Using an intersectional perspective allows for an examination of the impact of different aspects of identity and experiences with marginalization that create barriers to higher education, while allowing for opportunities to extend conversations on overcoming barriers and providing space for our field to become more diverse.

Race, Gender, Class, Education and the Juvenile Justice System – The Impact of Intersection

For me, some aspects of identity are inextricably tied to the way I have been perceived by others in a variety of contexts. Being young, white, and female ensured that I would be targeted in the streets, yet coming from poorer neighborhoods gave me an advantage in navigating my way around them. The first time I got locked up, kids that knew me from the neighborhood were there and they vouched for me. This helped ease my transition into the system. Yet, as a teenager and young adult, I found that the injustice of the system at times could be buffered by my complexion, my age, and my femininity.

At other times, it was a completely different experience. I was still young when I began to believe that the criminal justice system was the biggest set-up of all. From my vantage point, the streets merely fueled an economy that was built on poverty and a carceral system of injustice, taking human bodies and pushing them into jails and prisons like coal being shoveled into a blazing inferno. Except these bodies represented human lives – the lived experiences of men, women, and children who found themselves on the wrong side of the law.

Racial Identity and Culture

One of the first things that stood out to me when I came to Convict Criminology was its lack of racial diversity. When studying the criminal justice system, issues of racial disparities always show up. The overrepresentation of Black folx in the system is evident; in 2014, there were 6.8 million people overall in the correctional population, and over one-third of those individuals identified as African American or Black (NAACP, 2021a). In addition, a recent paper examining disparities in higher education finds that differences in access, completion, and future earnings persist for African Americans and Latinos (Carnevale & Strohl, 2013). I was not blind to the fact that throughout my college career, young Black men, in particular, were absent from my classes.

I have been analyzing racial issues as far back as I can remember. I grew up in a diverse home, surrounded by people from different ethnicities and different cultures. Issues of race have always dominated American society, and growing up in different interracial and diverse households gave me a first-hand view of hate and prejudice. By the time I started kindergarten, I began to realize that some people could not or would not like you solely based on the color of your skin. Racial issues were never a secret with my family and I remember the tough lessons I learned about how some people would treat me different simply because of who my mother loved.

Over the years, my racial identity has been continually questioned, my whiteness continually challenged. Grier and colleagues (2014) suggest that individuals who present as racially ambiguous do not afford others the opportunity to easily categorize them, leading to additional discriminatory practices. I have had boyfriends who did not know I was white until a conversation about race came up. For years my own children did not believe that I was "really" white, until they met my biological father. I have been cussed out when telling some folx that I was white and have had people argue with me about my own ethnicity. Since joining the academic environment, this has not gotten any easier for me. I have been told I was "nothing but a convict", an anomaly that people cannot figure out. I have been asked if I am a "wigger"[1] and I have heard that I "might be just a little too ghetto".

Recently, I have been told that I need to address my whiteness and the privilege that comes with it. Based on my lived experiences, this is not always easy. Yet, I understand the impetus for those who suggest it. As Potter (2015) points out, criminologists should examine how being white influences their experiences compared with those of other races. I have always analyzed, for my own understanding, differences in how people are treated in different places, based on identity. This is another reason that intersectionality makes so much sense to me, because in analyzing these experiences and watching others has allowed me to see that no one has the upper hand all of the time, but based on race, class, gender, age and sexuality, as well as other personal characteristics, some people do better in certain situations than others.

After all of these years, it has gotten harder for me to describe my own racial identity and to discuss the implications and experiences of being me, both positive and negative. I usually do not self-describe on questionnaires. For instance, I usually mark "other". In all honesty, I have never felt that I belonged to any racial group, feeling more like I was caught somewhere in the middle. Maybe my experience with identity and race are somewhat unique. Race defines so much of what we see happening in this world, and the criminal and juvenile justice systems are no exception. I have experienced the consequences of race on both sides of the coin, both positive and negative, and while racial issues surely impacted my life growing up, within the intersection of gender, age, and race, I found both burden and blessing.

Becoming a Woman

More women are locked up today than ever before. Recent reports show that women's incarceration rates in the US have continued to increase and have now reached a rate eight times higher than it was in 1980, an increase of over 700% (Kajstura & Immarigeon, 2018). Data from 2019 indicates that there were nearly a quarter of a million girls and women incarcerated in US jails and prisons (Kajstura, 2019). Research shows that nearly one in eight individuals released from prison and one in six jail releases in the US each year are women. This data reflects the fact that almost two million women are released annually from jails and prisons, and yet the availability of resources and programs focused on reentry for women is largely inadequate (Sawyer, 2019). Research on gendered pathways to crime consistently finds that women in prison have often been subjected to high levels of interpersonal violence in multiple forms, including physical, sexual, and mental abuse, in both childhood and adulthood (Fuentas, 2013). Reported abuse is a significant predictor for high levels of trauma among incarcerated girls and women (Mollard & Hudson, 2016). Women in jails are more likely to present with significant levels of anxiety, personality disorders, serious mental illness, and PTSD (Dehart et al., 2009; Drapalski et al., 2009; Green et al., 2016).

For me, my experience of gender is entwined with becoming a mother. I was in love with my daughter before she was even born, but I almost lost the opportunity to parent her. I had gotten in some trouble years before and, after going through pre-sentencing, I was told that I was going to be sentenced to prison. After breaking my ankle while out on bond and having surgery twice, my mother came to visit me. While I was still heavily medicated, she decided to take me back home. I left town before my court hearing, which meant that soon I had a warrant listed in the national database.

When I finally got caught and went to jail, I was almost three months pregnant. Everyone, including my lawyers, told me that I should plan on having someone come get my baby when she was born and that, if I did not, my baby would be placed into the child protective system (CPS). I knew this to be true from seeing the experience of other girls – jails separate 2.3 million mothers from their children each year (Sawyer & Bertram, 2013). I could not imagine the pain that this would cause me.

I ended up staying in jail for a large part of my pregnancy, and I was worried. I had heard horrific stories of the risks involved with being pregnant while locked up such as mothers left to suffer in cells during labor while waiting on transport to the hospital. I was not allowed to leave my cell during my pregnancy. I was denied both extra food and any exercise. I spent over six months sleeping on a thin mat on the floor. Unfortunately, studies continue to show that prisons and jails neglect the needs of pregnant women in their facilities (Daniel, 2019).

I prayed the whole time I was in there, locked up and pregnant, and stretched my faith like never before as I hoped for transformation in my life. By grace and mercy, I was released in time to prepare to have my baby girl. This changed me into a better person and, although I would still struggle in the process, this experience put me on a path to personal redemption. So, my identity as a woman, particularly becoming a new mother, motivated me to seek help through my faith. By then, I desperately wanted to change my life and be a better person for my baby. The study of love has been limited in the field of criminal justice. Rusu (2017) argued that there has been a "cold indifference" to the study of love in the inclusion of social research. I am convinced this is a mistake. I argue that love changes people. Perhaps this stems from my experiences as a woman and as a mother, but I do not believe my thoughts are unique. We know that relationships and the emotional ties of love can have a significant impact on our lives, and a primary source of this love we often find embedded within our familial relationships. Those who felt family was lacking to fulfill these needs in childhood often look forward to having children and starting their own family.

Juvenile Justice and System-Involved Youth

Even as incarceration rates slow in the US, mass incarceration practices have ensured the highest incarceration rates of any country. Comparative data shows that the US has nearly six times as many adolescents and young adults incarcerated in secure facilities as Australia, Canada, the UK, Germany, and Finland combined (Sickmund et al., 2017). On an average day in the US, almost 50,000 youth are confined in juvenile justice facilities, while another 7,500 youth are sitting in adult jails and prisons (Sawyer, 2019). African

American and Latino youth are disproportionally overrepresented in the juvenile justice system (Hockenberry et al., 2016).

It is well established that system-involved youth, both male and female, present with higher levels of trauma, neglect, and abuse compared to their peers (Siegel & Welsh, 2018). The juvenile justice system further exacerbates harm among youth through various practices and policies meant to punish and control them instead of offering healing and transformation. The physical, mental, and emotional trauma experienced by those in the system becomes evident if you pay attention. They say you do not need any studies to see these facts, because if you look closely, it is there…in their faces…you can see it in their eyes (Leyva and Bickel, 2010).

The experiences of system-involved youth significantly decrease the likelihood that they will transition into higher education, while also increasing the likelihood that they will transition into prison and jails. Nearly 70% of people incarcerated in state and federal prisons do not have a high school diploma. Research continually finds that one of the biggest impediments to higher education is prior experiences with incarceration (Suitts et al., 2014). Juveniles and young adults who have spent significant time during adolescence engaged with the system are most likely to suffer consequential trauma, and these youth become the least likely to effectively overcome the obstacles as they move through life (Youth.gov, n.d.). In addition, while protective factors can mitigate negative experiences in the system (e.g. positive relationships with parents, prosocial role models, stable housing, and access to quality education and employment opportunities), system-involved youth are less likely to have this support (Dannerbeck & Yan, 2011).

Experiencing incarceration often holds individuals back from educational opportunities, making it almost impossible for those folx to obtain the credentials they need to successfully integrate into society once they are released from prison (Couloute, 2018). When I got out of juvenile detention at fifteen years old, I tried going back to high school. Not only did I not fit in, but I was told because of my lack of proper education while in juvenile facilities, I did not have the necessary credits and would not be able to graduate until I was at least 21-years-old. After I turned 16, I was encouraged to take the GED and I thought that was a good idea. I tried to go to a community college, but I had spent years entangled in the juvenile justice system and I was still living the street life. From the time I was 13-years-old into my early twenties, I dealt with many different challenges.

I had become a mother, and yet I still struggled to break free of the system and the street life that I knew while working on getting my life straight. That is what I was doing when I enrolled in college courses the second time. I had already been doing work in the community and had even helped with the development of a transitional living house for women with children. Yet, I knew that I needed additional education. One day I found my way to the community college that was across the street from where I was working at the time. Maruna (2001) points out that individuals who have been incarcerated, and who have acknowledged creating harm through a deviant lifestyle, often feel the need to "make good", that is to use those experiences to share a transformed life with others, helping them avoid the same pitfalls. In the streets I often thought about how one day, when I got free from that life, I would use my experiences to make a difference in my community.

For many people – both men and women, youth and adults alike – coming out of the system and seeking changes in their life, faith helps them find a path to freedom and transformation (Irwin, 1985; Leyva & Bickel, 2010). Sometimes that may be all they have left. I know that was true for me, and at the end of the day I found out how much I needed that faith for my own journey. Without faith, I am sure I would not be here today.

Education and Opportunity – Class
Class, race, gender, and age differentially shape these struggles for youth already involved in the system. The accumulation of disadvantage can often be overwhelming. Every struggle increases the necessity of focusing on survival. Surviving homes, surviving the streets, and surviving the system, young people are just trying to make it another day, alive and free. Many juveniles going through the system, especially girls, are often guilty of having committed survival crimes (Sickmund et al., 2008). In the juvenile justice system, it is easy to see that most kids come from poorer neighborhoods and households, an exception being more serious criminal cases. Growing up, my family was poor and that was an identity I carried. I knew this affected how some people saw us, but I also knew I wanted something different, something more. I was sure education could help.

Yet, I was not so sure about my chances of success anywhere, much less in educational settings. Higher education can often seem like a luxury, an elusive dream. One study found that the probability of formerly incarcerated kids even applying to college was significantly lower compared to their peers (Kirk & Sampson, 2013). Education can be key in helping folx desist from a criminal lifestyle and overcome obstacles on a trajectory toward a healthy and productive life, and research has shown the value of education and its correlation with positive life outcomes, including employment and relationship opportunities. We also know that not everyone has the same access to education and growing up in poverty decreases the quality of one's education, especially for marginalized populations. The majority of the correctional population in the United States has not completed high school or obtained a GED, with incarcerated women slightly less likely to have these certifications, and minorities less likely to have graduated from high school or with their GED compared with whites (Harlow, 2003).

DISCUSSION

Growing up, I felt stigma attached to my identity at every turn. Whether it was race and culture, gender, class, or my experiences in foster care and the justice system, I continually felt the shame, stigma, and repercussions of a multiply marginalized identity. While I wanted to be able to talk about those experiences and to be free of the shame that stigmatized identities bring, I found that it was not that easy. My life had been significantly different from the lives of the people I sat next to in my classes.

I wanted to be honest and open about how my experiences influenced my perspective, but in academic settings – first as a student and then as a professor – I was often told that I should not share my experiences. Yet, I always believed that it was necessary to talk about my reality to help others who were on the path. Sometimes, though, it was easier to hide, to avoid the judgements that you know will quickly come once you come out as a Convict Criminologist. There is often not a lot of support for Convict Criminologists in the academy, and members of our group are not always welcomed into spaces dominated by traditional criminologists (DCC, 2021; Richards & Ross, 2013; Tietjen, 2013). It is no surprise that many members, while supporting and encouraging those who have "come out", choose to remain anonymous and to hide their real identities to avoid the very real personal and professional repercussions that almost certainly will come (Richards & Ross, 2001). These repercussions can impede everything from educational and research opportunities, inclusion on grant work and service projects, and prospective job opportunities and avenues for advancement.

Individuals coming out of the system deal with different multiply marginalized identities, and battle various struggles and situations while working to overcome traumatized and disrupted backgrounds. This often makes it so much harder to even make it to academic spaces in the first place (Custer et al., 2020), especially in graduate education. Because of these obstacles, it is imperative that mainstream criminologists who do have a voice in the academy use it to advocate not just for students, but for their fellow colleagues who are looking for the safety and security they need to "come out" and be honest about their own experiences with the justice system (Ross et al., 2011). As long as people like me are encouraged to keep our pasts hidden, as long as we are forced to conceal our personal identities to avoid negative consequences for our academic career, the less likely we will succeed in the attempt to bring more diverse voices to the table. Intersectional approaches to reflexivity in research can only broaden an understanding of the lived experiences of justice-impacted scholars.

Members of CC have spent considerable time and energy reaching out to those who have expressed interest in the group, and have provided a space and place for people like me and folx who have come out of the system, as juveniles and adults, from jails and prisons, presenting with diverse racial identities, gender identities, those who identify as LBGTQ, as well as those who do not wish to identify at all. This group continues to provide space for all of our allies who have loved ones, family and friends directly impacted by the justice system, and without them we would not be complete (Ross et al., 2016).

CONCLUSION

I realized at the intersection of personal and social identity that the stigma of being justice-involved was my greatest challenge and becoming an academic was my greatest achievement (aside from being a parent). While many colleges and universities continue to suffer from an overall lack of diversity, few criminal justice faculty members and/or administrators are willing to engage in the serious business of advocating for those from marginalized populations, especially when it comes to recruiting and supporting those who are formerly incarcerated or system-involved. Examining autoethnographic studies focused on reflexivity from an intersectional perspective can help address the impact on those experiencing multiply marginalized identities, while identifying pathways to overcoming barriers in higher education for FI and justice-impacted students.

I will admit that when I first got to graduate school and to Convict Criminology, I was scared to come out. It was an experience at the 2013 ASC conference that fundamentally changed the conversation for me. Victor Rios, a well-known scholar who writes about his gang experience as a juvenile, was at the conference. His work is inspiring for me, particularly his book *Punished: Policing the Lives of Black and Latino Boys* (Rios, 2011). When he caught my attention and walked over to where I was standing with a friend, I was eager to speak with him. Yet he had come to me with a question, and I was not sure I had an answer. He leaned over to tell me that he had noticed my jailhouse tattoo. Recognizing that I was with the Convict Criminology group, he had brought a young female student over with him and explained that she had been asking where the women in the group were.

As this young lady looked to me for answers, I realized two things. One, that the tattoo I got when I was 13-years-old might always be a giveaway about my past to those who knew about such things. While studies show that jail and prison tattoos can signal an experience that is laden with stigma, the renaissance in tattoo art has somewhat diminished the risk and the taboo of having ink, but a jailhouse tattoo is always recognizable by those with insider knowledge (Earle, 2018). Second, and more importantly, this was a defining moment for me. Over the years, I have realized how important it is for people to have space to talk about who they are, to express the truth about their unique identities and experiences, and the influence it has on their teaching and research, and to be able to do so without the fear of stigma and repercussions in the workplace. For me, I have found that as much as I might try, I could never really hide who I was and that, in reality, I should never even want to. Those experiences ensured that I would be able to encourage others, whether they were headed to higher education or involved in other pursuits, engaging their energy towards building a positive and successful life. That is all I ever really wanted. This is my way of making good.

ENDNOTES

[1]   This term appends the "w" in "white" to a derogatory term for Black people.

REFERENCES

Austin, James & John Irwin (2002) *It's About Time: America's Imprisonment Binge*, Belmont (CA): Wadsworth.

Barak, Gregg, Paul Leighton, & Allison M. Cotton (2018) *Class, Race, Gender, and Crime: The Social Realities of Justice in America*, London: Rowman & Littlefield.

Belknap, Joanne (2015) "The 2014 American Society of Criminology Presidential Address: Activist Criminology: Criminologists' Responsibility to Advocate for Social and Legal Justice", *Criminology*, 53(1): 1-22.

Carbado, Devin W. (2013) "Intersectionality: Theorizing Power, Empowering Theory", *Journal of Women in Culture and Society*, 38(4): 811-845.

Carnevale, Anthony P. & Jeff Strohl (2013) "How Higher Education Reinforces the Intergenerational Reproduction of White Racial Privilege", *Separate and Unequal* – July 30.

Carrington, Kerry, Joseph F. Donnermeyer & Walter S. DeKeseredy (2014) "Intersectionality, Rural Criminology, and Re-imaging the Boundaries of Critical Criminology", *Critical Criminology*, 22: 463-477.

Cho, Sumi, Kimberlé Williams Crenshaw & Leslie McCall (2013) "Toward a Field of Intersectionality Studies: Theory, Applications, and Praxis", *Signs: Journal of Women in Culture and Society*, 38(4): 785–810.

Collins, Patricia Hill (1993) "Toward a New Vision: Race, Class, and Gender as Categories of Analysis and Connection", *Race, Sex & Class*, 1(1): 25-45.

Collins, Patricia Hill (1989) "The Social Construction of Black Feminist Thought", *Signs: Journal of Women in Culture and Society*, 14(4): 745-773.

Copenhaver, Anna, Tina L. Edwards-Willey & Brian T. Byers (2007) "Journeys in Social Stigma: The Lives of Formerly Incarcerated Felons in Higher Education", *Journal of Correctional Education*, 58(3): 268-283.

Couloute, Lucius (2018) "Getting Back on Course: Educational Exclusion and Attainment among Formerly Incarcerated People", *Prison Policy Initiative* – October. Retrieved from https://www.prisonpolicy.org/reports/education.html

Crenshaw, Kimberlé (1991) "Mapping the Margins: Intersectionality, Identity Politics, and Violence against Women of Color", *Stanford Law Review*, 43(6): 1241-1299.

Crenshaw, Kimberlé (1989) "Demarginalizing the Intersection of Race and Sex: A Black Feminist Critique of Antidiscrimination Doctrine, Feminist Theory and Antiracist Politics", *University of Chicago Legal Forum,* 1: 139-167.

Custer, Bradley D., Michelle L. Malkin, & Gina Castillo (2020) "Criminal Justice System-Impacted Faculty: Motivations, Barriers, and Successes on the Academic Job Market", *Journal of Education Human Resources*, 38(2): 336-364.

Daniel, Roxanne (2019) "Prisons Neglect Pregnant Women in their Healthcare Policies", *Prison Policy Initiative* – December 5. Retrieved from https://www.prisonpolicy.org/blog/2019/12/05/pregnancy/

Dannerbeck, Anne & Jiahui Yan (2011) "Missouri's Crossover Youth: Examining the Relationship between their Maltreatment History and their Risk of Violence", *Journal of Juvenile Justice*, 1(1): 78-98.

DeHart, Dana, Shannon Lynch, Joanne Belknap, Priscilla Dass-Brailsford & Bonnie Green (2013) "Life History Models of Female Offending: The Roles of Serious

Mental Illness and Trauma in Women's Pathways to Jail", *Psychology of Women Quarterly*, 38(1): 138-151.

Division of Convict Criminology (2021) "Home", *American Society of Criminology.* Retrieved from https://concrim.org/

Drapalski, Amy L., Kerstin Youman, Jeff Stuewig & June Tangney (2009) "Gender Differences in Jail Inmates' Symptoms of Mental Illness, Treatment History and Treatment Seeking", *Criminal Behaviour and Mental Health*, 19(3): 193-206.

Earle, Rod (2017) *Convict Criminology: Inside and Out*, Bristol: Policy Press.

Esposito, Jennifer & Venus Evans-Winters (2022) *Introduction to Intersectional Qualitative Research*, New York: Sage Publishing.

Frana, John F., Michael Lenza & Ryan D. Schroeder (2012) "Convict Criminologists in the Classroom", *Journal of Prisoners on Prisons*, 21(1&2): 35-47.

Fuentas, Catherine Mitchell (2013) "Nobody's Child: The Role of Trauma and Interpersonal Violence in Women's Pathways to Incarceration and Resultant Service Needs", *Medical Anthropology Quarterly*, 28(1): 85-104.

Green, Bonnie L., Priscilla Dass-Brailsford, Alejandra Hurtado de Mendoza, Mihriye Mete, Shannon M. Lynch, Dana DeHart & Joanne Belknap (2016) "Trauma Experiences and Mental Health Among Incarcerated Women", *Psychological Trauma: Theory, Research, Practice, and Policy*, 8(4): 455-463.

Grier, Tiffanie, Carol Rambo & Marshall A. Taylor (2014) "'What are you?': Racial Ambiguity, Stigma, and the Racial Formation Project", *Deviant Behavior*, 35(12): 1006-1022.

Hancock, Ange-Marie (2007) "When Multiplication Doesn't Equal Quick Addition: Examining Intersectionality as a Research Paradigm", *Perspectives on Politics*, 5(1): 63-79.

Harlow, Caroline Wolf (2003) "Education and Correctional Populations", Washington (DC): Bureau of Justice Statistics – January. Retrieved from: https://bjs.ojp.gov/library/publications/education-and-correctional-populations

Henne, Kathryn & Emily Troshynski (2013) "Mapping the Margins of Intersectionality: Criminological Possibilities in a Transnational World", *Theoretical Criminology*, 17(4): 455-473.

Hockenberry, Sarah, Andrew Wachter & Anthony Sladky (2016) "Juvenile Residential Facility Census, 2014: Selected Findings", Washington (DC): Office of Juvenile Justice and Delinquency Prevention, US Department of Justice. Retrieved from https://www.ojjdp.gov/pubs/250123.pdf

Irwin, John (2005) *The Warehouse Prison: Disposal of the New Dangerous Class*, Los Angeles: Roxbury.

Irwin, John (1985) *The Jail: Managing the Underclass in American Society*, Berkeley: University of California Press.

Kajstura, Aleks (2019) "Women's Mass Incarceration: The Whole Pie 2019", *The Prison Policy Initiative*. Retrieved from https://www.prisonpolicy.org/reports/pie2019women.html

Kajstura, Aleks & Russ Immarigeon (2018) "States of Women's Incarceration: The Global Context 2018", *The Prison Policy Initiative*. Retrieved from: https://www.prisonpolicy.org/global/women/

Kirk, David S. & Robert J. Sampson (2013) "Juvenile Arrest and Collateral Educational Damage in the Transition to Adulthood", *Sociology of Education*, 86(1): 36-62.

Kreager, Derek A., Ross L. Matsueda & Elena A. Erosheva (2010) "Motherhood and Criminal Desistance in Disadvantaged Neighborhoods", *Criminology*, 48(1): 221-258.

Leyva, Martin & Christopher Bickel (2010) "From Corrections to College: The Value of a Convict's Voice", *Western Criminology Review*, 11(1): 50-60.

Maruna, Shadd (2001) *Making Good: How Ex-Convicts Reform and Rebuild Their Lives*, Washington (DC): American Psychological Association.

Miller, Jody & Kristin Carbone-Lopez (2015) "Beyond 'Doing Gender': Incorporating Race, Class, Place, and Life Transitions into Feminist Drug Research", *Substance Use and Misuse*, 50(6): 693-707.

Mollard, Elizabeth & Diane Brage Hudson (2016) "Nurse-Led Trauma-Informed Correctional Care for Women", *Perspectives in Psychiatric Care*, 52(3): 224-230.

Monazzam, Niki & Kristen M. Budd (2022) *Incarcerated Women and Girls*, New York: The Sentencing Project. Retrieved from https://www.sentencingproject.org/publications/incarcerated-women-and-girls/

Moore, Kelly E., Katherine C. Milam, Johanna B. Folk & June P. Tangney (2018) "Self-stigma among Criminal Offenders: Risk and Protective Factors", *Stigma and Health*, 3(3): 241-252.

Museus, Samuel D. & Kimberly A. Griffin (2011) "Mapping the Margins in Higher Education: On the Promise of Intersectionality Frameworks in Research and Discourse", *New Directions for Institutional Research*, 151: 5-13.

NAACP (2021a) *Criminal Justice Fact Sheet*. Retrieved from https://naacp.org/resources/criminal-justice-fact-sheet

NAACP (2021b) *Fair Chance Hiring Fact Sheet*. Retrieved from https://naacp.org/resources/fair-chance-hiring-fact-sheet

Paik, Leslie (2017) "Critical Perspectives on Intersectionality and Criminology: Introduction", *Theoretical Criminology*, 21(1): 4-10.

Potter, Hillary (2015) *Intersectionality and Criminology: Disrupting and Revolutionizing Studies of Crime*, London: Routledge.

Potter, Hillary (2013) "Intersectional Criminology: Interrogating Identity and Power in Criminological Research and Theory", *Critical Criminology*, 2(3): 305-318.

Reed-Danahay, Deborah (2017) "Bourdieu and Critical Autoethnography: Implications for Research, Writing, and Teaching", *International Journal of Multicultural Education*, 19(1): 144-154.

Richards, Stephen C. and Jeffrey Ian Ross (2001) "Introducing the New School of Convict Criminology", *Social Justice*, 28(1): 177-190.

Rios, Victor M. (2011) *Punished: Policing the Lives of Black and Latino Boys*, New York: NYU Press.

Ross, Jeffrey Ian, and Stephen C. Richards (2003) "What Is the New School of Convict Criminology?", in Jeffrey Ian Ross and Stephen C. Richards (eds.), *Convict Criminology*, Belmont (CA): Wadsworth, pp. 1-13.

Ross, Jeffrey Ian, Stephen C. Richards, Greg Newbold, Richard S. Jones, Michael Lenza, Daniel S. Murphy, Richard Hogan & G. David Curry (2011) "Knocking on the Ivory Tower's Door: The Experience of Ex-Convicts Applying for Tenure-Track University Positions", *Journal of Criminal Justice Education*, 22(2): 267-285.

Ross, Jeffrey Ian, Richard S. Jones, Mike Lenza & Stephen C. Richards (2016) "Convict Criminology and the Struggle for Inclusion", *Critical Criminology*, 24(4): 489-501.

Rusu, Mihai Stelian (2017) "Theorising Love in Sociological Thought: Classical Contributions to a Sociology of Love", *Journal of Classical Sociology*, 18(1): 3-20.

Sawyer, Wendy (2019a) "Who's Helping the 1.9 Million Women Released from Prisons and Jails Each Year?", *Prison Policy Initiative*. Retrieved from https://www.prisonpolicy.org/blog/2019/07/19/reentry/

Sawyer, Wendy (2019b) "Youth Confinement: The Whole Pie 2019", *Prison Policy Initiative*. Retrieved from https://www.prisonpolicy.org/reports/youth2019.html

Sawyer, Wendy & Wanda Bertram (2018) "Jail Will Separate 2.3 Million Mothers from their Children This Year", *Prison Policy Initiative*. Retrieved from: https://www.prisonpolicy.org/blog/2018/05/13/mothers-day-2018/

Scott, Joan W. (1991) "Experience as Evidence", *Critical Inquiry*, 17(4): 773-797.

Sickmund, Melissa, T.J. Sladky, Wei Kang & Charles Puzzanchera (2019) *Easy Access to the Census of Juveniles in Residential Placement*, Washington (DC): Office of Juvenile Justice and Delinquency Prevention. Retrieved from http://www.ojjdp.gov/ojstatbb/ezacjrp/

Siegel, Larry J. & Brandon C. Welsh (2018) *Juvenile Delinquency: Theory, Practice, and Law*, Boston: Cengage Learning.

Suitts, Steeve, Katherine Dunn & Nasheed Sabree (2014) *Just Learning: The Imperative to Transform Juvenile Justice Systems into Effective Educational Systems: A Study of Juvenile Justice Schools in the South and the Nation*, Atlanta: Southern Education Foundation.

Tietjen, Grant (2019) "Convict Criminology: Learning from the Past, Confronting the Present, Expanding for the Future", *Critical Criminology*, 27: 101-114.

Tietjen, Grant (2013) "The Inside's Influence on the Outside", *Journal of Prisoners on Prisons*, 22(2): 76-99.

Veenstra, Gerry (2012) "The Gendered Nature of Discriminatory Experiences by Race, Class, and Sexuality: A Comparison of Intersectionality Theory and the Subordinate Male Target Hypothesis", *Sex Roles*, 68(11-12): 646-659.

Warren-Gordon, Kiesha (2020) "Presidential Address: Examining Criminal Justice and Criminology through the Lens of Intersectionality", *Journal of Crime and Justice*, 43(4): 409-413.

Wesely, Jennifer K. & J. Mitchell Miller (2017) "Justice System Bias Perceptions of the Dually Marginalized: Observations from a Sample of Women Ex-Offenders", *Victims & Offenders*, 13(4): 451-470.

Williams, D. J., Debra Bischoff, Teresa Casey & James Burnett (2014) "'Mom, They Are Going to Kill My Dad!' A Personal Narrative on Capital Punishment from a Convict Criminology Perspective", *Critical Criminology*, 22(3): 389-401.

Witt, Charlotte (1995) "Anti-Essentialism in Feminist Theory", *Philosophical Topics*, 23(2): 321-344.

Woodall, Denise (2019) "We Are all Criminals: The Abolitionist Potential of Remembering", *Social Justice*, 45(4): 117-140.

Youth.gov (n.d.) *Youth Involved with the Juvenile Justice System*. Retrieved from: https://youth.gov/youth-topics/juvenile-justice/youth-involved-juvenile-justice-system

ABOUT THE AUTHOR

Dr. J. Renee Trombley is an Assistant Professor in Criminal Justice and Criminology at Metropolitan State University – Denver, where she also serves as a Faculty Fellow and is currently developing the Justice Impacted Scholars Alliance. Dr. Trombley is dedicated to building opportunities in higher education for justice impacted folx, both in the community and in prisons and jails. Her research interests include restorative justice, peacemaking criminology, convict criminology, violence and victimization among youth, and juvenile justice and delinquency, as well as the use of qualitative methods in academic research. Dr. Trombley has spent time writing, publishing, and presenting on issues related to trauma among youth, juvenile justice and schools, restorative justice and reentry, restorative justice in higher education, and convict criminology and identity.

Beyond the Ivory Tower:
The Need for Collective Activism in Convict Criminology
Jennifer Ortiz

ABSTRACT

In this essay, I argue that the Division of Convict Criminology must reject the academic status quo by engaging in collective activism. Academia convinces scholars that the primary goal of their work is individual accolades with little regard for creating substantive change in the world. In doing so, academia exploits marginalized populations, like convicts, by pillaging data while offering little meaningful assistance to marginalized groups. As Convict Criminology continues to expand its reach within academia, we have a duty to reject the academic status quo by adopting the scholarvist model that advocates for scholarship coupled with activism. It is our responsibility to combat the structural violence inherent in both academia and the criminal injustice system. This essay is a call for collective activism that targets the foundations of oppressive social institutions. The time has come for us to move beyond public statements and towards policy change that creates a more equitable society for current and future convicts.

> "The sooner we create our vision of all we desire, set our intention to implement it together, and put our individual capacities into collective action, the greater our chances of success".
>
> – Elisabet Sahtouris (2006, p. 41)

INTRODUCTION

The above quote from renowned biologist Dr. Elisabet Sahtouris effectively summarizes the main argument of this essay. I posit that there is a need for collective activism within American Convict Criminology with a specific focus on the newly developed Division of Convict Criminology (DCC) of the American Society of Criminology (ASC). In 2020, Convict Criminology (CC) in the United States became a formally recognized division of ASC. In doing so, the board members and the founding members of the collective previously known as Convict Criminology sought to establish a space to support and uplift convict scholars and other justice-impacted scholars.[1] The development of DCC was the first step in creating a more equitable and accepting academic space for scholars with direct criminal justice experience. However, it cannot be the last step. In this essay, I issue a call to action to all members and supporters of DCC. I posit that there is dire need to engage in collective activism.

Although many members of DCC are in the trenches fighting for the rights of marginalized persons, individual efforts are insufficient to create substantive change at the institutional and structural-level. Collective activism, rather than individual efforts, is required to break the chains that bind convicts to oppressive institutions. DCC must avoid becoming another complacent division that focuses on individual-level academic accolades. The Division must actively strive to demand and implement necessary changes so that future convict-scholars and justice-impacted scholars do not face the same discrimination experienced by the founding members of Convict Criminology in the United States.

ACADEMIC STATUS QUO

Academia trains us to become obedient to the publish or perish model that measures a scholar's value by the number of publications they have in top-tier journals (Vossen, 2017), rather than the impact they have on knowledge or humanity (Ortiz, 2021). Academia also teaches us to strive for academic accolades, including professional awards. However, top academic accolades are largely given to positivist, quantitative research because top-tier journals in criminology rarely publish qualitative or critical research (Copes et al., 2015; Tewksbury et al., 2010). Academics are also beholden to government grants to fund their research, which limits the use of critical theoretical or methodological frameworks in proposed studies (Ortiz, 2021). Thus, in striving to win academic accolades, the field pushes scholars away from critical research that critiques systems of oppression and towards research that perpetuates the status-quo in society. Adherence to this academic status quo is problematic for many reasons.

While publishing in top-tier journals and obtaining research grants ensures that we individually have illustrious and successful careers in criminology, we must acknowledge that these goals are largely meaningless in the fight for social justice. The reality is that most of our published works are never read by the stakeholders that have the power to create change both in academia and the world beyond the ivory tower. Our publications are individual achievements that distract us from the tireless work of developing a more inclusive world for marginalized people and scholars. The year 2020 is a prime example of how academic scholarship rarely translates to social change.

In 2020, following the brutal murders of George Floyd, Ahmaud Arbery, and Breonna Taylor we witnessed large scale performative allyship from institutions and individual scholars. Between March and August 2020, nearly every university and corporation in the United States issued public statements regarding the Black Lives Matter movement and the need to honor diversity. These public statements were not heartfelt commitments to combat structural issues, but rather served to assuage academic and corporate guilt without creating any real substantive change. Based on the return to silence on the part of most academic institutions, it appears they may believe that they solved racism with their public statements and life can return to normal in 2022. The status quo remains intact and marginalized people continue to be oppressed. Nothing has changed except the news cycle. If 2020 taught us anything, it should be that we need to reject the social and academic status quos. This is the call I issue to the Division of Convict Criminology.

REJECTING THE STATUS QUO

As a newly formed division of ASC and a division comprised of convict and justice-impacted scholars who experience marginalization both within and outside of the Ivory Tower, it behooves us to not only reject but directly challenge the academic status quo. We must engage in a deeper conversation that grapples with several moral questions. Why did we become a division? Was it to carve out a "new" space that demands conformity to the academic status quo? Or did we aim to challenge and disrupt the institutions that oppress us? The answers to these questions are imperative for determining how we move forward as a division. How are we going to be different from other divisions? How are we going to avoid becoming part of the problem?

The first step for DCC should be the development of clear goals for the next dime (Jones, et al., 2009). Current DCC members must begin to envision the legacy of the New School of Convict Criminology (Richards, 2013). We must take an inventory of our division and begin to develop initiatives to achieve our goals. Of primary importance to the DCC should be increasing and supporting diversity within our division. The academy has historically been an elitist institution that actively sought to exclude people of color, women, LGBTQ+ individuals, and convicts (Boustani & Taylor, 2020; Kennelly et al., 1999; Pierce et al., 2014). The DCC must actively engage with methods of combating that exclusion. The founders of DCC have expressed their commitment to this endeavor. One need only look at the diversity of the inaugural board to see that commitment in action (Convict Criminology, 2020). Moreover, when the board debated how much to charge for membership dues, we decided that justice-impacted students should not take on additional financial burdens. Thus, student membership in DCC is free to all current students (American Society of Criminology, 2020). This inclusionary practice directly rejects the notion that divisions should remain focused on fundraising. As the DCC continues to progress and develop, we must remain committed to active inclusion for all persons. We should expand our initiatives to ensure not just diversity but equity in our division.

When I envision the future of DCC, I see a division that offers scholarships to convict scholars whose criminal records render them ineligible for other scholarships. I also envision a Convict Criminology journal where the works of convict and system-impacted scholars from undergraduates to full professors are not only published, but are made freely available to the public and all stakeholders. In doing so, I see the DCC shattering the walls of the Ivory Tower and giving knowledge back to the people, where it belongs. Perhaps my loftiest goal for DCC is the development of our own conference where registration fees are optional and virtual presentations are welcomed. A DCC conference would eliminate the legal and financial barriers that inhibit convict scholars and other marginalized groups from participating in academic conferences. For example, virtual options would alleviate issues surrounding travel visas for individuals with criminal records. Such inclusionary practices would help DCC members combat the structural violence they experience in academia. Although my vision may seem lofty and some may dismiss them as idealistic, I want to remind members that at one point forming the DCC was viewed as a lofty goal. We can create change within our division that radically transforms the lives of convict and system-impacted scholars if we dare to dream big. However, if we want to avoid merely perpetuating or replicating the academic status quo, our work must extend beyond our division and to the real-world. We must reject the academic status quo and concentrate our privilege and power on activism. I believe this is only possible if the DCC moves towards collective activism.

BECOMING SCHOLARVISTS THROUGH COLLECTIVE ACTIVISM

Collective activism or collective action refers to when a group of people work in concert to challenge inequality, exclusion, and injustice to improve their collective social positions or experiences (Millward &Takhar, 2019). The term scholarvist combines the words scholar and activist, and refers to academics who prioritize using their scholarship and social capital to fight for social change (Green, 2018). In this section, I issue a call to action for collective activism as a mechanism for transforming DCC into a collective of scholarvists who reject the academic status quo. However, I want to first acknowledge our predecessors who worked tirelessly to carve out a space for convicts in criminology. I want to ensure that my words are not misconstrued as a dismissal of the foundational work written by scholars who fought to develop Convict Criminology within a field that actively rejects first-person narratives and autoethnographic research as 'unscientific'. I am truly grateful for the over ten years of work that allowed for the formation of the DCC (see Jones et al, 2009 and Richards, 2013 for overviews of this work). John Irwin's academic research (e.g. *The Felon*) and his role as a mentor for formerly incarcerated academics was pivotal to the formation of Convict Criminology. Still others like Jeffrey Ross, Charles Terry, Barbara Owen, and Stephen Richards provided a foundation for us to build upon. Their work was revolutionary and radical for its time, and I am truly grateful for the men and women who paved the road we find ourselves upon. However, now that we stand on a strong foundation, we must move beyond development and towards policy reform and abolition. As a Division we must be unafraid of academic retribution as we forge ahead in our collective battle for respect and empowerment. I acknowledge that those of us who are precariously employed or who fear retribution during tenure processes may be unable to join the battle at this time. However, those of us with career stability, including tenured members, must begin the work of developing our collective of activists.

There are substantial ways for the DCC to engage in collective activism. Of primary importance is demanding that academia and all its institutions Ban the Box (Craigie, 2020) on college admissions and employment applications to address the exclusion of scholars with criminal records (Stewart & Uggen, 2020; Ortiz et al., 2022). Again, I want to acknowledge that many scholars including members of DCC have advocated for this policy change. In 2021, the DCC issued a statement calling on universities to Ban the Box, however, public statements are insufficient to create change without additional collective action on our part. The DCC should engage in a concerted effort to communicate directly with universities and colleges to demand this change. We could write letters, request meetings, contact politicians, and work directly with grassroots organizations that are fighting to change this policy (e.g. Unlock Higher Education). Collectively, we must shake the foundation of the Ivory Tower until its oppressive structure crumbles. We must demand change no matter the costs. We must move beyond the individual need to be successful and work towards making "good trouble" (Lewis, 2020). In American history, change has never occurred without rocking the proverbial boat.

The DCC should also fight to make our scholarship publicly available so that it can be used to create change. The fact that with few exceptions (e.g. *Journal of Prisoners on Prisons*), we publish journal articles hidden behind paywalls is antithetical to who we are as a division. Every DCC member is here today because non-academics supported us along our journeys. We must remain cognizant of this fact so that we do not become complicit in academia. Knowledge belongs to the people, not to journal publishers and universities who profit from our marginalization. While I acknowledge the need for publications to ensure tenure, this does not preclude us also making that knowledge available in public. A simple method of ensuring our knowledge is publicly available is developing an online repository that contains one-page summaries of our research devoid of all the academic jargon and statistical charts. Such a repository could be shared with all members of the public including those in non-profit organizations, as well as public officials. In giving knowledge back to the people, we can move beyond academic accolades and towards a world where our research can make a difference.

Another area where DCC can begin to engage in collective activism is by rejecting academic elitism. Elitism permeates academia through financial barriers (Baum & Johnson, 2015), which at the graduate and faculty level includes professional organization membership fees, conference expenses, and publishing costs. DCC could begin to demand an end to these financial barriers, especially in the wake of the 2020 discussions of social justice. While this goal may seem unrealistic to those who are accustomed to passively accepting the academic status-quo, I beg to differ. One collective way to challenge these fees is to boycott our engagement with journals and conferences whose financial fees serve to exclude marginalized persons. A conference that has modeled inclusivity is the *New Directions in Critical Criminology Conference* that is free to all attendees. We could also issue public challenges to membership fees in organizations like ASC especially given the financial issues ASC faces in the wake of 2020. Why should one board of people, which has historically lacked diversity among its ranks, maintain control over our field? Why should justice-impacted scholars whose voices have been excluded from most conversations be beholden to an oppressive institution? I acknowledge the irony of both being a division of ASC and advocating for a boycott of its conference, however, consumer activism has a long history in the United States that led to radical changes in other social institutions (Glickman, 2009). Through collective consumer activism we can demand change that will alleviate the suffering of other convicts and marginalized scholars.

The DCC should also work to advocate for young scholars whose voices are marginalized and dismissed. In 2021, I witnessed another Twitter dispute in which a doctoral student at a top ten program in our field had her voice and experiences dismissed because she was 'just' a student. Furthermore, when I originally proposed a collected volume on gangs, the reviewers disagreed with our inclusion of graduate student pieces because they were 'not experts'. As Convict Criminologists, we must reject these elitist views of who is an expert and whose voice is worthy of acknowledgment. Many of the young scholars in DCC have more expertise on imprisonment and the carceral system than most self-proclaimed correctional experts. We must strive to highlight, promote, and support research by young scholars by creating spaces for undergraduate and graduate students. For example, at the 2017 ASC Conference I developed an undergraduate researcher panel where two of my students presented analyses they had conducted. This experience was transformational in the lives of both students, one of whom has now completed a master's degree and is applying to doctoral programs. Another way that we could promote and support young scholars is by developing an online repository where they can share their work. My institution publishes both an undergraduate and graduate journal annually. By creating a space for these young scholars to share their work, we help them become part of our collective action. Lastly, I believe we should support young scholars by developing a fund for those who want to attend conferences, but are unable to do so because of financial restraints. At our 2021 business meeting at the ASC Conference, the DCC board voted to establish an Early Career Travel scholarship and I have personally committed to contributing funds annually so that convict and system-impacted students have the same opportunities as privileged students.

Beyond academia, the DCC should strive to engage in political activism at the state and national level. We must use our social, political, and human capital to challenge oppressive policies especially within the criminal justice system. For example, we can engage in financial resistance by refusing to support institutions and corporations who support and maintain the status quo. Again, I know that some will dismiss this call as unrealistic or unlikely to create change. I disagree wholeheartedly. One need only look at the Montgomery Bus Boycott to see the power of financial violence committed against oppressive institutions (The History Channel, 2021; Glickman, 2009). A single voice will be drowned out, but thousands of voices cannot be silenced. Moving beyond boycotts, we can develop relationships with and support organizations run by formerly incarcerated individuals. For example, we could partner with Just Leadership USA, All of Us or None of Us, and other organizations that are actively fighting to address the needs of currently and formerly incarcerated individuals. We can also work to elect or remove politicians from office especially at the national level. We are the experts in corrections and the criminal justice system. They can ignore one of us, but collectively we can stir the foundation of the system that has taken so much from so many of us.

Regardless of which strategies we implore or which problems we choose to tackle, we must remember the power of collective action. A strategy in war is to divide armies so that they are weakened and easier to conquer. While I do not want to minimize the severity of war by drawing an analogy with our battle in academia, I do want us to remain cognizant of the fact that the easiest way to conquer a people is to divide them. Said differently, "The most common way people give up their power is by believing they have none" (Alice Walker quoted in Martin, 2004, p. 173). Our power to bring about change and to dismantle the oppressive structures in academia and society can only be manifested when we unite to combat the issue.

CONCLUSION

The Division of Convict Criminology has the social and political capital to create change if we reject the academic status quo and envision a division comprised of scholarvists who demand change and work tirelessly to create a better world for convict scholars, system-impacted scholars, and marginalized scholars. The onus is on us, the convict criminologists, to fight back against the system at all costs. We cannot wait for academia to cut the chains that bind us to its oppressive structure. Academia does not accept convicts as experts because our presence is a direct challenge to the institution's power. Academia did not willingly grant us admission to its elitist Ivory Tower; we overcame the structural violence inherent in academia to penetrate the heavily guarded gates that sought to exclude scholars like us. We infiltrated criminology and for twenty-five years the field has sought to discredit and dismiss Convict Criminology. Our cause cannot be demanding respect or acceptance within oppressive institutions like academia. Our cause must be dismantling these institutions and envisioning a space where all are welcome not because they conform, but precisely because they refuse to conform. In the words of Mahatma Gandhi, *"First they ignore you, then they ridicule you, then they fight you, and then you win"*.

ENDNOTES

[1] While original members of Convict Criminology all identified as convicts, within our current membership some individuals prefer to use terms like system-impacted because either the term is perceived as less stigmatizing or the term is inclusive of persons who did not serve time within a correctional facility. For a full discussion of language within Convict Criminology, see Ortiz and colleagues (2022).

REFERENCES

American Society of Criminology (2020) *ASC Division of Convict Criminology*. Retrieved from https://asc41.com/divisions/dcc/.

Baum, Sandy & Martha Johnson (2015) *Financing Public Higher Education: The Evolution of State Funding*, Washington (DC): Urban Institute of Justice.

Boustami, Karim & Kirk Taylor (2020) "Navigating LGBTQ+ Discrimination in Academia: Where Do We Go From Here?", *Biochemist*, 42(3): 16-20.

Convict Criminology (2020) "Officers and committees", *American Society of Criminology*. Retrieved from https://www.concrim.org/officers-committees.

Copes, Heith, Richards Tewksbury & Sveinung Sandberg (2016) "Publishing Qualitative Research in Criminology and Criminal Justice Journals", *Journal of Criminal Justice Education,* 27(1): 121-139.

Craigie, Terry-Ann (2020) "Ban the Box, Convictions, and Public Employment", *Economic Inquiry*, 58(1): 425-445.

Glickman, Lawrence B. (2009) *Buying Power: A History of Consumer Activism in America*, Chicago: University of Chicago Press.

Green, C.M. (2018). *Against Criminalization and Pathology: The Making of a Black Achievement Praxis*, unpublished doctoral dissertation, New York: CUNY Graduate Center. Retrieved from https://academicworks.cuny.edu/cgi/viewcontent.cgi?article=3981&context=gc_etds

History Channel (2021) *The Montgomery Bus Boycott*. Retrieved from https://www.history.com/topics/black-history/montgomery-bus-boycott

Jones, Richard S., Jeffrey Ian Ross, Stephen C. Richards & Daniel S. Murphy (2009) "First Dime: A Decade of Convict Criminology", *The Prison Journal,* 89(2): 151-171.

Kennelly, Ivy, Joya Misra & Marina Karides (1999) "The Historical Context of Gender, Race, & Class in the Academic Labor Market", *Interdisciplinary Issues on Race,* 6(3): 125-155.

Lewis, J. (2020). *Speech at National Constitutional Convention – July 29*. Retrieved from https://www.youtube.com/watch?v=e-8DThtP36Q

Martin, William P. (2004) *The Best Liberal Quotes Ever: Why the Left is Right*, Naperville: Sourcebooks.

Millward, Peter & Shaminder Takhar (2019) "Social Movements, Collective Action and Activism", *Sociology*, *53*(3): NP1–NP12.

Ortiz, Jennifer (2021) "Doxa is Dangerous: How Academic Doxa Inhibits Prison Gang Research", in David C. Brotherton & Rafael J. Gude (eds.), *International Handbook of Critical Gang Studies*, New York: Routledge, pp. 624-632.

Ortiz, Jennifer M., Alison Cox, Daniel Ryan Kavish & Grant Tietjen (2022) "Let the Convicts Speak: A Critical Conversation of the Ongoing Language Debate in Convict Criminology", *Criminal Justice Studies*, 35(3): 255-273.

Pierce, Mathiew W., Carol W. Runyan & Shirkant I. Bangdiwala (2014) "The Use of Criminal History Information in College Admissions Decisions", *Journal of School Violence,* 13(4): 359-376.

Richards, Stephen C. (2013) "The New School of Convict Criminology Thrives and Matures", *Critical Criminology,* 21(2): 375-387.

Sahtouris, Elisabet (2006) "Seven Reasons Why I Remain an Optimist", *Shift: At the Frontiers of Consciousness,* 11: 34-41.

Stewart, Robert & Christopher Uggen (2020) "Criminal Records and College Admissions: A Modified Experimental Audit", *Criminology,* 58(1): 156-188.

Tewksbury, Richard, Dean A. Dabney & Heith Copes (2010) "The Prominence of Qualitative Research in Criminology and Criminal Justice", *Journal of Criminal Justice Education*, 21(4): 391-411.

Vossen, Emma (2017) "Publish and Perish: On Publishing, Precarity and Poverty in Academia", *Journal of Working-Class Studies*, 2(2): 121-135.

ABOUT THE AUTHOR

Jennifer Ortiz, PhD is an Associate Professor of Criminology at The College of New Jersey. She earned her doctorate in Criminal Justice from John Jay College of Criminal Justice in New York City. Her research interests center on structural violence within the criminal justice system with a focus on reentry post-incarceration and gangs. Dr. Ortiz is currently the Division Chair for the American Society of Criminology's Division of Convict Criminology and Book Review Editor for *Critical Criminology*. She previously served as President of the New Albany, Indiana Human Rights Commission and as an executive board member for Mission Behind Bars and Beyond, a Kentucky-based non-profit reentry organization. She can be reached via email at Ortizje@tcnj.edu or by mail at the following address:

Jennifer Ortiz, PhD
The College of New Jersey
2000 Pennington Road, SSB 333
Ewing Township, NJ 08628

Every Picture Tells a Story: Framing and Understanding the Activism of Convict Criminology

Jeffrey Ian Ross and Grant Tietjen

ABSTRACT

Convict Criminology (CC) consists of three major initiatives. Although scholarship and mentoring have been dominant activities, understanding the activism/policymaking of CC is less well known. This paper reviews the primary United States based activities that CC has done in this area and suggests what it needs to do to assist the interests of individuals who are behind bars and those who are formerly incarcerated, as well as work towards the mission of the CC organization as a whole. Some of the areas where CC has participated politically include the news-making we have done (i.e. interviews with the news media) and the periodic statements released on social media by the American Society of Criminology's Division of Convict Criminology. This paper will also consider the notion of praxis as applied to CC, in that some members consider their research, public speaking, and mentorship to be political actions worthy to be considered political activity.

INTRODUCTION

Most people are uncertain about what politics and political activity encompasses. For them, the political process primarily involves either voting or attending a protest (Ginsberg, 1981). However, there are numerous behaviors that the public can engage in that can have a political and social impact, including letter-writing, social media activities, donations to political campaigns, etc. (Hirsch, 1993: Doherty et al., 2015; Rhodes et al., 2018). When ostensibly apolitical organizations, like those built around scholarship, formally and informally engage in political activities, things become complex. The boundaries between scholarship and activism may be fuzzy. Moreover, there is a tendency to associate activism only with left-wing politics. This perception, however, is incorrect. Clearly, activism exists across the entire political spectrum and can be observed in all major academic fields.

Over the past 25 years, Convict Criminology (CC) (Ross & Richards, 2003) – variously called a group, organization, theoretical approach, or network – "recognized that the convict voice was typically ignored in current research and policymaking in the fields of criminology and criminal justice in general, and corrections in particular" (Ross, 2021, p. 606). Although none of the previous critiques of CC (e.g. Larsen & Piché, 2012; Newbold & Ross, 2013; Belknap, 2015) have pointed out that Convict Criminology has not engaged in enough activism, there has been some internal discussion about the need to do more in this area.

Some of the work of CC encompasses what some scholars (e.g. Uggen & Inderbitzin, 2010; Loader & Sparks, 2010) call Public Criminology. This involves attempts to bring the findings of criminological research to audiences beyond academic criminologists. Part of the mission of CC is to engage with the public, politicians, and the news media. This is done not only in the classroom and conferences, but engaging with a variety of media, by serving as sources for articles that reporters are writing, consenting to be interviewed, and writing op eds.

To provide a better understanding of the role of activism, the authors, both insiders to the Convict Criminology network and Division of Convict Criminology, reflect upon this important aspect of CC. We know that many people affiliated with the CC perspective have long been engaged in progressive-leaning political actions in support of CC in one way or another. It is important to critically examine this activity to take inventory of what members and supporters have done, where they have made contributions, and ways that improvement can be achieved. In sum, this paper will explore, but is not limited to, different political aspects of CC praxis (Aresti & Darke, 2016; Aresti, Darke, & Manlow, 2016; Cann & DeMeulenaere, 2020; Smith, 2020; Smith & Kinzel, 2020). It primarily reviews and contextualizes CC activist activities in the United States.

WHAT IS ACTIVISM? WHY IS IT IMPORTANT FOR CONVICT CRIMINOLOGY?

To begin, a handful of scholars (e.g. LeBel, 2007, 2008, 2009; Ross, 2018) have noted that many formerly incarcerated individuals engage in activism. This work is both a way that they have dealt with stigma of a criminal conviction and have found their participation in this kind of activity is therapeutic, if not transformational.

Many professors and academic administrators consider activism by scholars to be controversial and even frown upon this activity. Why? Academia lacks clear-cut guidelines about the role that activism can or should play in professors' activities. Also, some professors and administrators believe that scholars should spend more time doing research and teaching, rather than engaging in political activities. They do not want the proverbial boat to be rocked and possibly draw negative attention to universities. Most importantly, system-impacted scholars may find themselves more susceptible to status fragility when they engage in activism. Participating in activism is risky for many scholars, particularly those who occupy precarious positions of employment (Tietjen & Kavish, 2021).

Some professors argue that their scholarship and teaching is a form of activism and/or praxis (i.e. turning theory into action). On the one hand, the activism aspect of CC is not very well developed, frequently functioning as the most nebulous and neglected element of the organization (e.g. Smith, 2020; Smith & Kinzel, 2020). On the other hand, attempting to provide a widely agreed-upon definition of activism in CC may not be possible. Why? Merely considering activism actions is too simplistic. For example, the formation of CC, member engagement in universities, including bringing CC ideas to classrooms and faculty committees, and advocating for system-impacted students can be offered as evidence of activism.

Thus, the definition of activism within CC may depend on which Convict Criminologist you speak to. And there are a variety of different types of members from students to professors, from formerly incarcerated (FI) individuals to people who are considered to be allies of CC.

To begin with, some may consider the creation of Convict Criminology in 1997 and the establishment of the Division of Convict Criminology in 2020 as acts of activism in and of themselves. Much of the sentiment behind the founding of CC was born out of a desire to stand up against the bias that FI people experienced and to elevate the system-impacted voice in post-secondary education and scholarship circles. As Richards (2013, p. 377) explains:

> Convict Criminology was born of the frustration ex-convict graduate students and ex- convict professors felt reading the academic literature on prisons. In our view, most academic textbooks and journal articles reflected the ideas of prison administrators, while largely ignoring what convicts knew about the day-to-day realities of imprisonment.

Thus, if someone identifies with CC and engages in scholarship from a CC perspective, this could also potentially be regarded as activism.

A Brief History of Activism in Convict Criminology?

Before the creation of the Division of Convict Criminology (DCC) within the American Society of Criminology (ASC), the CC group functioned as an informal network of scholars, students, academics, and activists in varying levels of engagement with CC advocacy. As new people joined the group and others left, the type and amount of activism changed. For example, in the early years, few of the members were interested in prison abolition, but now the CC network can count among themselves a handful who do.[1] Similarly, the new, diverse, and expanded membership of CC (Ross et al., 2016) is engaging more with underrepresented and marginalized populations (i.e. LGTBQIA, feminists, African-Americans, etc.) and the issues that directly impact these groups (e.g. Woodall & Boeri, 2014; Malkin & DeJong, 2019). In addition, CC activist work continues to broaden its focus, to also include foreign academics (from the United Kingdom, Italy, South America, and Australia) whose scholarship and other activities aligned with the CC mission (Ross & Darke, 2018; Ross & Vianello, 2021; Veigh Weiss, 2021). It may be helpful to identify the range of activities that CC members and the group in general engage in. Three specific categories of activism can be seen in the CC space: activist scholarship, mentorship as activism, and direct activism.

Activist Scholarship

The most common form of activism performed within CC might be called activist scholarship. CC's research functions as a form of scholarly activism that sheds light on the experiences of directly-impacted people, who are often disregarded or unseen in conventional criminological research (Smith & Kinzel, 2020; Tietjen, 2022). Due to the direct criminal justice contact of many CC scholars, they possess a unique potential to illuminate the value of lived experiences within the discipline of criminological research, which can lean heavily towards lifeless datasets. As Aresti and colleagues (2016, p. 6) explain:

> Through its combining of insider and critical research action perspectives on penality, it is our contention that Convict Criminology is well equipped

to challenge public misconceptions on prisons and prisoners. Further, by insisting on the need to privilege the knowledge and standpoint of those with firsthand experience of prison, convict criminologists find themselves in a strong position to resist institutional pressure to produce quantitative, hypothesis-testing (voodoo, positivistic) research.

While it might be easy for some critics of CC to argue that lived-experience scholarship is too biased and, thus, does not have any "activist" value within criminology, Newbold and colleagues (2014) point out that as long as the lived-experience perspective does not excessively influence the researcher's objectivity, it can have a valuable place within a criminological study. Newbold and colleagues (2014), referencing Jewkes (2012), emphasize that the insider's views can add "color, context, and contour" (p. 6) to scholarly findings.

One major question overshadows the others: does the scholarship get into the hands of the people who can best use it, including other relevant prison activists or policy makers and practitioners? There is no guarantee that even if these individuals are given the articles and books we write that they will read this material or do anything different with the information. Also keep in mind that scholarship is not limited to researching, writing, reviewing, and publishing, but it can also involve the transmission of knowledge at conferences, where attendees such as FI and justice-impacted individuals attend and discuss CC ideas, and can be motivated by them.

In short, the type of work that CC does can be considered "scholarvism" (Green, 2018). It is a collaborative-activist scholarship that involves credentialed experts whose activist work is based on rigorous, refereed research and scholarship. This might include Vianello's research team's work and her role in establishing/directing the M.A. in Critical Criminology program at University of Padova. In the spirit of CC, her involvement in these activities has created opportunities for system-impacted scholars to earn graduate degrees, as well as contribute research to the field of criminology and the like.

Mentorship as Activism

Since its formation CC has actively attempted to mentor people who are interested in this perspective. This includes individuals who are incarcerated (Darke & Aresti, 2016; Ross et al., 2011; Ross et al., 2015; Ross, 2019; Tewksbury & Ross, 2019) and those who are formerly incarcerated. Some of these people are considering starting a bachelor's degree, while others have academic positions. This mentorship includes conducting research together, collaboratively presenting findings on panels, co-authoring/co-editing papers for publication, and offering advisement on the academic job market, including writing letters of recommendation and providing feedback on departmental/college/university politics. We have performed many of the typical tasks pursued by undergraduate and graduate advisors. As testimony to this perspective, FI research participants in the study by Tietjen and colleagues (2021) spoke about the mentorship they received from CC mentors, who provided them with the tools and knowledge to "harness the value of his own lived experiences through higher education" (p. 7).

DIRECT ACTIVISM

The last type of activism involves the carcerally-impacted scholars, students, and allies who not only created CC, but who through the reclaiming of the word *Convict* (Ortiz et al., 2022) took a stand against mainstream criminologists (whom many CC scholars saw as having been coopted by the criminal justice system) and the criminal justice system itself (Richards, 2001; Ross & Richards, 2003). More than just bringing the voices of those convicted of crimes to the criminological discipline, CC expanded the utility of the lived-experience autoethnography as a means to both augment and challenge the managerial scholarship of conventional criminology (Earle, 2021).

Direct activism also includes more concrete and less symbolic kinds of behavior. CC members have participated in this kind of activity. This engagement includes a number of major activities: writing news articles or op-eds (e.g. Kalica, 2021); functioning as credible sources for reporters who are writing stories about corrections- and CC-related research (e.g. Tietjen, 2017); participating on Institutional Review Boards (IRBs); delivering public lectures and periodic public statements from the ASC DCC executive; and participating in protest activism, supporting Black Lives Matter, critical resistance, and so on.

CC Engaging in Newsmaking Criminology

Over the past three decades, motivated in part by Barak's (1988) classic article on news-making criminology, CC scholars have written op-eds about correctional issues and have become informed sources to the news media. They have actively made connections with reporters and editors of news organizations, and with the increasing proliferation of blogs, podcasts, and the use of YouTube, they have disseminated information about the challenges of the criminal justice system in general and corrections in particular.

Participating as Prisoner Representatives on IRBs
or Panels Examining Corrections

Some CC members have served on important committees that are relevant to this field. For example, in the 1990s Greg Newbold engaged in consulting research on the introduction of private prisons to New Zealand (Newbold & Smith, 1996). In 2008 and 2009, Jeffrey Ian Ross and Daniel Murphy served on the prisoner liaison committee for the National Institute of Health/ National Institute of Medicine task force, when these institutes were revising their protocols on testing practices involving prisoners (Ross & Hornblum, 2009). Miguel Zaldivar, an undergraduate formerly associated with of CC, served as a prisoner representative on an IRB with the University of Miami. From 2011 to 2013, Grant Tietjen served as an IRB representative for correctional research at the University of Nebraska-Lincoln. Also, Francesca Vianello has served on numerous commissions charged with making recommendations for the reform of the Italian penitentiary system. Moreover, Daniel Kavish and Adrian Heurta serve as board members for the Carceral Studies Consortium (https://architecture.ou.edu/csc/) with Kavish serving as a Core Affiliate Board Member and Huerta as an Affiliate Board member. Although having formerly incarcerated individuals on IRBs may appear to be lip service or tokenism, in most cases CC members are able to assist these bodies do a better (more thoughtful) job.

Serving on Editorial Boards

A handful of CC scholars serve on the editorial boards of criminology/ criminal justice journals and/or actively participate in the peer-review process. This activity can assist these journals when other editorial board members or reviewers of papers are unfamiliar or poorly informed about CC, its history, and CC's body of scholarship.

The ASC Division of Convict Criminology Periodic Public Statements

Shortly after CC became an official division of the ASC, the Executive of the DCC, using Twitter and Facebook, released a number of statements. The first was in reaction to the death of George Floyd, the 41-year-old African-American man who was killed by a white Minneapolis police officer in May 2020. This was followed a month later by a statement regarding the presence of COVID-19 in our country's correctional facilities, and the failure of state, local, and federal governments to properly respond. In January 2021, the DCC Executive launched its third public statement condemning the insurrection at the United States Capitol. Later in January 2021, the DCC also released a statement addressing Ban the Box.

Participating in Contemporary Progressive Activist Movements
Many members of CC are passionate about allied progressive activist causes. They frequently see connections between what CC does and these larger contemporary movements. They actively participate in activism surrounding Black Lives Matter, LGBTQIA rights, the rights of incarcerated and FI people, and the prison abolition movement – all of which bleed into the formal and informal discussions that CC members engage in. These issues arise during scholarly panels and at social events. Other activities include organizing and attending rallies and public meetings, and participating on diversity committees at various universities. On a related note, other engagement includes actively lobbying against the building of correctional facilities.

More concretely, CC has been identified as a good organization to serve as a "Haven for Radical Racial Exploration" (Wilson, 2021). Although "carcerality" is a central theme in Convict Criminology, is it not limited to incarceration experiences only. Rather, as Williams (2021, p. 13) argued, it is important to incorporate an intersectional lens when examining carceral experiences, to account for the "carcerality of Blackness" in the United States, institutions of higher education, and the criminal legal system.

Although these examples are important, they must also be placed in context. Just because a scholar is sympathetic to the Convict Criminology perspective and sits on an academic board, committee, and the like does not necessarily mean that they are engaging in activism. Instead, their activities may rightly be called service. The degree of meaningful participation is what is important here. Either way, they have the potential of engaging in activism, especially drawing attention to the convict voice, advocating for the rights of prisoners and ex-prisoners for example, and minimizing the resort to mass incarceration.

CONCLUSION

Summing up, CC incorporates activist scholarship, activism through mentorship, and direct activism. That being said, the activism in CC has varied over time, and individuals have struggled with how, when, and why they should engage in this activity. Why is this so? Formerly incarcerated CC members may struggle with personal traumas and stresses from incarceration and difficult pasts (Kirk & Wakefield, 2018), and are doing their best to work through the difficulties and the injustices they have endured, while learning to be more impactful/effective activists. Alternatively, they may be using activism in an attempt to "take ownership" of their trauma and stress (and thereby overcome it). On the other hand, members who are not formerly incarcerated or justice impacted may be unaware of the most effective way/s to engage in activism with this group.

Both types of individuals may have competing obligations. They may want to be scholars, instructors, and good citizens in their universities and communities, but they may also have parental or caregiver obligations. In addition, many people who have aligned themselves with CC are trying to complete a doctorate or earn tenure. In this case, the focus of their efforts is often on publishing a considerable amount of scholarship and focusing on teaching, and not protesting in the streets and joining the barricades in public demonstrations. With this in mind, the more established members of CC or other individuals and groups may be in a better position to engage in the activism we do. On the other hand, the newer and younger members of the CC group frequently find their way to the CC organization through their involvement in activism. In sum, it is a long and sometimes difficult learning curve for many CC members and those aligned with the mission to learn to effectively balance the two roles of activist and scholar.

CC needs to continue to engage with its respective audiences (i.e. fellow criminologists, students, community groups they are part of or interact with, and the news media). It is important to understand and reach out to the people new to the CC group who may be interested in the broad span of ideas relevant to corrections and reentry in general and CC in particular.

ACKNOWLEDGEMENTS

Special thanks to the anonymous reviewers for comments on an earlier draft of this paper.

ENDNOTES

[1] This trend may also be tied to the increased acceptance and popularity of the prison abolition concept.

REFERENCES

Aresti, Andreas & Sacha Darke (2016) "Practicing Convict Criminology: Lessons Learned from British Academic Activism", *Critical Criminology*, 24(4): 533-547.

Aresti, Andreas, Sacha Darke & David Manlow (2016) "Bridging the Gap: Giving Public Voice to Prisoners and Former Prisoners through Research Activism", *Prison Service Journal*, 224: 3-13.

Barak, Gregg (1988) "Newsmaking Criminology: Reflections of the Media, Intellectuals, and Crime", *Justice Quarterly*, 5(4): 565-587.

Belknap, Joanne (2015) "Activist Criminology: Criminologists' Responsibility to Advocate for Social and Legal Justice, The 2014 American Society of Criminology Presidential Address", *Criminology*, 53(1): 1-22.

Cann, Colette & Eric DeMeulenaere (2020) *The Activist Academic: Engaged Scholarship for Resistance, Hope and Social Change*, Gorham (ME): Myers Education Press.

Darke, Sacha & Andreas Aresti (2016) "Connecting Prisons and Universities Through Higher Education", *Prison Service Journal*, 225: 26-32.

Doherty, Carroll, Jocelyn Kiley, Alec Tyson & Bridget Jameson (2015) "Beyond Distrust: How Americans View Their Government", *Pew Research Center* – November 23. Retrieved from https://www.pewresearch.org/politics/2015/11/23/beyond-distrust-how-americans-view-their-government/

Earle, Rod (2021) "Exploring Narrative, Convictions and Autoethnography as a Convict Criminologist", *Tijdschrift over Cultuur & Criminaliteit*, 2020(3): 80–96.

Ginsberg, Benjamin (1981) *The Consequences of Consent: Elections, Citizen Control, and Popular Acquiescence*, Reading: Addison Wesley Publishing.

Green, C.M. (2018). *Against Criminalization and Pathology: The Making of a Black Achievement Praxis*, unpublished doctoral dissertation, New York: CUNY Graduate Center. Retrieved from https://academicworks.cuny.edu/cgi/viewcontent.cgi?article=3981&context=gc_etds

Hirsch, Debora J. (1993) "Politics Through Action: Student Service and Activism in the 90s", *Change: The Magazine of Higher Learning*, 25(5): 32-36.

Jewkes, Yvonne (2012) "Autoethnography and Emotion as Intellectual Resources: Doing Prison Research Differently", *Qualitative Inquiry*, 18(1): 63-75.

Jones, Richard S., Jeffrey Ian Ross, Stephen C. Richards & Daniel S. Murphy (2009) "The First Dime: A Decade of Convict Criminology", *The Prison Journal*, 89(2): 151-171.

Kalica, Elton (2021) "Convict Counter-information to Contest Crime-press Disinformation", in Jeffrey Ian Ross & Francesca Vianello (eds.), *Convict Criminology for the Future*, New York: Routledge, pp. 50-65.

Kirk, David S. & Sara Wakefield (2018) "Collateral Consequences of Punishment: A Critical Review and Path Forward", *Annual Review of Criminology*, 1: 171-194.

Larsen, Mike & Justin Piché (2012) "A Challenge from and Challenge to Convict Criminology", *Journal of Prisoners on Prison*, 21(1&2): 199-202.

LeBel, Thomas P. (2009) "Formerly Incarcerated Persons Use of Advocacy/Activism as a Coping Orientation in the Reintegration Process", in Bonita M. Veysey, Johnna Christian & Damian J. Martinez, (eds.), *How Offenders Transform Their Lives*, Cullompton (UK): Willan, pp. 165–187.

LeBel, Thomas P. (2008) "Perceptions of and Responses to Stigma", *Sociology Compass*, 2(2): 409-432.

LeBel, Thomas P. (2007) "An Examination of the Impact of Formerly Incarcerated Persons Helping Others", *Journal of Offender Rehabilitation*, 46(1/2): 1–24.

Loader, Ian & Richard Sparks (2010) "What Is To Be Done With Public Criminology?", *Criminology and Public Policy*, 9(4): 771-781.

Malkin, Michelle L. & Christina DeJong (2019) "Protections for Transgender Inmates Under PREA: A Comparison of State Correctional Policies in the United States", *Sexuality Research and Social Policy*, 16(4): 393-407

Newbold, Greg & Jefferey Ian Ross (2013) "Convict Criminology at the Crossroads", *The Prison Journal*, 93(1): 3-10.

Newbold, Greg & Merv Smith (1996) "Privatization of Corrections in New Zealand", in G. Larry Mays & Tara Gray (eds.), *Privatization and the Provision of Correctional Services: Context and Consequences*, Cincinnati: Anderson Publishing Co., pp. 75-86.

Newbold, Greg, Jefferey Ian Ross, Richard S. Jones, Stephen C. Richards & Michael Lenza (2014) "Prison Research from the Inside: The Role of Convict Autoethnography", *Qualitative Inquiry*, 20(4): 439-448.

Ortiz, Jennifer M., Alison Cox, Daniel Ryan Kavish & Grant Tietjen (2022) "Let the Convicts Speak: A Critical Conversation of the Ongoing Language Debate in Convict Criminology", *Criminal Justice Studies*, 35(3): 255-273.

Richards, Stephen C. (2013) "The New School of Convict Criminology Thrives and Matures", *Critical Criminology*, 21(3): 375–387.

Rhodes, Carl, Christopher Wright & Alison Pullen (2018) "Changing the World? The Politics of Activism and Impact in the Neoliberal University", *Organization*, 25(1): 139–147.

Ross, Jeffrey Ian (2019) "Getting a Second Chance with a University Education: Barriers & Opportunities", *Interchange: A Quarterly Review of Education*, 50(2): 175-186.

Ross, Jeffrey Ian (2018) "Prison Activism", in Vidisha B. Worley & Robert M. Worley (eds.), *American Prisons and Jails: An Encyclopedia of Controversies and Trends*, Santa Barbara: ABC-Clio Reference, pp. 5-9.

Ross, Jeffrey Ian & Sacha Darke (2018) "Interpreting the Development and Growth of Convict Criminology in South America", *Journal of Prisoners on Prisons*, 27(2): 108-117

Ross, Jeffrey Ian, Sacha Darke, Andreas Aresti, Greg Newbold & Rod Earle (2014) "Developing Convict Criminology Beyond North America", *International Criminal Justice Review*, 24(2): 121-133.

Ross, Jeffrey Ian & Allen M. Hornblum (2009) "No Prison Guinea Pigs: President Obama Should Act Now to Ensure Prisoners Aren't Used For Medical Research", *Prison Legal News*, 20(2): 55.

Ross, Jeffrey Ian, Richard S. Jones, Michael Lenza & Stephen C. Richards (2016) "Convict Criminology and the Struggle for Inclusion", *Critical Criminology*, 24(4): 489–501.

Ross, Jeffrey Ian & Stephen C. Richards (eds.) (2003) *Convict Criminology*, Belmont (CA): Wadsworth Publishing.

Ross, Jeffrey Ian, Stephen C. Richards, Greg Newbold, Richard S. Jones, Michael Lenza, Daniel S. Murphy, Richard Hogan & G. David Curry (2011) "Knocking on the Ivory Tower's Door: The Experience of Ex-Convicts Applying for Tenure-Track University Positions", *Journal of Criminal Justice Education*, 22(2): 267-285.

Ross, Jeffrey Ian & Francesca Vianello (eds.) (2021) *Convict Criminology for the Future*, New York: Routledge.

Ross, Jeffrey Ian, Miguel Zaldivar & Richard Tewksbury (2015) "Breaking Out of Prison and Into Print? Rationales and Strategies to Assist Educated Convicts Conduct Scholarly Research and Writing Behind Bars", *Critical Criminology*, 23(1): 73-83.

Smith, Justin M. (2020) "The Formerly Incarcerated, Advocacy, Activism, and Community Reintegration", *Contemporary Justice Review,* 24(1): 43-63.

Smith, Justin M. & Aaron Kinzel (2020) "Carceral Citizenship as Strength: Formerly Incarcerated Activists, Civic Engagement, and Criminal Justice Transformation", *Critical Criminology,* 29(1): 93-110.

Tewksbury, Richard & Jeffrey Ian Ross (2019) "Instructing and Mentoring Ex-Con University Students in Departments of Criminology and Criminal Justice", *Corrections: Policy, Practice and Research,* 4(2): 79-88.

Tietjen, Grant (under review) *Justice Lessons: The Rise of System Affected Academic Groups.*

Tietjen, Grant (2019) "Convict Criminology: Learning from the Past, Confronting the Present, Expanding for the Future", *Critical Criminology*, 27(1): 101-114.

Tietjen, Grant (2017) "In Interviews With 122 Rapists, Student Pursues Not-So-Simple Question: Why?" (interviewed by Kamala Thiagarajan), *National Public Radio* – December 16. Retrieved from https://www.npr.org/sections/goatsandsoda/2017/12/16/570827107/in-interviews-with-122-rapists-student-pursues-not-so-simple-question-why

Tietjen, Grant, James Burnett & Bernadette Olson Jessie (2021) "Onward and Upward: The Significance of Mentorship for Formerly Incarcerated Students and Academics", *Critical Criminology*, 29: 633–64.

Tietjen, Grant & Daniel Kavish (2021) "In the Pool Without a Life Jacket: Status Fragility and Convict Criminology", in Jeffrey Ian Ross & Francesca Vianello (eds.), *Convict Criminology for the Future*, New York: Routledge, pp. 66-81.

Uggen, Christopher & Michelle Inderbitzin (2010) "Public Criminologies", *Criminology & Public Policy*, 9(4): 725–749.

Wilson-Edge, E. & J. Burkhardt (2017) "Chris Beasley Builds a Pipeline". Retrieved from https://www.tacoma.uw.edu/news/article/chris-beasley-builds-pipeline

Woodall, Denise & Miriam Boeri (2014) "When You Got Friends in Low Places, You Stay Low Social Networks and Access to Resources for Female Methamphetamine Users in Low-Income Suburban Communities", *Journal of Drug Issues*, 44(3): 321-333.

Vegh Weiss, Valeria (2021) "It's Time! Towards a Southern Convict Criminology", in Jeffrey Ian Ross & Francesca Vianello (eds.), *Convict Criminology for the Future*, New York: Routledge, pp. 112-126.

ABOUT THE AUTHORS

Jeffrey Ian Ross, PhD is a Professor in the School of Criminal Justice, College of Public Affairs, and a Research Fellow in the Center for International and Comparative Law, and the Schaefer Center for Public Policy at the University of Baltimore. He has been a Visiting Professor at Ruhr-Universität Bochum in Germany and the University of Padua in Italy. Professor Ross has researched, written, and lectured primarily on corrections, policing, political crime, state crime, crimes of the powerful, violence, street culture, as well as crime and justice in American Indian communities for over two decades. His work has appeared in many academic journals and books, including most recently the *Routledge Handbook of Street Culture* (2021) and *Convict Criminology for the Future* (2021). Ross is a respected subject matter expert for local, regional, national and international news media. He has made live appearances on CNN, CNBC, Fox News Network, MSNBC, and NBC. Additionally, Ross has written op-eds for *The (Baltimore) Sun*, the *Baltimore Examiner*, *The (Maryland) Daily Record*, *The Gazette*, *The Hill*, *Inside Higher Ed*, and *The Tampa Tribune*. Professor Ross is the co-founder of Convict Criminology, and the former co-chair/chair of the Division of Critical Criminology and Social Justice (2014-2017) of the American Society of Criminology. In 2018, Ross was given the Hans W. Mattick Award, "for an individual who has made a distinguished contribution to the field of Criminology & Criminal Justice practice", from the University of Illinois at Chicago. In 2020, he received the John Howard Award from the Academy of Criminal Justice Sciences' Division of Corrections. The award is the ACJS Corrections Section's most prestigious award, and was given because of his "outstanding research and service to the field of corrections". In 2020, he was honored with the John Keith Irwin Distinguished Professor Award from the ASC Division of Convict Criminology. During the early 1980s, Jeff worked for almost four years in a correctional institution.

Grant E. Tietjen, PhD is an Associate Professor in the Criminal Justice Program at the School of Social Work and Criminal Justice at the University of Washington – Tacoma (UWT). He earned his PhD from the Department of Sociology at the University of Nebraska – Lincoln (UNL) in 2013. Dr. Tietjen has written, researched, and lectured on convict criminology, mass incarceration, class inequality, criminological theory, and pathways to correctional/postcorrectional education. He has published in multiple peer reviewed papers in journals and edited volumes, including most recently in *Humanity and Society*, *Social Justice: A Journal of Crime, Conflict & World Order*, and *Criminal Justice Studies*. He is the author of *Justice Lessons: The Rise of the System Affect Academic Movement*, with the University of California Press, slated for publication in 2024. Dr. Tietjen works closely with multiple System Affected Academic organizations, including Huskies Post Prison Pathways (HP3) at UWT and the Division Convict Criminology (DCC) in the American Society of Criminology (ASC). HP3 is a support program for formerly-incarcerated students. As part of UWT HP3, he is a member of the Steering Committee for this growing initiative. He has also been involved with the CC discipline since 2005, mentoring new CC members, and serving as the group's Co-Chair from 2017-2019. During this time, Tietjen has worked with many other dedicated CC members to strengthen the CC organization. In 2020, he was appointed as the inaugural Chair of the newly formed American Society of Criminology Division of Convict Criminology, and currently serves as DCC Vice-Chair. Dr. Tietjen can be reached for questions at grantt5@uw.edu.

Continuing the Interactionist Tradition: Examining the Relationship Between Juvenile Delinquency, Formal Labeling, and Adult Criminal Behavior
Daniel Ryan Kavish

INTRODUCTION

The legacy of the Convict Criminology movement in the United States is closely tied to the work of two scholars: John Keith Irwin and Frank Tannenbaum. Irwin and Tannenbaum both championed a symbolic interactionist perspective (Carceral & Flaherty, 2022; Earle, 2016; Yeager, 2011, 2015; also see Irwin, 1987). For instance, in *Convict Criminology: Inside and Out*, Rod Earle notes that "At the heart of Tannenbaum's (1938) analysis of crime is the nature of social conflict, reaction, and social interaction" (Earle, 2016, p. 29). Likewise, Irwin (1987) explicitly stated that he found people, especially people with felony conviction records, to be "symbolic interacting human beings" (pp. 45-46). The "self" is of paramount importance to the interactionist perspective and Shadd Maruna, the current president of the American Society of Criminology, has stated "Convict Criminology is, of course, an ideal example of a Criminology of the Self" (p. xiii, as cited in Earle, 2016). As such, contemporary scholars with lived-carceral-experience carry on the interactionist tradition of Convict Criminology each time they produce theoretical and empirical scholarship on stigma, identity, and labeling theory.

Staying true to the legacy of Tannenbaum, Irwin, and the interactionist perspective, this paper seeks to provide answers to the questions: Who is formally labeled, and what are the effects of formal labeling on subsequent criminality? However, the current study breaks from the largely qualitative tradition of convict criminology by utilizing quantitative methods to examine interactionist labeling and the relationship between behavior and formal contact with the criminal justice system. An interactionist labeling model of juvenile delinquency that incorporates parental labeling, school labeling, and respondents' levels of self-control is presented. Structural Equation Modeling (SEM) is used to predict levels of juvenile delinquency, the application of formal labels, and adult criminality among a nationally representative sample of American adolescents: three waves of the National Longitudinal Study of Adolescent Health (2009).

THEORETICAL BACKGROUND

Tannenbaum's (1938) "dramatization of evil" describes the process by which offenders acquire deviant labels from members of society. If an act has been characterized as evil by society, then the offender will be simultaneously associated with the act and labeled as deviant. Thus, deviant labels are acquired from formal labeling experiences such as arrests, prosecutions, or convictions (Barrick, 2014). Paternoster and Iovanni (1989) hypothesized that there are mechanisms that intervene in the relationship between negative labeling and subsequent behavior. Formal labels may influence crime and delinquency due to their relationship with intervening non-criminal measures such as involvement with deviant peers (Becker, 1963; Bernburg et al., 2006), pro-social expectations (Restivo & Lanier, 2013), procedural justice (Slocum et al., 2016), perceptions of care (Kavish et al., 2016), structural impediments and blocked access to conventional opportunities (Bernburg & Krohn, 2003; Chiricos et al., 2007), delinquent identities (Becker, 1963; Paternoster & Iovanni, 1989), as well as redemption programs and rite of passage ceremonies (Maruna, 2001; 2011; Maruna et al., 2004; Rocque et al., 2016).

Following labeling theory, Chiricos and colleagues (2007) claimed that a formal labeling experience may lead to the transformation of an individual's identity and could increase subsequent involvement in crime. Additionally, they viewed the collateral consequences of felony convictions as "structural impediments". Structural impediments encountered after a formal labeling experience can have a dramatic impact on an individual's self-image and identity because those impediments continually and consistently reinforce negatively applied labels. In fact, Burton and colleagues (1986) described the collateral consequences of felony convictions as "persistent punishments" (p. 52) that follow individuals long after their sentences are completed. A person is reminded of their criminal past each time they are denied employment, housing, or the opportunity to vote. This constant reminder of their past reinforces the initial application of the negative formal label surely takes a toll on their concept of self.

It is also possible that other formal labels, such as an official arrest or prosecution, could have dramatic implications similar to the structural impediments related to criminal convictions that were outlined by Chiricos and colleagues (2007). Even though some individuals do not receive a formal criminal conviction, the process of being arrested and prosecuted is likely to lead to the development of negative informal labels and a litany of other negative life-course outcomes (Chiricos et al., 2007; Pratt et al., 2016). As argued by Mead (1934), we see ourselves as others see us. If this is correct, then each time people are restricted by the collateral consequences of arrests and convictions, then they are reminded that others view them as criminal, deviant, or dangerous. In turn, this can reinforce deviant identities (see also Sherman, 2014). Simple tasks such as voting, finding housing, or filling out job applications become nerve-racking activities for labeled individuals.

Labeling theorists have primarily focused on formal labeling measured by criminal convictions and adjudications, but aggressive early intervention policies and police in schools may also be having negative impacts on the delinquency trajectories. Therefore, it is important to examine all types of labeling experiences. Conceptualizing formal labeling as an arrest is in line with other labeling research that treats arrests as formal labeling experiences (Huizinga & Henry, 2008; Kavish et al., 2016; Lopes et al., 2012; Restivo & Lanier, 2013; Slocum et al., 2016; Wiley & Esbensen, 2013).

Application of Labels
Labeling can occur when there is conflict between youth and their parents, peers, teachers, or formal social control agents. Labeling theory states that labels are differentially applied based on sources of social conflict such as gender, race, and class. Thus, labeling theory proposes that law is not uniformly imposed upon the public, and that formal agents of social control selectively apply labels. For instance, Becker (1963) suggested that economically disadvantaged individuals and people not racialized as white are more likely than others to have labels applied to them. In more general conflict terms, members of society with fewer resources are more susceptible to labeling, less able to defend themselves against the application of labels, and have less influence on the definition of social norms.

Chambliss' (1973) qualitative work established that it is possible that markers of socioeconomic status influence the likelihood of experiencing negative labeling events. Chambliss (1994) specifically argued that police organizations seek to maximize rewards and minimize strains, and that "...the powerless, the poor, and those who fit the public stereotype of "the criminal" are the human resources needed by law enforcement agencies to maximize rewards and minimize strains" (p. 192). Alternatively, others have argued that members of more privileged groups with a greater stake in conformity are more subject to the power of a formal label in self-image construction (see Sherman et al., 1992). Addressing both points, and in line with a conflict tradition, contemporary labeling research proposes that the application of labels and the effect of those labels on individuals varies by socio-demographic characteristics (see Barrick, 2014).

In sum, labeling theorists assert that definitions of deviance and crime, and social responses, are created within specific social contexts. Literature suggests that socio-demographic characteristics, deviant peer associations, where police patrol, levels of racial profiling, status differences between individuals, and how much behavior deviates from social norms all may influence the application of a deviant label (Becker, 1963; Chambliss, 1973, 1994; Schur, 1971). This is why it is just as important to know who is labeled and how they were labeled, as it is to understand the impact of that label.

Labeling, Interaction and Self-Control

Low self-control is closely linked with one's concept of self (Brownfield & Thompson, 2008). Brownfield and Thompson (2005, 2008) began a line of research that examined the relationships between reflected appraisals, delinquent self-concepts, and delinquency. They examined whether control, labeling, and interactionist variables were correlates of a deviant self-concept and juvenile delinquency. They were specifically concerned about how a delinquent identity is actually created. Brownfield and Thompson (2008) found that measures of self-control are compatible with interactionist labeling approaches because measurements of self-control are closely linked to the self-concept.

While interactionists may disagree with Gottfredson and Hirschi's (1990) description of self-control as a stable personality trait, there is little to no debate of a properly constructed self-control measure's usefulness in predicting criminal or delinquent behavior. Braithwaite (1989) clearly viewed control and labeling perspectives as compatible for theoretical integration as both theories were incorporated into Braithwaite's (1989) theory of reintegrative shaming (p. 16). Likewise, Higgins and colleagues (2006) integrated concepts of self-control and social learning to explain digital piracy. Elements of Hirschi's (1969) social bonding theory have been routinely integrated with self-control theory (Doherty, 2006; Wright et al., 1999). Turanovic and Pratt (2013) integrated elements of strain and self-control theory to explain the relationship between victimization, substance use, and criminal violence. Thus, it is apparent that many criminologists have sought to integrate Gottfredson and Hirschi's (1990) general theory of crime with other theoretical perspectives.

Self-control appears to be an important component of the interaction process and should be included in future examinations of interactionist labeling (Brownfield & Thompson, 2008). This study seeks to do just that, by incorporating a measure of self-control into the analysis. Though research on integrating self-control with the view of the self as dynamic is in its infancy, Pratt (2016) recently outlined how self-control and life-course theories could be theoretically integrated. Many of his points can easily be incorporated into interactionist labeling perspectives of delinquency and criminal behavior. One of his theoretical propositions was to view self-control as a selection variable of sorts. Thus, controlling for self-control in interactionist labeling models of delinquency and crime is just another way of avoiding selection bias as originally outlined by Smith and Paternoster (1990).

DATA AND METHODS

Sample

The sample used is derived from the National Longitudinal Study of Adolescent Health (2009).[1] Add Health is a nationally representative sample of adolescents in grades 7-12 from the United States starting in the 1994-95 school year. The current study utilizes waves 1, 2, and 3 of the Add Health data. Wave 2 data was collected in 1996 and wave 3 was collected in 2001. This means that respondents had reached adulthood at the third data collection point but were no older than the age of twenty-seven. For the purposes of this study, variables were constructed using each wave's in-home questionnaire and the wave 1 parent questionnaire. For a more detailed description of the collection procedures and data, see Harris and colleagues' (2009) full description of the Add Health data. The final sample used is limited to survey respondents who had valid statistical weights and observed pairwise-present data (n=8439).[2]

The primary advantages of this data set are that it is a large nationally representative sample, and it includes a wide variety of possible variables to be used in a criminological analysis. The panel design of the study further allows researchers to examine variables at different time points. One disadvantage of the data is that it is not particularly concerned with labeling events, labeling dynamics, or labeling theory. This shortcoming prevents the current study from properly testing reflected appraisals as originally outlined by Matsueda (1992). However, the survey does provide enough valid measures of key concepts for a test of labeling theory.

Variables

Endogenous Variables

Delinquency/Criminal Behavior. Latent variables, incorporating both violent and non-violent delinquent acts, were constructed using confirmatory factor analysis (CFA) to be used as endogenous measures. Observed variables asked respondents how often, in the past 12 months, they deliberately damaged property that did not belong to them, stole something worth more than $50, stole something worth less than $50, went into a house or building to steal something, used or threatened to use a weapon to get something from someone, and sold marijuana or other drugs. In waves one and three, respondents were asked about their frequencies of engaging in the aforementioned behaviors. Response categories were "never" (0), "1 or 2 times" (1), "3 or 4 times" (2), and "5 or more times" (3). This CFA process is done once for wave one observed measures, and again for wave three observed measures. Therefore, latent variables are created for early manifestations of delinquency, and for subsequent criminal behavior that occurs long after potential labeling experiences.

Formal Labeling. Official formal labeling was measured by retroactively tracking self-reported arrests listed by respondents in wave 3. This was necessary because the questions concerned with formal labeling were not posed to respondents in the first two waves. Follow-up items were asked that inquired about date of the arrest. These follow-up items could then be compared with the dates that surveys were completed. Arrest dates were compared to survey dates to ensure that labeled individuals were labeled after the first wave of surveys and at least one year prior to the date they completed the surveys at wave 3. Thus, individuals were coded as being formally labeled if they indicated that they had been arrested after wave 1 but one year prior to the date that they completed the wave 3 survey. The final analytical variable used is a dichotomous variable with "yes" responses (yes=1) denoting that the respondent was formally labeled by the criminal justice system. "No" (no=0) responses indicate that an individual was not formally labeled.

Exogenous Variables and Controls

Age. The age cohort of the respondent was expressed as the respondent's age in years at the time of the survey's first wave.

Non-White. Race was measured with a single dichotomous variable. The variable indicates whether the respondent identifies *primarily* as non-white (non-white=1; white=0).

Male. Biological sex was measured with a single dummy variable (male=1; female=0).

SES. The variables concerned with the education level of the respondent's residential parents served as a proxy for socioeconomic status (*SES*) in the current study.[3] The survey items were asked as part of the wave one parent questionnaire and were concerned with the highest degree completed by each of the respondents' residential parents. The items were collapsed into five distinct levels of educational attainment: (1) no high school diploma, (2) high school diploma or G.E.D., (3) Some college but no degree, (4) undergraduate college degree, (5) education beyond an undergraduate college degree. If only one residential parent was listed, then that parent's education level was used as the respondent's SES. If two parents were available, then their education levels were averaged. Higher scores represent higher levels of educational attainment (Range: 1-5).

Public Assistance. Public assistance was measured using a single survey item from the parent questionnaire at wave one. The respondent's parents were asked if they were recipients of public assistance. The variable used was a dichotomous variable with "yes" responses (yes=1) denoting that the respondent's parents answered that they were receiving public assistance or welfare. "No" (no=0) responses indicate that an individual's parents answered that they were not receiving public assistance or welfare.

Family Type. The role of the family in delinquency involvement has a rich history in delinquency research and debate (Gove & Crutchfield,

1982; Mack et al., 2007; Rankin, 1983; Tannenbaum, 1925). Therefore, it is important for this study to control for the role of different family types when examining the impact of formal labeling on subsequent delinquency. Respondents' family type was measured with a single dummy variable indicating the family type structure in which the respondent lives. Respondents were categorized based on whether they indicated that they lived in traditional two-parent households, or whether they were a part of some other family type at wave one.[4] This binary measure is coded as a "1" if respondents indicated that they live with two biological parents or two adoptive parents, and coded as a "0" if respondents indicated that they did not live in a traditional two-parent household.

School Labeling. Respondents' school labeling experiences were measured by using multiple survey items indicating stigmatizing school experiences and the grades that these experiences occurred. Respondents were asked whether they had ever been suspended or been expelled. These questions were followed up with items inquiring about the grade the respondent was in for their most recent suspension and expulsion. Consequently, the final analytical variable capturing school labeling is coded as "1" if any of the aforementioned survey responses were coded as a "1" and the experience happened at least one grade prior to the grade they were in at wave 1.

Parental Labeling. The parental labeling measure captures parental perceptions of their child's temperament and behavior. Each item is pulled from the wave 1 in-home parent questionnaire. The survey items used asked parents whether their child: has a bad temper; is doing well in life; is trustworthy; smokes regularly; and drinks regularly.[5] The item inquiring about how the child's life is going was originally measured on a scale of 1 (very well) to 4 (not well at all). Responses of "not so well" and "not well at all" were recoded as "1", with the remaining responses coded as "0". Similarly, the item inquiring about the child's trustworthiness asked parents how often their child was trustworthy and was originally measured on a scale 1 (always) to 5 (never). Responses of "never" and "seldom" were recoded as "1", with the other responses coded as "0". The remaining survey items were binary, and as such, were coded so that "Yes" responses (yes=1) denote that the respondent's parent believes that the child has a bad temper, smokes regularly, or drinks regularly. Likewise, "No" (no=0) responses indicate that the parent does not believe that their child has a bad temper, smokes regularly, or drinks regularly. The study is chiefly concerned with whether a parental figure labels their child as deviant or not. Consequently, parental labeling is coded as "1" if any of the aforementioned survey responses were coded as a "1". The final analytical variable used indicates whether or not parents perceived their child as a "rule violator" or "distressed". The items used are also consistent with Matsueda's (1992) constructs of a perceived "rule violator" and "distressed" juvenile (Rocheleau & Chavez, 2015).

Low Self-Control. In the first wave, respondents were asked whether they had trouble getting along with their teachers, trouble paying attention, trouble keeping their mind focused, and trouble finishing their homework. A fifth question asked respondents to indicate whether they felt that they did everything just right. The responses to these items were summed together to form a low self-control scale (α= 0.6682). The scale was coded so that higher values represent lower levels of self-control (range: 1-20).

Perceptions of Care. Youth perceptions of care were measured by constructing three variables derived from wave two survey items. These survey items asked respondents how much they felt teachers, parents, and friends cared about them. Responses ranged from "not at all" to "very much". The variables were reverse coded (5= "not at all"; 1= "very much"). Thus, a higher score represents a more negative perception of how much respondents felt teachers, parents, and friends cared about them.

Plan of Analysis
Structural equation modeling (SEM) is the primary analytic strategy used for the current examination of juvenile delinquency, application of formal labels, and adult criminality. Individual measures of observed variables pertaining to different types of delinquent behavior serve as indicators of the underlying latent construct defined as "delinquency." Confirmatory factor analysis (CFA) process is done once for wave one observed delinquency measures, and again for wave three observed criminal behavior measures. Therefore, latent variables are created for early manifestations of delinquency, and for subsequent criminal behavior that occurs after potential labeling experiences. Both latent variables, along with the observed variable of formal labeling, will serve as endogenous variables. All other observed

variables included in the model will serve as exogenous variables. The results of the tests of mediation coupled with the overall model fit indices of the structural model are used to establish or reject statistical mediation effects. Furthermore, criminological theory and temporal ordering of variables allow the current study to tentatively confirm or reject the actual existence of mediation.

FINDINGS

Sample Characteristics

The sample's basic characteristics are presented in Table 1. The percentages displayed are weighted proportions. The mean age of the sample at wave 1 was approximately 15 years old. Roughly half of the sample was male (50.22%) and just over half of the respondents came from traditional two-parent family types (57.65%). The mean level of educational attainment by respondents' parents was a high school diploma but no college degree. The racial makeup of the sample closely mirrors national numbers reported in the 2010 census (Humes et al., 2011). A small weighted proportion of the sample was formally labeled (8.37%). Likewise, a similar proportion of the sample was suspended or expelled from school (8.35%). A higher proportion of respondents was informally labeled by parents (36.45%). Respondents, on average, reported more negative perceptions of care from teachers than from friends or parents. This finding is expected due to the social distance between respondents and parents or friends compared to the social distance between respondents and their teachers (Waller, 1932).

Assessing the Measurement Model

Figures 1 and 2 show the impact of the latent variables on their corresponding observed variables. CFA confirms that all of the indicators loaded high on the delinquency latent variables. The results show that the factor loadings on the first-order factors from observed wave 1 delinquency variables are significant and above 0.500, indicating that the observed measures adequately reflect the latent factor of delinquency ($\chi^2 = 74.84$, 7, $p < 0.000$; TLI = 0.98; CFI = 0.98; RMSEA = 0.030). Likewise, the factor loadings on the first-order factors from observed wave 3 criminal behavior variables are significant and above 0.500, indicating that the observed measures adequately reflect the latent factor of criminal behavior ($\chi^2 = 59.18$, 7, $p <$

0.000; TLI = 0.98; CFI = 0.98; RMSEA = 0.026). Therefore, delinquency and criminal behavior are single latent factors accurately representing their corresponding observed measures.

Assessing the Structural Model
As shown in table 2, the goodness-of-fit indices indicate that the structural model predicting wave 1 delinquency, formal labeling, and wave 3 criminal behavior provided an acceptable fit to the data (χ^2 = 190.01, 52, p < 0.000; TLI = 0.95; CFI = 0.95; RMSEA = 0.017).[6] The TLI and CFI indices for the current study are right at the threshold (TLI = 0.952; CFI = 0.950) for an acceptable fit (Hu & Bentler, 1998). The current study's RMSEA measures are very close to their suggested cutoff of 0.01 for exceptional models.[7] As expected due to the size of the sample, the χ^2 test statistic is significant, but the other model fit indices point to an acceptable fitting structural model.

First, as depicted in *Figure 3*, the structural model predicted wave 1 delinquency using the observed wave 1 exogenous variables. Individuals that were labeled by parents, labeled by schools, had higher SES scores, had lower levels of self-control, men, and non-white respondents were all found to have significantly higher levels of delinquency involvement at wave 1. Likewise, those on public assistance and from traditional two parent households were found to have significantly lower levels of delinquency involvement at wave 1. The unstandardized estimates listed in table 2 are probit coefficients. The model R^2 for the latent juvenile delinquency factor is the variance explained for the continuous latent response variable (y*), rather than the observed ordinal dependent variable (y) (Bollen, 1989b).

Standardized results indicate that low self-control had the strongest effect on early delinquency involvement, followed by biological sex, parental labeling, race, SES, school labeling, family type, and public assistance. For one standard deviation increase in low self-control, wave 1 delinquency increased by 0.393 standard deviations. Men were found to be more delinquent than women by 0.194 standard deviations. Respondents labeled by their parents were found to be more delinquent at wave 1 than their non-labeled peers by 0.100 standard deviations. Non-whites were significantly more delinquent than others by 0.085 standard deviations.

For each standard deviation increase in SES, wave 1 delinquency increased by 0.074 standard deviations. Those labeled by school officials were 0.068 standard deviations more delinquent at wave 1 than their non-labeled peers. Respondents from traditional two-parent households were less delinquent at wave 1 than those not from traditional two-parent households by 0.051 standard deviations. Finally, individuals that received public assistance were less delinquent at wave 1 than those not receiving public assistance by 0.047 standard deviations. The model accounts for about 25% of the variance in juvenile delinquency.

Next, as depicted in *Figure 4*, the structural model predicted formal labeling using the observed wave 1 exogenous variables and wave 1 delinquency. Older respondents, men, individuals labeled delinquent or distressed by their parents, and those with higher levels of early delinquency involvement were all significantly more likely than others to be formally labeled. Respondents from households with two biological parents were significantly less likely than others to be formally labeled. Sex was the strongest predictor of formal labeling, followed in turn by early delinquency involvement, age, parental labeling, and family type. While low self-control was strongly and significantly predictive of early delinquency, it had no significant impact on formal labeling. Likewise, school labeling, race, public assistance, and SES were found to have no significant influence on societal reaction to delinquency involvement through formal labeling processes. The model accounts for about 20% of the variance in formal labeling.

Finally, as depicted in *Figure 5*, the structural model predicted subsequent criminal behavior at wave 3 using the observed exogenous variables from waves 1 and 2, and the endogenous variables wave 1 delinquency and formal labeling. Seven variables were predictive of future criminal behavior. Older individuals were significantly less involved in criminal behavior at wave 3. This is to be expected as respondents begin to "age out" of criminal behavior as they reach adulthood. Formal labeling, prior delinquency at wave 1, sex, SES, and negative perceptions of care from teachers were all found to significantly increase wave 3 criminal involvement. Conversely, parental labeling was found to significantly decrease wave 3 involvement in criminal behavior. School labeling, low self-control, public assistance, race, family type, along with negative perceptions of care from parents and friends were all found to be insignificant in the prediction of wave 3 criminal behavior.

Standardized estimates indicate that formal labeling was the strongest predictor of wave 3 involvement in criminal behavior. One standard deviation increase in formal labeling increased wave 3 criminal behavior by 0.323 standard deviations. Prior delinquency involvement was the second most predictive measure of wave 3 criminal behavior. One standard deviation increase in wave 1 delinquency increased wave 3 criminal behavior by 0.291 standard deviations. Age was the third most predictive measure of wave 3 criminal behavior. One standard deviation increase in age decreased wave 3 criminal behavior by 0.176 standard deviations. Following age, sex was the next variable most predictive of future criminal behavior as men were significantly more involved in criminalized behavior than women at wave 3. Men were 0.166 standard deviations more criminally involved than women. Following sex, SES was the next measure most predictive of wave 3 criminal behavior. For each standard deviation increase in SES, wave 3 criminal behavior increased by 0.131 standard deviations. For each standard deviation increase of negative perceptions of care from teachers, an important interactionist labeling variable, wave 3 criminal behavior increased by 0.092 standard deviations. Finally, parental labeling was predictive of future criminal behavior, but not in the expected direction. Respondents labeled as delinquent or distressed by their parents at wave 1 were significantly less criminally involved than unlabeled respondents by 0.042 standard deviations. The structural model accounts for about 40% of the variance in wave 3 criminal behavior.

Assessing Mediation

One final aspect of the current study was to examine whether formal labeling mediates the relationship between prior delinquency and subsequent delinquency. Likewise, the study sought to investigate whether formal labeling mediated the relationship between low self-control and future criminal behavior. As aforementioned, the results clearly indicate that wave 1 delinquency is predictive of formal labeling and subsequent criminal behavior measured at wave 3. Likewise, formal labeling is significantly and directly associated with future criminal behavior. In fact, standardized estimates indicate that formal labeling is the most predictive measure of subsequent criminal behavior in this model. That being said, the findings also indicate that formal labeling exerts a mediating influence between prior delinquency and subsequent criminal involvement. To be clear, formal labeling mediated the effect of prior delinquency on subsequent criminal behavior by 0.081 standard deviations.

The causal steps approach was the primary method used to statistically establish the existence of a mediation effect between prior delinquency and criminal behavior. To ease the interpretation of findings, the results of the coefficients relevant to these steps are presented in Table 3. According to the causal steps approach (Baron & Kenny, 1986; see also MacKinnon et al., 2007), these results tentatively indicate that formal labels mediate the relationship between prior delinquency and subsequent delinquency. The same causal steps approach was repeated to examine the relationship between low self-control, formal labeling, and future criminal behavior. The lack of significant results for the first two causal steps indicates that there is no relationship between low self-control and future criminal behavior for formal labeling to mediate.

Multiple additional steps beyond Baron and Kenny's (1986) causal steps approach were undertaken to further justify the statistical mediating effect of formal labeling between prior delinquency and subsequent criminal behavior. First, a joint test of significance was conducted using the statistical program "*R*" because MacKinnon and colleagues (2002) found it to be the best test of mediation hypotheses. Furthermore, the product of coefficients approach was used by conducting four variations of the Sobel test: the Delta method (Muthen & Muthen, 1998-2010), the Sobel (1982) first-order solution, the Aroian (1944) second-order exact solution, and the Goodman (1960) unbiased solution (see also MacKinnon et al., 2002). All five of the aforementioned statistical tests indicated that formal labeling was a statistically significant intervening variable between prior delinquency and future criminal behavior. The results of the causal steps approach, the aforementioned tests of significance, and the overall model fit indices of the structural model provide strong support for the hypothesis that formal labeling statistically mediates the relationship between prior delinquency and future criminal behavior.

DISCUSSION

Formal Labeling

Formal labeling significantly increased subsequent criminal behavior. Not only did formal labeling have the strongest significant relationship with subsequent criminal behavior, but it also partially mediated the influence of prior delinquency on future involvement in criminal behavior. This is a strong indication that formal labeling has a significant and substantial impact on subsequent criminality, and that this relationship is not just an artifact of prior delinquent behavior. The findings provide confirmation of the deviance amplification hypothesis, and the mediation effect provides further support for the notion that sanctions and labeling experiences influence future involvement with crime independent of prior behavior.

Some formally labeled individuals do not subsequently become more involved in criminal behavior (Morris & Piquero, 2013). This can likely be explained by the mechanisms labeling theorists assert intervene in the relationship between formal labels and subsequent criminalized behavior (Becker, 1963; Barrick, 2014). Individuals may be formally labeled, but deviance amplification should not be expected if the label does not result in increased deviant peer associations, employment and education failures, or changes to identities. For instance, individuals may be formally labeled, but may not increase their involvement in crime if criminal identities are unimportant to them (Chassin et al., 1981), they do not seek out deviant peers, or they are able to achieve employment or educational success.

The mechanisms that labeling scholars claim intervene in the relationship between formal labeling and subsequent behavior are important because prior research suggests that there are strong associations between them and involvement in crime and delinquency. Association with deviant peers and peer reflected appraisals as delinquent are consistently related to increased delinquency involvement (Adams, 1996; Haynie, 2001; 2002; Haynie & Osgood, 2005; Heimer & Matsueda, 1994). More specifically, and most relevant to the current findings, Adams (1996) found that the effects of labeling were mediated by associations with deviant peers. Formal labeling has been found to be significantly related to education failures (Sweeten, 2006). This is troubling because prior research also shows a strong relationship between educational attainment and reduced recidivism (Chappell, 2004; Dennison, 2019; Gordon & Weldon, 2003; MacKenzie & Hickman, 1998; Mercer, 2009). Likewise, employment has been found to be associated with reduced recidivism (Berg & Huebner, 2011; MacKenzie & Hickman, 1998; Skardhamar & Telle, 2012; Visher et al., 2008; Yahner & Visher, 2008), especially for older individuals (Uggen, 2000). Together, these studies indicate that peer associations, education, and employment are all important predictors of desistance and reintegration success after labeling experiences.

Identity and Low Self-Control

A key aspect of this study was the inclusion of low self-control in the structural model. It is interesting to note that low self-control did not have a significant impact on formal labeling or subsequent criminal involvement. The former finding is in stark contrast to the findings of Beaver and his colleagues (2009) and Longshore and Turner (1998), which both found that self-control was linked to arrest experiences. However, low self-control was the strongest predictor of delinquency involvement. These findings indicate that while low self-control is a theoretically important variable in predicting initial involvement in delinquency, it is much less important in the prediction of formal labeling and adult criminal behavior. This reinforces that formal labeling is a selective social reaction not based on stable personality traits. It also suggests that formal labeling is much more important in predicting secondary deviance than low self-control.

Low self-control is likely influencing early delinquency, which in turn, impacts dynamic self-concepts. Conceptually, self-control is likely a correlate of identity. In other words, personality traits such as impulsivity and risk-taking influence others' perceptions of individuals, which in turn, influence identity measures like reflected appraisals and self-appraisals. These delinquent identities may then influence subsequent criminality. Therefore, as prior scholars have already found (Brownfield & Thompson, 2008), formal contact with police in the form of an arrest likely has a greater impact on delinquent identities than low self-control. Similarly, delinquent identities likely have a greater influence on the development of criminal behavior than self-control. Brownfield and Thompson's (2008) research indicates that low-self-control plays an important role in the development of delinquent identities, but official arrests were more predictive of delinquent identities and the current study further revealed formal labeling to be the most influential variable for predicting future criminal behavior. Taken together, the current study and the work of Brownfield and Thompson (2008) suggests that low self-control is merely one dimension of a dynamic interactionist relationship between juvenile delinquency, self-concepts, and subsequent criminality (also see Brownfield & Thompson, 2005).

In sum, formal labeling's influence on subsequent criminal behavior was stronger than the influence of prior delinquency or any other variable in the analyses. Furthermore, what influence prior delinquency did have on future criminal behavior was partly mediated by formal labeling.

This study contends that this mediation effect is likely the product of important unmeasured intervening variables such as blocked opportunities, associations with deviant peers, and identity changes. Future research should seek to use longitudinal data collected at many different time points, and include measures of these potential intervening mechanisms, to further investigate and disentangle the relationship between formal labels, non-criminal outcomes, and subsequent involvement in criminalized behavior.

Stakes in Conformity

The findings pertaining to negative perceptions of care from teachers suggest that teachers may play an important role in the development of criminal behavior. In line with prior research (Kavish et al., 2016), respondents with more negative perceptions of care from teachers were more involved in criminal behavior as young adults. This finding appears to add weight to the notion that stakes in conformity play a role in the labeling process (see Barrick, 2014; also see Sherman et al., 1992). In other words, it may be that how much one believes their teacher cares about them could influence how much impact an official formal label will have on subsequent behavior. If adolescents perceive their teachers to not care about them, an unsaid negative informal label, then that weakens the bond between youth and the institution of education. Thereby, making them more prone to the effects of formal labels. Conversely, if individuals perceive their teachers to care for them, an unsaid positive informal label, then this may reduce the influence of formal labeling on future outcomes.[8] Essentially, it is possible that positive perceptions of care from teachers could serve as a protective factor from the deviance amplifying effects of formal labels. While this is not a direct test of positive labeling, it does lend support to the notion that positive labels may have a positive relationship with desistance from crime.

Positive labels can come in many forms. For the purposes of encouraging desistance from criminal or delinquent behavior though, pro-social (as opposed to antisocial) labels may serve to replace stigmatizing labels of "delinquent" or "felon" (Maruna et al., 2004). Arrests, official adjudications, and convictions serve as degradation ceremonies that apply formal negative labels (Garfinkel, 1956; also see Maruna et al., 2004). Therefore, an official ceremony or process that applies pro-social labels may be necessary to replace such negative labels, and in turn, encourage desistance. In fact, Maruna and colleagues (2004) noted that until individuals see that others view them as "success stories" (p.277), they are not likely to view themselves as such. Similarly, they pointed out how it is well established that individuals that have desisted tend to rely on people of "good moral standing" (p. 275) to vouch for their character (also see Maruna, 2001). You can see the value and importance of "personal vouchers" on desistance in Convict Criminology's emphasis on mutual support, mentorship, and desistance narratives (Catoe, 2021; Maruna & Liem, 2021; Tietjen & Kavish, 2020).

LIMITATIONS

This paper is not without its methodological limitations. The sample and data used only allow the findings to be generalized to adolescents attending school in the United States. Since truancy is a status offense that could evoke informal and formal social responses, this study is unable to generalize its findings to a small but important segment of the nation's adolescent population. Additionally, the data itself was not particularly concerned with labeling events or processes. It is strongly suggested that future surveys strive to include the items needed for a proper test of labeling theory. In fact, for the purposes of improving criminological research, social surveys of adolescents should begin including items considered to be the most pertinent among all types of criminology. This would allow research of all types to improve and would simultaneously foster a new wave of theoretical elaboration and integration.

Another limitation of the current study is that only one formal label was examined. This paper operationalized formal labeling as a self-reported arrest. An arrest, arguably, is a weak measure of formal labeling because there are fewer "structural impediments" after being arrested than after being officially adjudicated and sanctioned.[9] That being said, contemporary research has found that even being stopped and detained by police, rather than being arrested, can have deviance amplifying effects (Slocum et al., 2016; Wiley & Esbensen, 2013; Wiley et al., 2013). Thus, research seems to indicate that any type of contact with law enforcement or the criminal justice system can have deviance amplifying effects.

Existing criminological and criminal justice research shows that there are other noteworthy formal labels that could influence criminalized behavior and future criminal justice outcomes. For example, Quinn (2010) examined the relationship between a formal "gang member" label and juvenile justice dispositions. Still yet, other studies have operationalized formal labeling as an official conviction (Chiricos et al., 2007). To compound this limitation, all labels do not impact or influence an individual's life equally. Becker (1963) made this clear when he described the idea of a "master status." Not all labels are negative and specific labels can hold more or less weight for certain individuals.[10] Future research should make a greater attempt to elaborate conceptually on Becker's (1963) notion of a "master status" and to better explain how different types of labels specifically affect different types of people.

Similarly, this study did not account for the influence of positive labels on delinquency or formal labeling. Thompson (2014) suggested that labeling theory could be extended to explain how labels could function positively. Becker (1963) stated that labels motivate our behavior, and the bulk of labeling research has focused on how negative labels motivate criminalized behavior. That being said, Thompson (2014) clearly demonstrated that a positive label could motivate a positive change in behavior. Future research should consider discussing how positive labeling, whether formal or informal, could possibly motivate desistance from crime and delinquency.

Another limitation of this study was that temporal precedence was not established for the prediction of early juvenile delinquency. The current study was unable to distinguish the exact relationship between parental labeling and juvenile delinquency. Parental labeling was significantly linked to juvenile delinquency, but the direction of this relationship cannot be definitively established by this research. However, temporal precedence was established for the prediction of criminal behavior, so this limitation had no impact on the study's focal analysis of deviance amplification. Overall, it is hoped that any deficiencies and limitations found in this analysis of labeling theory might be remedied by future criminological research by using even more statistically sound techniques of analysis, different datasets, or other innovative research strategies.

CONCLUSION

This paper presented an interactionist labeling model that incorporates respondents' levels of self-control to explain juvenile delinquency, formal labeling, and criminal behavior among a nationally representative sample of American adolescents. This contributes to existing criminological research by providing a contemporary test of labeling theory using a nationally-representative and longitudinal data set, and by continuing a new and innovative conceptual approach towards labels and criminalized behavior (see Kavish et al., 2016). This study was multivariate, controlled for prior delinquent behavior and low self-control, included variables for respondent's perceptions of care, examined a large nationally representative sample, and had an extensive follow-up period between wave 1 and wave 3. According to Barrick (2014), these attributes qualify it as one of the more methodologically rigorous tests of labeling theory. Future research should seek to follow Barrick's (2014) guidelines and suggestions for the most theoretically informed labeling theory studies because her research found that the most methodologically rigorous tests of labeling theory happened to also be the tests most likely to be supportive of labeling theory. This means that tests of labeling theory should use multivariate statistical techniques, include intervening mechanisms such as delinquent peers, employment and educational success, and identity changes, investigate potential contingencies and stakes in conformity, as well as control for important confounding variables such as prior delinquency and low self-control. Doing so will allow future research to better decipher when and how sanctions will lead to desistance or deviance amplification.

The findings of this study provide the context for a couple policy implications. Only a small portion of arrested juveniles are dealt with in an informal manner such as restorative justice programs, family counseling programs, or a transfer to some other social welfare agency (Puzzanchera, 2014). More programs and policies could be implemented to allow local jurisdictions to process juveniles and young adults informally, instead of arresting them. Processing people informally allows for the avoidance of further labeling, stigmatization, and more specifically in the case of older adolescents and young adults, the collateral consequences of official convictions. Though these programs could trigger further negative labeling, the label would be less formal than further official processing, less severe than official adjudications, and could be spearheaded by local community organizations. Furthermore, these programs could also provide opportunities for redemption, forgiveness, mentorship, and possibly an opportunity to de-label arrested individuals.

The findings of this study can also be viewed as supportive of marijuana decriminalization policies. In some instances, laws actually allow for police officers to more freely exercise their discretionary arrest powers.

For instance, in Illinois, a city ordinance allowed Springfield police officers to treat possession of marijuana as a simple ordinance violation rather than arresting an individual according to state law (Rushton, 2012). Then Springfield alderman, Gail Simpson, proposed the city ordinance as a way of helping teenagers avoid "a lasting stigma" of a drug arrest or conviction (Olsen, 2015). The findings of this study lend credence to the alderman's idea that decriminalizing such drug arrests helps individuals avoid stigma and future involvement in the criminal justice system.

The criminal stigma associated with being formally labeled has been found to impact nearly every facet of a person's life and contributes to a cycle of captivity within society (Gundur & Kavish, 2022). As such, policy initiatives should limit the proliferation of formal labels, provide access to de-labeling opportunities, and address the intervening mechanisms that interactionists claim reinforce deviant identities and contribute to deviance amplification. For instance, policies and programs could be put in place that reduce prison and jail populations, end the "war on drugs", demilitarize police, increase the use of deferred adjudication in sentencing, restore voting rights for people with felony convictions, reduce the scope and number of collateral consequences associated with arrests and felony convictions, restore access and funding for higher education in all prisons, increase employment opportunities, reduce housing discrimination, and greatly expand reentry programs such as Project Rebound and other community-centered resources (Chowdhury & Butler, 2019; Richards et al., 2012; Wilson, 2019).

Petrich and colleagues (Petrich et al., 2021) asserted that skeptics have long claimed that sanctions, especially custodial sanctions, may have an amplifying effect of subsequent criminalized behavior. Their meta-analysis concluded, quite simply, that "The skeptics were right" (Petrich et al., 2021, p. 51). To that point, I'd point out that proponents of Convict Criminology have been some of the biggest skeptics of deterrence theory and any idea that crime can be reduced through the increased use or harshness of punishment. The legacy of Convict Criminology is one of staunch resistance to any notion that punishment, deprivation, or dehumanization could possibly lead to crime reductions (Ross & Richards, 2003; Ross & Vianello, 2020; Tannenbaum, 1922; Tietjen, 2019).

In sum, this study's findings are in line with a wide body of evidence suggesting that the stigmatizing impact of criminal justice sanctions can have an amplifying effect on subsequent criminalized behavior (Kavish et al., 2016; Petrich, et al., 2021; Pratt et al., 2020; Slocum et al., 2016; Wiley et al., 2013). It followed the tradition of one of the original skeptics, Frank Tannenbaum, and used an interactionist labeling model to explain juvenile delinquency, the application of deviant labels, and adult criminal behavior. The findings indicated that while low self-control was the strongest significant predictor of early delinquency involvement, formal labeling was the strongest significant predictor of future criminal behavior and partially mediated the influence of prior delinquency on subsequent behavior.

ENDNOTES

[1]   This research uses data from Add Health, a program project directed by Kathleen Mullan Harris and designed by J. Richard Udry, Peter S. Bearman, and Kathleen Mullan Harris at the University of North Carolina at Chapel Hill, and funded by grant P01-HD31921 from the Eunice Kennedy Shriver National Institute of Child Health and Human Development, with cooperative funding from 23 other federal agencies and foundations. Special acknowledgment is due to Ronald R. Rindfuss and Barbara Entwisle for assistance in the original design. Information on how to obtain the Add Health data files is available on the Add Health website (see http://www.cpc.unc.edu/addhealth). No direct support was received from grant P01-HD31921 for this analysis.

[2]   This strategy preserves the overall integrity and maintains the nationally representative nature of the data. This strategy is optimal because deleted non-weighted cases were selected outside of the framework used for the core Add Health sample. The majority of the deleted cases had missing data for the three variables derived from the parent questionnaire. All other variables ranged from no missing responses to only 3% missing. Additionally, as a sensitivity test, missing values were replaced and the same models presented below were duplicated. The imputed models resulted in no significant differences in outcomes.

[3]   Using the income of the respondents' residential parents as a proxy for SES was initially considered for the study. However, the data collectors and other scholars found the income measures to be highly unreliable. To be more specific, there is a substantial amount of missing data pertaining to parental income. Recent studies have concluded that these missing data may not be random, but rather, represent a distinct subset of the study's population (see Harris et al., 2009).

[4]   Kressierer and Bryant (1996) stated that adoptive relationships might be stigmatizing due to the social expectation that parents would prefer having biological children. Because of this, this study considered treating adoptive parents differently than biological parents. However, the final variable was operationalized to reflect families with two biological parents or two adoptive parents. There are two reasons for this operationalization. Firstly, there were only a small number of children with two adoptive parents (n=141). Secondly, as a sensitivity analysis, respondents that did

have two adoptive parents were coded as not having two biological parents. There were no significant differences in findings between the two coding options, which suggests there is no difference between having two biological parents and two adoptive parents.

[5] The survey items used for the parental labeling variable were measured at the same time as delinquency measures (wave 1), but these same survey items have been previously operationalized as measures of self-control (Beaver et al., 2009). Therefore, it is assumed that these labels were applied at an early age. Measuring self-control using parental appraisals is relatively commonplace in self-control research (Beaver et al., 2009; Wright et al., 1999; see also Duckworth & Kern, 2011), but because the items used to construct this variable are parental appraisals, the items used are also consistent with Matsueda's (1992) constructs of a perceived "rule violator" and "distressed" juvenile (Rocheleau & Chavez, 2015).

[6] The χ^2 value and degrees of freedom are corrected for using the WLSMV estimator. Only the p-value should be interpreted for model fit (Muthen and Muthen, 1998-2010). The χ^2 test statistic is significant for the measurement and structural models suggesting a poor model fit, but Schermelleh-Engel and colleagues (2003) cautioned scholars from putting too much emphasis on the χ^2 test because of its known dependence on sample size. This test statistic is dependent on sample size because the χ^2 value increases with sample size while the degrees of freedom remains constant. Essentially, sample sizes above 400 tend to always be statistically significant (Kenny, 2015). While the problem of sample size dependence cannot be eliminated, Jöreskog and Sörbom (1993) suggested that researchers compare the ratio between the χ^2 value and degrees of freedom to better gauge model fit (χ^2/df). This ratio should be as low as possible, but there is no agreed upon standard for gauging a model's fit using this technique. However, a ratio of about three is generally considered an acceptable fit (Kenny, 2015).

[7] Three other goodness-of-fit indices based on the χ^2 statistic and degrees of freedom were used in conjunction with the χ^2 test statistic to assess the overall fit of the structural and measurement models: the comparative fit index (CFI), the Tucker-Lewis index (TLI), and the root mean square error approximation (RMSEA). These alternative indices are necessary because researchers, such as Bollen (1989a), have noted that one fit measure alone does not determine whether a model is valid. Hu and Bentler (1998) concluded that TLI and CFI indices that have scores close to or higher than 0.95 are indicative of a reasonably good fit between theorized models and observed data. MacCallum and colleagues (1996) suggested that a RMSEA fit measure of 0.01 is an exceptional model fit score, and a measure of 0.05 represents a good fit.

[8] An interaction term and tests for mediation were considered to examine the relationship with future criminal behavior between perceptions of care from teachers and formal labeling. However, temporal precedence could not be established and the temporal ordering of variables was not possible due to the unique way in which formal labeling was measured. In essence, there was no way to distinguish whether negative perceptions of care came before, simultaneously, or after formal labels.

[9] Formal convictions and adjudications were considered for use as formal labels in this study, but there were too few respondents with these outcomes to construct a

reliable measure of formal labeling. Essentially, arrest was used because this was the best formal label available in the dataset.

[10] Status is typically distinguished by one important trait that dictates who belongs and who does not belong. Similar to skin color, the label of "deviant" is a master status. A master status is one that transcends other auxiliary status traits. Becker (1963) argued that a deviant status transcends other status traits. Through stereotyping, auxiliary status traits are often "informally expected" (Becker, 1963, p. 32) to accompany a master status. Thus, those labeled as deviant are expected to not respect or value laws and be likely to engage in behavior that may have preceded the initial application of a deviant label (Becker, 1963; see also Schur, 1971). Becker (1963) argued that these generalizations and social expectations result in self-fulfilling prophecies for labeled individuals, and they ignore that individuals may value other statuses and roles that conflict with a socially applied label.

REFERENCES

Adams, Mike S. (1996) "Labeling and Differential Association: Towards a General Social Learning Theory of Crime and Deviance", *American Journal of Criminal Justice*, 20(2): 147-164.

Aroian, Leo A. (1944) "The Probability Function of the Product of Two Normally Distributed Variables", *Annals of Mathematical Statistics*, 18: 265-271.

Barrick, Kelle (2014) "A Review of Prior Tests of Labeling Theory", in David P. Farrington & Joseph Murray (eds.), *Labeling Theory: Empirical Tests*, New Brunswick (NJ): Transaction, pp. 89-112.

Baron, Reuben M. & David A. Kenny (1986) "The Moderator-mediator Variable Distinction in Social Psychological Research: Conceptual, Strategic, and Statistical Considerations", *Journal of Personality and Social Psychology*, 51: 1173-1182.

Beaver, Kevin M., Matt DeLisi, Daniel P. Mears & Eric Stewart (2009) "Low Self-control and Contact with the Criminal Justice System in a Nationally Representative Sample of Males", *Justice Quarterly*, 26(4): 695-715.

Becker, Howard S. (1963) *Outsiders*, New York: Free Press.

Berg, Mark T. & Beth M. Huebner (2011) "Reentry and the Ties that Bind: An Examination of Social Ties, Employment and Recidivism", *Justice Quarterly*, 28(2): 382-410.

Bernburg, Jón Gunnar & Marvin D. Krohn (2003) "Labeling, Life Chances, and Adult Crime: The Direct and Indirect Effects of Official Intervention in Adolescence on Crime in Early Adulthood", *Criminology*, 41(4): 1287-1318.

Bernburg, Jón Gunnar, Marvin D. Krohn & Craig J. Rivera (2006) "Official Labeling, Criminal Embeddedness, and Subsequent Delinquency: A Longitudinal Test of Labeling Theory", *Journal of Research in Crime and Delinquency*, 43(1): 67-88.

Bollen, Kenneth A. (1989a) "A New Incremental Fit Index for General Structural Equation Models", *Sociological Methods & Research*, 17(3): 303-316.

Bollen, Kenneth A. (1989b) *Structural Equations with Latent Variables*, New York: Wiley.

Braithwaite, John (1989) *Crime, Shame, and Reintegration*, New York: Cambridge.

Brownfield, David & Kevin Thompson (2008) "Correlates of Delinquent Identity: Testing Interactionist, Labeling, and Control Theory", *International Journal of Criminal Justice Sciences*, 3(1): 44-53.

Brownfield, David & Kevin Thompson (2005) "Self-concept and Delinquency: The Effects of Reflected Appraisals by Parents and Peers", *Western Criminology Review*, 6(1): 22-29.

Burton, Velmer S., Francis T. Cullen & Lawrence F. Travis (1986) "The Collateral Consequences of a Felony Conviction: A National Study of State Statutes", *Federal Probation*, 51(3): 52-60.

Carceral, K. C. & Michael G. Flaherty (2022) *The Cage of Days: Time and Temporal Experience in Prison*, New York: Columbia University Press.

Catoe, Kristen (2021) *How Convict Criminologists Navigate Stigma*, Greensboro: The University of North Carolina.

Chambliss, William J. (1994) "Policing the Ghetto Underclass: The Politics of Law and Law Enforcement", *Social Problems*, 41(2): 177-194.

Chambliss, William J. (1973) "The Saints and the Roughnecks", *Society*, 11(1): 24-31.

Chappell, Catherine A. (2004) "Post-secondary Correctional Education and Recidivism: A Meta-analysis of Research Conducted 1990-1999", *Journal of Correctional Education*, 55(2): 148-169.

Chassin, Laurie, Clark C. Presson., Richard David Young & Roger Light (1981) "Self-concepts of Institutionalized Adolescents: A Framework for Conceptualizing Labeling Effects", *Journal of Abnormal Psychology*, 90: 143-151.

Chiricos, Ted, Kelle Barrick, William Bales & Stephanie Bontrager (2007) "The Labeling of Convicted Felons and Its Consequences for Recidivism", *Criminology*, 45(3): 547-581.

Chowdhury, Lisa & Rashanna Butler (2019) "Laying the Foundation of Punishment Against Black Males", in Jason M. Williams & Steven Kniffley (eds.), *Black Males and the Criminal Justice System*, New York: Routledge, pp. 1-10.

Dennison, Christopher R. (2019) "The Crime-reducing Benefits of a College Degree: Evidence from a Nationally Representative US sample", *Criminal Justice Studies*, 32(4): 297-316.

Doherty, Elaine Eggleston (2006) "Self-control, Social Bonds, and Desistance: A Test of Life-course Interdependence", *Criminology*, 44(4): 807-833.

Duckworth, Angela Lee & Margaret L. Kern (2011) "A Meta-analysis of the Convergent Validity of Self-control Measures", *Journal of Research in Personality*, 45(3): 259-268.

Earle, Rod (2016) *Convict Criminology: Inside and Out*, Bristol: Policy Press.

Garfinkel, Harold (1956) "Conditions of Successful Degradation Ceremonies", *American Journal of Sociology*, 61(5): 420-424.

Goodman, Leo A. (1960) "On the Exact Variance of Products", *Journal of the American Statistical Association*, 55(292): 708-713.

Gordon, Haward & Bracie Weldon (2003) "The Impact of Career and Technical Education Programs on Adult Offenders: Learning Behind Bars", *Journal of Correctional Education*, 54(4): 200-209.

Gottfredson, Michael R. & Travis Hirschi (1990) *A General Theory of Crime*, Stanford: Stanford University Press.

Gove, Walter R. & Robert D. Crutchfield (1982) "The Family and Juvenile Delinquency", *Sociological Quarterly*, 23(3): 301-319.

Gundur, Rajeev V. & Daniel R. Kavish (2022) "Captives in Society: The Role of Race in the Carceral Cycle", in Ben Crewe, Andrew Goldsmith & Mark Halsey (eds.), *Power and Pain in the Modern Prison*, New York: Oxford University Press, pp. 235-250.

Harris, Kathleen Mullan, Carolyn Tucker Halpern, Eric A. Whitsel, Jon M. Hussey, Ley A. Killeya-Jones, Joyce Tabor, & Sarah C. Dean (2009) *The National Longitudinal Study of Adolescent Health: Research Design*. Retrieved from http://www.cpc.unc.edu/projects/addhealth/design

Haynie, Dana L. (2002) "Friendship Networks and Delinquency: The Relative Nature of Peer Delinquency", *Journal of Quantitative Criminology*, 18(2): 99-134.

Haynie, Dana L. (2001) "Delinquent Peers Revisited: Does Network Structure Matter?", *American Journal of Sociology*, 106(4): 1013-1057.

Haynie, Dana L. & D. Wayne Osgood (2005) "Reconsidering Peers and Delinquency: How Do Peers Matter?", *Social Forces*, 84(2): 1109-1130.

Heimer, Karen & Ross L. Matsueda (1994) "Role-taking, Role Commitment, and Delinquency: A Theory of Differential Social Control", *American Sociological Review*, 59(3): 365-390.

Higgins, George E., Brian D. Fell & Abby L. Wilson (2006) "Digital Piracy: Assessing the Contributions of an Integrated Self-control Theory and Social Learning Theory Using Structural Equation Modeling", *Criminal Justice Studies*, 19(1): 3-22.

Hirschi, Travis (1969) *Causes of Delinquency*, Berkeley: University of California Press.

Hu, Li-tze & Peter M. Bentler (1998) "Fit Indices in Covariance Structure Modeling: Sensitivity to Underparameterized Model Misspecification", *Psychological Methods*, 3(4): 424-453.

Huizinga, David & Kimberly L. Henry (2008) "The Effect of Arrest and Justice System Sanctions on Subsequent Behavior: Findings from Longitudinal and Other Studies", in Akiva M. Liberman (ed.), *The Long View of Crime: A Synthesis of Longitudinal Research*, New York: Springer, pp. 220-254.

Humes, Karen R., Nicholas A. Jones & Roberto R. Ramirez (2011) "Overview of Race and Hispanic Origins: 2010", *2010 Census Briefs*, 1-23.

Irwin, John (1987) "Reflections on Ethnography", *Journal of Contemporary Ethnography*, 16(1): 41-48.

Jöreskog, Karl G. & Dag Sörbom (1993) *LISREL 8: Structural Equation Modeling with the SIMPLIS Command Language*, Hillsdale: Erlbaum.

Kavish, Daniel Ryan, Christopher W. Mullins & Danielle A. Soto (2016) "Interactionist Labeling: Formal and Informal Labeling's Effects on Juvenile Delinquency", *Crime & Delinquency*, 62(10): 1313-1336.

Kenny, David A. (2015). *Measuring Model Fit* – November 24. Retrieved from http://davidakenny.net/cm/fit.htm

Kressierer, Dana Katherine & Clifton D. Bryant (1996) "Adoption as Deviance: Socially Constructed Parent-child Kinship as a Stigmatized and Legally Burdened Relationship", *Deviant Behavior*, 17: 391-415.

Longshore, Douglas & Susan Turner (1998) "Self-control and Criminal Opportunity: Cross-sectional Test of the General Theory of Crime", *Criminal Justice and Behavior*, 25(1): 81-98.

Lopes, Gina, Marvin D. Krohn, Alan J. Lizotte, Nicole M. Schmidt, Bob Edward Vasquez & Jón Gunnar Bernburg (2012) "Labeling and Cumulative Disadvantage: The Impact of Formal Police Intervention on Life Chances and Crime During Emerging Adulthood", *Crime & Delinquency,* 58(3): 456-488.

MacCallum, Robert C., Michael W. Browne & Hazuki M. Sugawara (1996) "Power Analysis and Determination of Sample Size for Covariance Structure Modeling", *Psychological Methods,* 1(2): 130-149.

Mack, Kristin Y., Michael J. Leiber, Richard A. Featherstone & Maria A. Monserud (2007) "Reassessing the Family-delinquency Association: Do Family Type, Family Processes, and Economic Factors Make a Difference?", *Journal of Criminal Justice*, 35(1): 51-67.

MacKenzie, Doris Layton & L. J. Hickman (1998) *What Works in Corrections? An Examination of the Effectiveness of the Type of Rehabilitation Programs Offered by Washington Department of Corrections – Report to the State of Washington Legislature Joint Adult and Review Committee*, College Park: University of Maryland.

MacKinnon, David P., Amanda J. Fairchild & Matthew S. Fritz (2007) "Mediation Analysis", *Annual Review of Psychology*, 58: 593-614.

MacKinnon, David P., Chondra M. Lockwood, Jeanne M. Hoffman, Stephen G. West & Virgil Sheets (2002) "A Comparison of Methods to Test Mediation and Other Intervening Variable Effects", *Psychological Methods*, 7(1): 83-104.

Maruna, Shadd. (2011) "Reentry as a Rite of Passage", *Punishment & Society*, 13(1): 3-28.

Maruna, Shadd (2001) *Making Good: How Ex-convicts Reform and Rebuild Their Lives*, Washington (DC): American Psychological Association.

Maruna, Shadd, Thomas P. Lebel, Nick Mitchell & Michelle Naples (2004) "Pygmalion in the Reintegration Process: Desistance from Crime through the Looking Glass", *Psychology, Crime & Law*, 10: 271-281.

Maruna, Shadd & Marieke Liem (2021) "Where Is This Story Going? A Critical Analysis of the Emerging Field of Narrative Criminology", *Annual Review of Criminology*, 4: 125-146.

Matsueda, Ross L. (1992) "Reflected Appraisals, Parental Labeling, and Delinquency: Specifying a Symbolic Interactionist Theory", *American Journal of Sociology,* 97(6): 1577-1611.

Mead, George Herbert (1934) *Mind, Self, and Society*, Chicago: University of Chicago Press.

Mercer, Kerri Russo (2009) "The Importance of Funding Postsecondary Correctional Educational Programs", *Community College Review*, 37(2): 153-164.

Morris, Robert G. & Alex R. Piquero (2013) "For Whom Do Sanctions Deter and Label?", *Justice Quarterly*, 30(5): 837-868.

Muthén, Linda K & Bengt O. Muthen (1998-2010) *Mplus User's Guide*, Los Angeles: Muthen and Muthen.

Olsen, D. (2015) "City of Springfield may tweak marijuana possession ordinance if Rauner signs bill", *The State Journal-Register* – June 27. Retrieved from http://www.sj-r.com/article/20150627/NEWS/150629549/?Start=1

Paternoster, Raymond & Leeann Iovanni (1989) "The Labeling Perspective and Delinquency: An Elaboration of the Theory and An Assessment of the Evidence", *Justice Quarterly*, 6(3): 359-394.

Petrich, Damon M., Travis C. Pratt, Cheryl Leo Jonson & Francis T. Cullen (2021) "Custodial Sanctions and Reoffending: A Meta-analytic Review", *Crime and Justice*, 50(1): 353-424.

Pratt, Travis C. (2016) "A Self-control/Life-course Theory of Criminal Behavior", *European Journal of Criminology*, 13(1): 129-146.

Pratt, Travis C., Teresa May & Lisa Kan (2020) "Increasing Pretrial Releases and Reducing Felony Convictions for Defendants: Implications for Desistance from Crime", *Canadian Journal of Criminology and Criminal Justice*, 62(3): 51-70.

Puzzanchera, Charles (2014) *Juvenile Arrests 2012*, Washington (DC): Department of Justice, Office of Juvenile Justice and Delinquency Prevention – *December*. *Retrieved from* https://ojjdp.ojp.gov/sites/g/files/xyckuh176/files/pubs/248513.pdf

Quinn, Susan Theresa (2010) "The Gang Member Label and Juvenile Justice Decision-making", *Electronic Theses, Treatises, and Dissertations*, Tallahassee: Florida State University, pp. 1-154.

Rankin, Joseph H. (1983) "The Family Context of Delinquency", *Social Problems*, 30(4): 466-479.

Restivo, Emily & Mark M. Lanier (2015) "Measuring the Contextual Effects and Mitigating Factors of Labeling Theory", *Justice Quarterly*, 32(1): 116-141.

Richards, Stephen C., Jeffrey Ian Ross, Greg Newbold, Michael Lenza, Richard S. Jones, Daniel S. Murphy & Robert S. Grigsby (2012) "Convict Criminology, Prisoner Reentry and Public Policy Recommendations", *Journal of Prisoners on Prisons*, 21(1&2): 16-34.

Rocheleau, Gregory C. & Jorge M. Chavez (2015) "Guilt by Association: The Relationship Between Deviant Peers and Deviant Labels", *Deviant Behavior*, 36(3): 167-186.

Rocque, Michael, Chad Posick & Ray Paternoster (2016) "Identities Through Time: An Exploration of Identity Change as a Cause of Desistance", *Justice Quarterly*, 33(1): 45-72.

Ross, Jeffrey Ian & Stephen C. Richards (2003) *Convict Criminology*, Belmont (CA): Wadsworth/Thomson Learning.

Ross, Jeffrey Ian & Francesca Vianello (eds.) (2020) *Convict Criminology for the Future*, New York: Routledge.

Rushton, Bruce (2012) "The war on weed: Prohibition costs Illinois big bucks", *The State Journal-Register*. Retrieved from http://illinoistimes.com/article-9633-the-war-on-weed.html

Schermelleh-Engel, Karin, Helfried Moosbrugger & Hans Muller (2003) "Evaluating the Fit of Structural Equation Models: Tests of Significance and Descriptive Goodness-of-fit Measures", *Methods of Psychological Research*, 8(2): 23-74.

Schur, Edwin M. (1971) *Labeling Deviant Behavior: Its Sociological Implications*, New York: Harper & Row.

Sherman, Lawrence W. (2014) "Experiments in Criminal Sanctions: Labeling, Deterrence, and Restorative Justice", in David P. Farrington & Joseph Murray (eds.), *Labeling Theory: Empirical tests*, New Brunswick (NJ): Transaction, pp. 149-176.

Sherman, Lawrence W., Douglas A. Smith., Janell D. Schmidt & Dennis P. Rogan (1992) "Crime, Punishment, and Stake in Conformity: Legal and Informal Control of Domestic Violence", *American Sociological Review*, 57(5): 680-690.

Skardhamar, Torbjørn & Kjetil Telle (2012) "Post-release Employment and Recidivism in Norway", *Journal of Quantitative Criminology*, 28(4): 629-649.

Slocum, Lee Ann, Stephanie Ann Wiley & Finn-Aage Esbensen (2016) "The Importance of Being Satisfied: A Longitudinal Exploration of Police Contact, Procedural Injustice, and Subsequent Delinquency", *Criminal Justice and Behavior*, 43(1): 7-26.

Smith, Douglas A. & Raymond Paternoster (1990) "Formal Processing and Future Delinquency: Deviance Amplification as Selection Artifact", *Law & Society Review*, 24(5): 1109-1131.

Sobel, Michael E. (1982) "Asymptotic Confidence Intervals for Indirect Effects in Structural Equation Models", *Sociological Methodology*, 13: 290-312.

Sweeten, Gary (2006) "Who Will Graduate? Disruption of High School Education by Arrest and Court Involvement", *Justice Quarterly*, 23(4): 462-480.

Tannenbaum, Frank (1938) *Crime and Community*, New York: Columbia University Press.

Tannenbaum, Frank (1925) "The Professional Criminal: An Inquiry Into the Making of Criminals", *Century Magazine*, 110: 577-588.

Tannenbaum, Frank (1922) *Wall Shadows: A Study in American Prisons*, New York: GP Putnam's Sons.

Thompson, Gregory A. (2014) "Labeling in Interactional Practice: Applying Labeling Theory to Interactions and Interactional Analysis to Labeling", *Symbolic Interaction*, 37(4): 458-482.

Tietjen, Grant (2019) "Convict Criminology: Learning from the Past, Confronting the Present, Expanding for the Future", *Critical Criminology*, 27: 101-114.

Tietjen, Grant & Daniel Kavish (2020) "In the Pool Without a Life Jacket: Status Fragility and Convict Criminology in the Current Criminological Era", in Jeffrey Ian Ross & Francesca Vianello (eds.), *Convict Criminology for the Future*, New York: Routledge, pp. 66-81.

Turanovic, Jillian J. & Travis C. Pratt (2013) "The Consequences of Maladaptive Coping: Integrating General Strain and Self-control Theories to Specify a Causal Pathway Between Victimization and Offending", *Journal of Quantitative Criminology*, 29: 321-345.

Uggen, Christopher (2000) "Work as a Turning Point in the Life Course of Criminals: A Duration Model of Age, Employment, and Recidivism", *American Sociological Review*, 65(4): 529-546.

Visher, Christy, Sara Debus & Jennifer Yahner (2008) *Employment After Prison: A Longitudinal Study of Releasees in Three States*, Research Brief – Washington (DC): Urban Institute, Justice Policy Center. Retrieved from https://search.issuelab.org/resources/7153/7153.pdf

Waller, Willard (1932) *The Sociology of Teaching*, New York: Wiley.

Wiley, Stephanie & Finn-Aage Esbensen (2013) "The Effect of Police Contact: Does Official Intervention Result in Deviance Amplification", *Crime & Delinquency*, 62(3): 283-307.

Wiley, Stephanie, Lee Ann Slocum & Finn-Aage Esbensen (2013) "The Unintended Consequences of Being Stopped or Arrested: An Exploration of the Labeling Mechanisms Through Which Police Contact Leads to Subsequent Delinquency", *Criminology*, 51(4): 927-966.

Wilson, Sean (2019) "Failures of Reintegration and the Return to Prison", in Jason M. Williams & Steven Kniffley (eds.), *Black Males and the Criminal Justice System*, New York: Routledge, pp. 85-94.

Wright, Bradley. R., Avshalom Caspi, Terrie E. Moffit & Phil A. Silva (1999) "Low Self-control, Social Bonds, and Crime: Social Causation, Social Selection, or Both?", *Criminology*, 37(3): 479-514.

Yahner, Jennifer & Christy Visher (2008) *Illinois Prisoners' Reentry Success Three Years After Release*, Research Brief – Washington (DC): Urban Institute, Justice Policy Center. Retrieved from https://www.issuelab.org/resources/7346/7346.pdf

Yeager, Matthew G. (2015) *Frank Tannenbaum: The Making of a Convict Criminologist*, New York: Routledge.

Yeager, Matthew G. (2011) "Frank Tannenbaum: The Making of a Convict Criminologist", *The Prison Journal*, 91(2): 177-197.

APPENDIX

Table 1: Descriptive Statistics

	Variables	Range	Mean	Standard Error[2]
			(n = 10,828)	
1	MALE	0-1	0.502	0.006
2	AGE (W1)	11-21	15.077	0.113
	RACE			
3	NON-WHITE	0-1	0.344	0.028
	FAMILY TYPE			
4	TRADITIONAL TWO-PARENT	0-1	0.577	0.013
5	SES	1-5	2.698	0.052
6	PUBLIC ASSISTANCE	0-1	0.096	0.009
	PERCEPTIONS OF CARE (W2)			
7	TEACHER	1-5	2.462	0.024
8	PARENT	1-5	1.236	0.012
9	FRIEND	1-5	1.689	0.016
10	LOW SELF-CONTROL	1-20	6.394	0.066
11	PARENTAL LABELING	0-1	0.365	0.010
12	SCHOOL LABELING	0-1	0.084	0.007
13	FORMAL LABELING	0-1	0.084	0.005
	DELINQUENCY (W1)			
14	PROPERTY DAMAGE	0-3	0.247	0.010
15	STEAL 50 OR MORE	0-3	0.069	0.005
16	BURGLARY	0-3	0.070	0.005
17	ROBBERY	0-3	0.056	0.005
18	SELL DRUGS	0-3	0.131	0.010
19	STEAL 50 OR LESS	0-3	0.328	0.014
	CRIMINAL BEHAVIOR (W3)			
20	PROPERTY DAMAGE	0-3	0.120	0.006
21	STEAL 50 OR MORE	0-3	0.049	0.004
22	BURGLARY	0-3	0.027	0.003
23	ROBBERY	0-3	0.026	0.003
24	SELL DRUGS	0-3	0.187	0.011
25	STEAL 50 OR LESS	0-3	0.118	0.009

[1] Weighted means are reported
[2] Standard errors adjusted for survey design features of Add Health

Table 2: Structural Model Predicting Juvenile Delinquency, Formal Labeling, and Criminal Behavior

Variables	Delinquency (Wave 1)			Formal Labeling			Criminal Behavior (Wave 3)			Criminal Behavior (Wave 3)		
	b	SE	B	b	SE	B	b	SE	B	b	SE	B
Formal Label (W1)	-	-	-	-	-	-	-	-	-	0.246 ***	0.032	0.323
Delinquency (W1)	-	-	-	0.333 ***	0.055	0.251	0.378 ***	0.037	0.372	0.294 ***	0.040	0.291
Parental Label	0.171 ***	0.037	0.100	0.143 *	0.057	0.063	-0.038	0.036	-0.022	-0.073 *	0.035	-0.042
School Labell	0.224 **	0.080	0.068	-0.039	0.099	-0.009	0.009	0.067	0.003	0.019	0.064	0.006
Low Self-Control	0.102 ***	0.005	0.393	0.003	0.012	0.007	-0.006	0.007	-0.023	-0.007	0.007	-0.026
Male	0.318 ***	0.037	0.194	0.636 ***	0.070	0.293	0.433 ***	0.043	0.260	0.274 ***	0.047	0.166
Age	-0.018	0.012	-0.035	-0.048 *	0.019	-0.070	-0.105 ***	0.012	-0.199	-0.092 ***	0.013	-0.176
SES	0.055 ***	0.016	0.074	0.017	0.028	0.017	0.105 ***	0.018	0.100	0.100 ***	0.017	0.131
Public Assistance	-0.135 *	0.058	-0.047	-0.020	0.092	-0.005	0.014	0.076	0.020	0.020	0.071	0.007
Family Type	-0.085 **	0.033	-0.051	-0.105 *	0.050	-0.048	0.046	0.045	0.071	0.071	0.045	0.042
Race - Non-White	0.149 ***	0.043	0.085	-0.056	0.061	-0.024	-0.020		-0.006	-0.011	0.042	-0.004
Negative Perceptions of Care (W2)												
Teacher	-	-	-	-	-	-	0.075 ***	0.018	0.091	0.075 ***	0.018	0.092
Parent	-	-	-	-	-	-	0.016	0.037	0.011	0.016	0.036	0.011
Friend	-	-	-	-	-	-	-0.017	0.028	-0.016	-0.017	0.028	-0.016
Formal Labeling - Indirect[a]	-	-	-	-	-	-	-	-	-	0.082 ***	0.015	0.081
R^2	0.251			0.201			0.314			0.403		

X^2 (*p*-value)	182.441 (0.000)
df	52[b]
TLI	0.952
CFI	0.950
RMSEA	0.017

Note. All estimates corrected and standard errors adjusted for survey design features of AddHealth ($N = 8,439$)

[a] This is the indirect effect of formal labeling from wave 1 delinquency to wave 3 delinquency

[b] The x2 value and degrees of freedom are corrected for using the WSLMV estimator. Only the *P*-value should be interpreted for model fit (Muthen & Muthen. 1998-2010)

* p ≤ .05   ** p ≤ .01   *** p ≤ .001

Table 3: Causal Steps Approach to Mediation

Variables	b		SE	B
Juvenile Delinquency (X --> Y)	0.378	***	0.037	0.372
Juvenile Delinquency (X --> M)	0.333	***	0.055	0.251
Juvenile Delinquency (X --> Y, Controlling for M)	0.294	***	0.040	0.291
Low Self-Control (X --> Y)	-0.006		0.007	-0.023
Low Self-Control (X --> M)	0.003		0.012	0.007
Low Self-Control (X --> Y, Controlling for M)	-0.007		0.007	-0.026

Note. All estimates corrected and standard errors adjusted for survey design features of the Add Health.

X= Independent Variable (Juvenile Delinquency or Low Self-Control), M= Mediating Variable (Formal Labeling), Y=Dependent Variable (Criminal Behavior).

Formal Labeling in Full Model (b= 0.246, SE= 0.032, B= 0.323)
* $p \le .05$ ** $p \le .01$ *** $p \le .001$

Figure 1: Measurement Model for Juvenile Delinquency

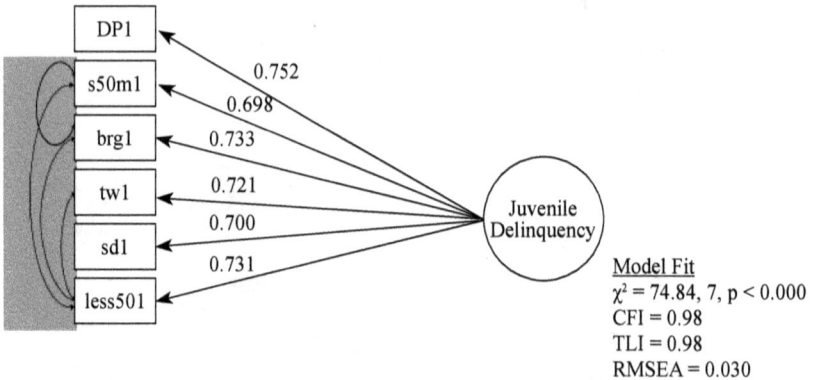

Model Fit
$\chi^2 = 74.84$, 7, p < 0.000
CFI = 0.98
TLI = 0.98
RMSEA = 0.030

Notes: All paths are significant. The small double-headed arrows are error terms.
The χ^2 value and degrees of freedom are corrected for using the MLSMV estimator.
Only the p-value should be interpreted for model fit (Muthen and Muthen, 1998-2010).

Figure 2: Measurement Model of Criminal Behavior

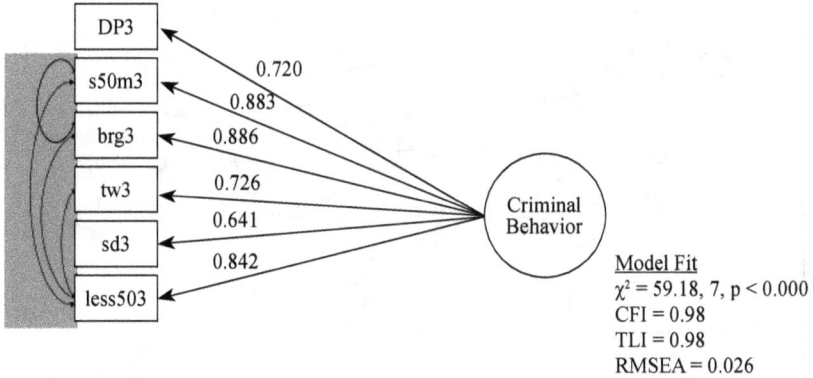

Notes: All paths are significant. The small double-headed arrows are error terms.
The χ² value and degrees of freedom are corrected for using the MLSMV estimator.
Only the p-value should be interpreted for model fit (Muthen and Muthen, 1998-2010).

Figure 3: Structural Model of Juvenile Delinquency

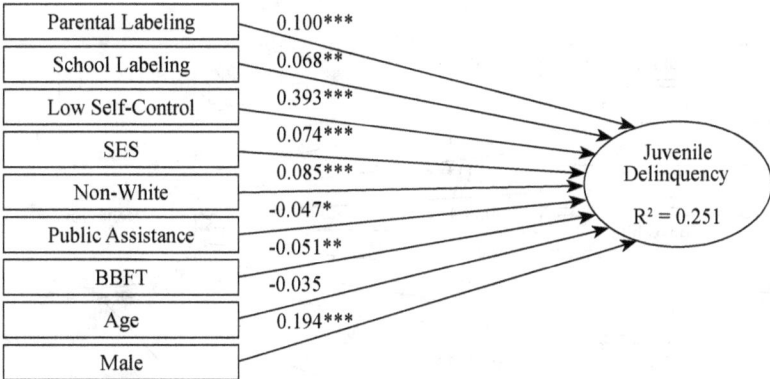

Notes: Standardized estimates reported. * p ≤ .05   ** p ≤ .01   *** p ≤ .001

Figure 4: Structural Model of Formal Labeling

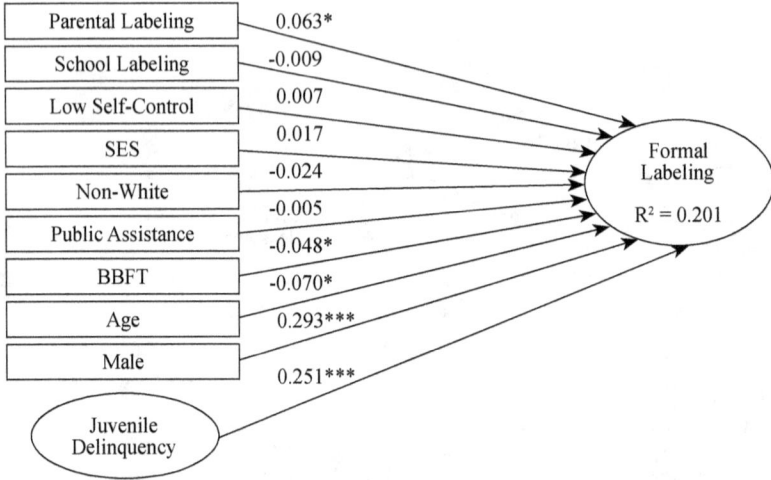

Notes: Standardized estimates reported. * p ≤ .05   ** p ≤ .01   *** p ≤ .001

Figure 5: Structural Model of Criminal Behavior

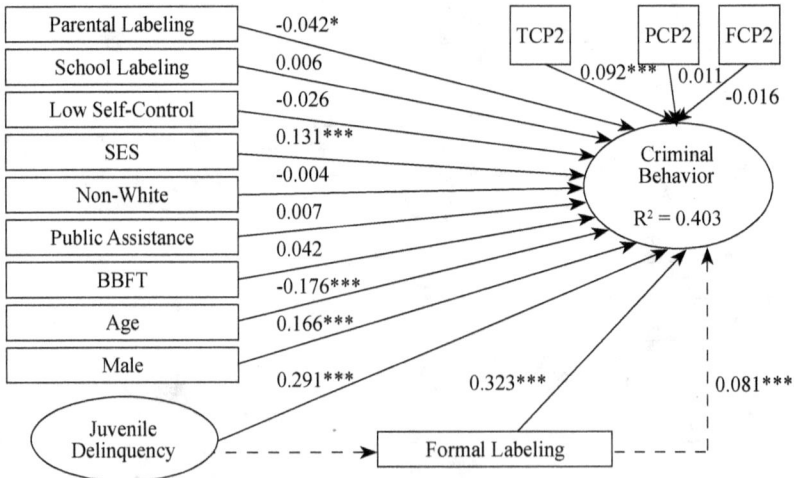

Notes: Standardized estimates reported. * p ≤ .05   ** p ≤ .01   *** p ≤ .001

ABOUT THE AUTHOR

Daniel Ryan Kavish, PhD is an Associate Professor of Sociology and Criminal Justice at Southwestern Oklahoma State University. Professor Kavish earned his PhD from the Department of Criminology and Criminal Justice at Southern Illinois University Carbondale (SIUC). He is one of the co-founders of the American Society of Criminology's Division of Convict Criminology and serves as co-editor of the division's official newsletter, *Criminology with Conviction*. His research interests include criminological theory, deviant subcultures, masculinity, collateral consequences, stigma, desistance, and the scholarly contributions of formerly incarcerated researchers. Professor Kavish's research and book reviews have been published in peer-reviewed journals such as *Crime & Delinquency*, *Criminal Justice Studies*, the *Journal of Qualitative Criminal Justice and Criminology*, *Critical Issues in Justice and Politics*, *Contemporary Justice Review*, and the *Canadian Journal of Criminology and Criminal Justice*.

RESPONSES

Thinking Critically About the Next Decade of Convict Criminology
Jeffrey Ian Ross

ABSTRACT

Convict Criminology (CC) is a quarter-century old. During those years, this combined approach, group, organization, school, theory, and network has produced scholarly literature and mentored actual and aspiring doctoral students who have been incarcerated and released from carceral custody, assisting them in their careers and engaging in corrections-related policy debates and activism. As the academic fields and real-world practice of Corrections and Critical Criminology have changed, and the people who have been involved in CC have come and gone, Convict Criminology has evolved. This paper briefly reviews the aims and history of CC, then applies a strength, weaknesses, opportunities, and threats (SWOT) analysis to Convict Criminology with the goal of suggesting ways that the leadership, members, and allies of the CC approach might best further its mission.

INTRODUCTION

The Convict Criminology (CC) idea was born over a quarter of a century ago. It started out as a series of conversations between Stephen C. Richards and Jeffrey Ian Ross, then morphed through a number of panels held at academic conferences, the production of scholarly studies, and the development into a worldwide global approach, collective, field, group, movement, network, organization, school, and theory.[1]

Given an appropriate quantity and quality of resources (including interest), the implications of each of these different labels, the relative suitability of them, and their advantages and disadvantages could be traced. We might even be able to set up a rough heuristic by which to judge them under those circumstances, but this path would probably not be much more than a temporary distraction. In reality, CC is a little of each of these things. In other words, it fits into each one of these categories just a bit, and that is why CC is a somewhat difficult to categorize and for those not familiar with it to understand.

Undoubtedly, whichever label is applied to CC will inevitably beg a number of questions. Most importantly, what are the implications of using one label over another, and how should we measure the success or failure of this kind of entity? Again, this effort would likely turn out to be a rabbit hole, with minimal gains to be achieved. That being said, it is probably a good idea to clarify the original aims of CC. When the movement began in the mid-1990s, its founders shared a general overall belief that the convict/ ex-convict voice was ignored, if not at least marginalized, in the academic fields of criminology, criminal justice, and corrections, in addition to policy-making contexts (Ross & Richards, 2003). CC also sought to help individuals who had been incarcerated, as well as those who had been released from jails or prisons who were interested in pursuing graduate degrees and perhaps careers in academia.

CC also attempted to engage in prison and criminal justice/legal activism and policy work, as a means to reform and transform corrections and the criminal justice system. Originally this kind of activity was difficult to do as older, former or original members of CC were too occupied and focused on organizational maintenance and development (Ross & Tietjen, this issue). Many individuals currently associated with Convict Criminology feel that correctional reform is a treadmill and a futile endeavor; they want to do more than reform and transform, wishing to change what the criminal justice/legal system looks like and how it operates, with a much stronger focus on de-carceration/prison abolition (Kalicia, 2018) and a greater commitment to social justice. This focus may reflect the kinds of literature the newer generation of CC members were exposed to versus the older one, which includes, but is not limited to concentrations on popular Black feminist research, and sluggish criminal justice and correctional reforms.[2] It may also be a reflection of exposure to popular social and cultural movements like Black Lives Matter and the #metoo movement. These subtle changes in CC's overall direction may also be the result of an increased awareness of these issues.

Meanwhile, Convict Criminology was and still remains global in scope (e.g. Ross & Vianello, 2021), and this approach has recently boomed due to an influx of new and more diverse members. In other words, the CC approach could be applied to any country that locks up their citizens, and not simply the locations where CC emerged.

Another thing to keep in mind is that CC was not established exclusively for convicts and ex-cons, but also for people who were justice-involved or justice-impacted, and individuals who might be considered or self-identify as prison activists (Tietjen, 2019). Why? There are a significant number of individuals who, because of prior suspected or actual criminal activity committed by themselves or by a loved one, had close contact with the criminal justice system, but were never charged, convicted, or incarcerated. This experience affected these colleagues deeply, thus they support the overall CC mission, sharing its goals and vision.

Regardless, both the objectives of CC and the people who have been drawn to the network were and remain relatively disparate, committed, and ambitious. The growth of CC, much like negotiating traffic whether as a pedestrian, bicyclist, or motorist, has been at times exciting, frustrating, and fun. On the plus side, CC has granted those affiliated with the group the opportunity to play a small part in advising those released from correctional custody through their bachelors and graduate degrees and into the professional job search process. On the other hand, it can often be challenging to encounter those individuals whose sole purpose seems to be to disrupt and challenge, rather than to build.

A BRIEF HISTORY OF THE CONVICT CRIMINOLOGY NETWORK

We could trace the history of the CC network in a variety of ways. For instance, we might choose to look at the larger structural forces that were conducive to the formation of CC (Ross, 2021b). Alternatively, we could examine the network through the paths of the various individuals who have come in and out of the group via the numerous panels and conferences held at different venues where CC members attended and presented papers (e.g. Ross & Vianello, 2021; Ross & Tietjen, 2022). Although this historical knowledge base is important and helps provide a context, this kind of information is available elsewhere,[3] thus it is not necessary to review it again here. On the other hand, it might be valuable to ask why it is important to explore where CC currently is as a network and where it is going.

WHY IS IT IMPORTANT TO HAVE A SENSE OF WHERE CONVICT CRIMINOLOGY IS NOW AND THE FUTURE OF THE NETWORK?

Although one might wish to distinguish between the CC network and the official ASC Division of Convict Criminology, for the sake of simplicity, these two groups are comingled. In sum, this exercise can help us with the strategic planning process. CC has limited resources (e.g. time, social capital, etc.), so it is wise to consider carefully their appropriate application and choose approaches that will minimize wastefulness. This strategic planning will also assist CC in adapting to current circumstances and enabling the network to achieve its stated goals.

HOW DO WE GO ABOUT GETTING A SENSE OF THE FUTURE OF CONVICT CRIMINOLOGY?

It is difficult to predict the future. This notion is even more salient when the world experiences black-swan events, such as the global COVID-19 pandemic. Nevertheless, experts have developed numerous qualitative and quantitative methods to assist them in trying to determine what the future might look like for a variety of situations and organizations. Choosing an appropriate method among these options depends upon a number of factors, including the quality of the data and the resources that are available to perform the analysis.[4]

Before trying to forecast the future of CC, selecting publicly available information may prove helpful to shaping our analysis. This includes the conclusions of major books on CC and the critiques of CC. Perhaps there is some merit in consulting the relatively short conclusions of the major CC texts such as books by Ross and Richards (2003), Earle (2016), and Ross and Vianello (2021). Examining these three works, we find, however, that although the last chapters of the monographs predictably review or summarize the contents of the studies, only the two edited books by Ross and Richards (2003), and Ross and Vianello (2021) prognosticate about the future.

That being said, although Richards and Ross (2003) outline what they believe needs to be done to improve or reform the field of corrections, they do not make specific predictions or recommendations about what is in store for CC.[5] Vianello and Ross (2021), on the other hand, basically argue that the network should continue to do what it is doing, and they outline five "practical suggestions" (p. 214-216). They are:

- "CC panels must be organized to accommodate the growing interest in the group" (p. 215);
- "strengthen our active involvement in prisoner education" (p. 215);

- develop and increase "contacts within the nonprofit sector (e.g., Foundations) and among prisoner support groups which advocate for prisoner rights and criminal reform and carry out awareness-raising campaigns" (p. 215);
- "take seriously the challenges of internationalization..." (p. 216); and
- "develop new opportunities inside the university environment (visiting professorships and exchanges for Ph.D. students) dedicated to former prisoners (which also means finding the funding for this purpose" (p. 216).

These recommendations were published approximately one year ago. Some attention could be spent determining where CC is with each of these suggestions, but I think that this might be a little premature. Instead, I will leave this analysis to someone else who is suitably motivated.

Critiques of Convict Criminology
Meanwhile, a handful of critiques of Convict Criminology have been published (e.g. Larsen & Piché, 2012; Newbold & Ross, 2013; Belknap, 2015). In short, these evaluations point to three primary shortcomings within the CC framework: the CC methodology is not sufficiently rigorous; CC seems to be unnecessarily exclusive; and CC needs to do more to include women, ethnic minorities, and members of the LGBTQ community. Some of these criticisms are legitimate, whereas others are unfounded or based on a poor understanding of CC (Ross et al., 2016).[6] Currently, however, I believe that the most helpful approach to move CC forward is to perform a SWOT analysis.

STRENGTHS, WEAKNESSES, OPPORTUNITIES AND THREATS ANALYSIS

One of the prominent ways to determine the status of an organization and where it is going is the SWOT analysis method. Although observers may be aware of the flaws of this technique and, thus, disinclined to utilize this analytical approach, which is relatively easy to perform, it is an appropriate place to start this examination. If it stimulates some productive conversations, then it will have served its purpose. In my SWOT analysis, I focus primarily on the CC network, though I also comingle my review with the field of corrections. In outlining what I believe are CC's current strengths, weaknesses, opportunities, and threats, issues might spill over from one category to another.

Strengths

Compared to other recent approaches to understanding and reforming corrections, CC remains a realistic policy-oriented approach to improving the lives of the many men and women who are incarcerated or released from correctional custody. Convict Criminology has close to twenty-five years of scholarship, mentorship, activism, and experience to draw on, which includes providing a realistic picture of life behind bars, life upon re-entry, and the fight to end mass incarceration, both in the United States and elsewhere. CC has assisted numerous formerly incarcerated people through their bachelors, masters, and doctoral degrees. CC has also connected with a relatively large number of people who are interested in the subject and network. These individuals are not simply scholars, but are also students (at different levels of their formal education), people who are or were incarcerated, and supportive people who have not had direct contact with the criminal justice system.

In terms of scholarship, one of the more exciting developments has been the translation of Ross and Vianello's *Convict Criminology for the Future* into Portuguese and its publication as *A Criminologia dos Condenados E O Futuro* by Brazilian publisher Tirant Lo Branch. Now that the book has been translated, it will be most useful to Portuguese-speaking students and scholars of criminology/criminal justice and corrections, journalists, prison activists, and relevant policy makers, legislators, and practitioners (i.e. especially individuals who work in correctional facilities) or those who are incarcerated. Among the ten countries where Portuguese is the principal language, the book may find its greatest utility in Brazil and Portugal, countries that have some of the highest numbers of people who are incarcerated in the world.

Over the past decade, various Brazilian criminologists and lawyers have been introduced to Convict Criminology scholarship and pedagogy. Hopefully *A Criminologia dos Condenados E O Futuro* will be useful for them. The translation of the book into Portuguese will increase discussions regarding not just the role of convicts and ex-convicts in the scholarly study of criminology/criminal justice, including much needed reforms, as well as serve as a catalyst to greater cross-national co-operation in addressing the challenges faced by incarcerated individuals who are pursuing postgraduate studies behind bars and upon release.

CC is now an official division of the American Society of Criminology (ASC). The Division of Convict Criminology (DCC) also has a significant number of members. By latest counts, the division has 80 members in good standing (i.e. members who are officially registered). Panels are well attended, as are the social and dinner that the division sponsors.

Why is this a good number? The division was granted official status during the pandemic, and the DCC now has more members than a handful of other divisions of the ASC that were also recently started.[7] The DCC also has excellent relationships with other ASC divisions, including the divisions of Critical Criminology and Social Justice, Queer Criminology, Victimology, and Women and Crime.

At least 75 percent of the eight-member executive board of the DCC is diverse in terms of gender and race, and at least half of the membership is composed of women. A similar pattern exists in terms of the six committees that report directly to the board. In short, CC has social capital. In a broader sense, no nation has yet to abolish its carceral facilities nor is this going to happen any time soon. Furthermore, at least in the United States, the number of individuals who are being sent to jails and prisons is decreasing (Gramlich, 2021), while due to COVID a greater number appear to have been released. Many of these individuals wish to complete not just a bachelor's degree, but advanced degrees as well. In the United States and Canada, at least, academia represents a real option for those individuals who will re-enter society. In other words, they may not be able to get a job in a trade, especially one that requires state licensing, but they may be able to secure a job and excel at teaching in a community college or university.

Weaknesses

With respect to weaknesses, there continues to be a number of people who make and hold unfounded assumptions about CC. These beliefs are often based on rumors, incomplete information, or a poor understanding about the aims of CC and what CC does. Why is this the case? I suspect it has something to do with the following factors:

- the so-called death of expertise (e.g., Nichols, 2018);
- the exponential increase in the presence of and reliance on social media;
- confusion and poor understanding surrounding the role of lived experiences, and some people's and organizations' commitment to reifying the "lived experience"; and
- a disinclination, not just by the general public, but by many of our criminology colleagues, to avoid reading peer-reviewed research and properly understanding it.

Why is this bad? CC constantly wages a battle against misinformation, and this becomes exhausting and frustrating. Many CC members appear to be burned out from continually having to explain CC concepts, ideas, and the purpose of this approach to critics who have read very little or no CC scholarship/literature at all. Since members of the network often juggle competing teaching, scholarship, service and family demands, this struggle becomes an additional burden. Closely connected to this last point is the fact that many formerly incarcerated people seem to disengage with the CC network once they get out of prison or reach one or more educational milestones (i.e. bachelors, masters, or doctoral degrees) (Ross & Tietjen, 2022).

Opportunities
The creation of the Division of Convict Criminology represents a true opportunity. When the founders and their allies got together almost twenty-five years ago, they had very modest goals, which transitioned over time. One of them was to not become a division of the American Society of Criminology. In fact, there was quite a bit of opposition to this specific engagement, but over time, this position softened.

On a related note, at no point in time has CC had as diverse a leadership group as it currently does. CC has also managed to attract a large number of energetic and curious graduate students. Furthermore, CC possesses a very strong intellectual scholarly base (of peer-reviewed articles, chapters, and books) to draw on (Ross & Tietjen, 2022). One aspect of this effort has been a strong attachment to the *Journal of Prisoners on Prisons* (www.jpp.org), which specializes in publishing convict authors in a peer-reviewed academic journal.

Threats

Convict Criminology will have to face a number of challenges in both the near- and long-term. These cluster around the field, the division, universities, and society in general. To begin with, there is a tendency to get sidelined and wander down rabbit holes. One of these tangents is the perennial discussion regarding changing the network's name, as well as that of the ASC division. In response, this issue was addressed in a joint article (Ortiz et al., 2022) that critically analyzed the ownership of the term *convict*. All organizations, learned or otherwise, will encounter obstacles both internally and externally, and CC is no different. In general, six prominent considerations need to be addressed.

The academic field of criminology/criminal justice has a tendency to start new types or branches. Every few years, it seems that a new iteration of criminology emerges (e.g. Cultural, Environmental, Ghost, Green, Rural, etc.). This creates distracting and competing pressure for our time, especially in this attention-strapped economy.

Both carceral institutions and public universities continue to cut back on the funds they spend on academic activities. In the academic world, this results in less money being made available to faculty and students to attend conferences, conduct research, and graduate student stipends, and the like.

The Convict Criminology network has always had difficulty organizing people (not just those who are incarcerated) who share the CC mission, but are diverse and geographically spread out. This is especially true in terms of recently released people, who for valid reasons often prefer to fly below the radar. Also, they may or may not have access to financial sources to enroll in schools or attend conferences, plus like all of us, they have competing demands.

We also have struggled with people interested in CC not wanting to attend academic events. Formerly incarcerated members are often reluctant to tell people that they were formerly incarcerated, particularly in public settings, and CC never compels anyone to reveal their prior criminal or incarceration history. This is a totally personal decision. Having a criminal record, however, prevents the formerly incarcerated from doing numerous things. This is part of the collateral consequences of incarceration. Members closely affiliated with CC understand this dilemma, which affects the degree and quality of participation among people who are on the margins of CC.

As mentioned above, from the beginning, a considerable amount of misinformation or misperceptions about CC has proliferated, including what CC is and what its goals are.[8] In general, this is not intentionally malicious, though the group has tried to diminish this misinformation through the creation of a website, the launching of an official ASC division, the effective use of social media, the publishing of high quality, peer-reviewed research, and regular participation at criminology conferences.

Finally, CC and the DCC periodically have to deal with a handful of so-called bomb throwers and contrarians. Some individuals come to DCC meetings (though often with a superficial knowledge of CC and its history), but due to a variety of dynamics, their primary goal often seems to be to disrupt, seek attention, or engage in intellectual one-upmanship. The actions of these individuals can have a debilitating effect on recruitment and retention, thus becoming a distracting influence (Ross & Tietjen, 2022).

SUGGESTIONS FOR THE FUTURE OF CONVICT CRIMINOLOGY

There is no shortage of ideas to further the agenda and mission of Convict Criminology – members of the network talk about these possible initiatives on a regular basis. Moving forward involves being aware of the weaknesses and threats confronting CC and successfully marshalling the organization's strengths to make optimal use of its opportunities. Below are ten major suggestions for the future that are reviewed from least to most pressing. However, before considering them, I wish to mention one direction that I do not think would be useful.

CC Presence in Other Learned Organizations

Many of the large scholarly criminology organizations have divisions on corrections, but lack Convict Criminology sections. For example, similar to what happened with the ASC Division of Critical Criminology and Social Justice, we might consider opening a division of Convict Criminology at the Academy of Criminal Justice Sciences. This might be helpful, but it is not pressing, since it may drain resources that could be best spent assisting the newly formed DCC. More useful are the following approaches and initiatives.

Better Tracking of CC Accomplishments

Many CC members engage in considerable scholarship, mentoring, and activism, but this is rarely tracked or communicated to others. This step is often ignored because it is boring, time consuming, distracting, or perceived as pretentious. By the same token, this kind of effort is necessary for members of the group to learn how to improve what they do and to demonstrate to external audiences our productivity and the breadth of our engagement.

Continuously Engage in Self-reflection

If the CC network is going to grow and flourish, both the members and leadership must engage in self-reflection, listen to its membership, and actively seek out the membership's desires, wants, and needs. It should also remain attuned to the fact that the person shouting the loudest may not necessarily reflect the best direction that the organization should take or be attuned to what is going on at a deeper level.

Regularly Release CC-relevant Communications

To fulfill the activism mission of CC, the executive needs to release regular statements about issues that are currently or will affect its membership and constituency. In support of this initiative, the DCC produced its very first newsletter in the fall of 2021. This is a resource-intensive exercise, but the DCC should now strive to release newsletters twice a year.

Periodically Hold Conferences Separate from the American Society of Criminology

It is important for members of the Convict Criminology network to meet on a regular basis to exchange scholarly communications, mentor junior colleagues, and develop a sense of community. This is why the annual conferences of the American Society of Criminology are so important to the maintenance of the CC approach. Also helpful are periodic meetings for people who are interested in CC but who may not live in the United States, where the majority of the ASC meetings take place. Examples of this kind of engagement were the Tampere, Finland (2010) and Padua, Italy

(2019) conferences. There was also some discussion about holding a CC conference in London in 2020, but then the pandemic hit. We should re-examine the possibility of holding a CC conference in South America (Ross & Darke, 2018; Vegh Weiss, 2021), for which Rio di Janero or São Paulo, Brazil might be good locations. Why? Darke and Aresti have developed strong connections to a number of Brazilian criminologists and doctoral students there, and *Convict Criminology for the Future* (Ross & Vianello, 2021) was recently translated into Portuguese (Ross & Vianello, 2021b).

Reconsider the Necessity of Separate National CC Groups

When CC originated, there was a belief that because the practice of corrections is slightly different in each country (Aresti & Darke, 2016; Earle, 2018) and because formerly incarcerated people often experience international travel restrictions, it might be wise to create separate CC organizations in places like the United Kingdom, Australia, and New Zealand (Carey et al., 2022). Over time, because of the ebb and flow of people who have come into the group and improvements in web-based electronic communications (e.g., Facetime, Skype, Zoom, etc.), the need and desire to form country-specific divisions or chapters seems less important now than it once did.

Adopt New Communication Technologies

Closely connected to the previous point, conferences are expensive to attend, frequently requiring flights and hotel stays, as well as conference fees. They are also very time-consuming. One way to counter these costs is to increase the use of online conferences. To do that, people in the CC network need to master communication strategies like Zoom or other web-based conference applications. For example, this method was successfully utilized during the 2021 ASC annual conference that was held in Chicago. At this venue, the DCC customized a system using personal Zoom presentations that were then streamed to individual computers.

Organize Special Issues of Relevant Academic Journals

Over the history of CC, the *Journal of Prisoners on Prisons* has published three special issues devoted to the network. The very first was edited by Stephen Richards and Mike Lenza, and the second by Andy Aresti and Sacha Darke, while the third was managed by Grant Tietjen, J. Renee Trombley, and

Alison Cox. Each team has brought with it a set of unique knowledge and skills, attracting and mentoring new people to CC through their networks.[9]

Battle Misinformation

It is important to identify specious arguments advanced about corrections in general and CC in particular by individuals who have minimal contact and understanding of Convict Criminology. Often these people show up at CC panels and meetings, or make unfounded claims about CC. If these individuals are amenable, CC representatives should spend the necessary resources trying to educate them. This requires sending these individuals articles and chapters to read, as well as walking them through their arguments in a systematic, but nonthreatening manner.

Boost Ongoing Mentoring Efforts

Finally, and most importantly, there is an ongoing need to recruit the next generation into the CC field. This requires proper mentoring (Tietjen et al., 2021). In the past, various members of CC have tried to launch an essay-writing program, but the responses were lackluster. Part of the reason for this failure was that many CC members are graduate students who have numerous obligations and limited resources (e.g. free time). Also, some people do not know the potential of the group. Thus, CC needs dedicated and rational leaders that will step up to meet that challenge by continuing to disseminate the framework's ideas and mentoring a younger generation. This could easily be done in the context of conferences, papers, and publications (Ross et al., 2015).

CONCLUSION

The way forward for CC is anything but clear. Convict Criminology has contributed to the scholarly literature (Ross & Copes, 2022), mentored numerous people from incarceration through release (and throughout the completion of undergraduate, masters, and doctoral degrees), and advocated for prison reform.

Newer members of the ASC Division of Convict Criminology are accomplishing a considerable amount of interesting scholarship, mentorship, and activism. And the diversity of the CC group bodes well for the network's attempts to expand its base and outreach. Ultimately, the future of CC depends on the commitment of its members, and the skills and personalities of its leaders. The future will also be shaped, to some extent, by the group's relationship to the American Society of Criminology. Changes taking place in the wider field of corrections will also have an influence on future directions of CC.

However, if CC and the DCC can be strategic about the environment in which they operate, the people who are interested in this field and their goals, they will be able to make a positive contribution to the academic fields of critical criminology, criminology, and corrections by assisting individuals who are incarcerated and recently-released to earn bachelors, masters, and doctoral degrees, and to take their place in academia. Likewise, an individual does not need to be formerly incarcerated to identify with the CC perspective, nor must one be a member of the ASC Division of Convict Criminology to be considered a Convict Criminologist (Ross et al., 2016).

CC would like others to participate in its journey, to be part of its story, and to ultimately improve the lives of people who are or were once incarcerated, as well as the lives of their loved ones. The hope is to assist them in successfully re-entering society, earning degrees, and making valuable contributions to their communities.

Like all academic fields and specialties, the future of CC is unknown. Part of its success will be tied to its ability to achieve its modest goals. CC has a great and energetic leadership that is diverse and vested in the success of the organization. CC will also need to create meaningful feedback loops with its membership and audience, while remaining committed to deliberately pursuing goals in a more strategic way. CC also needs to do a better job encouraging people to read their scholarship and to not simply jump to conclusions about what they think they know about the field. Other things CC should do in the future are to be mindful of inclusion, as well as prevent the naysayers and bomb throwers from distracting it from achieving its mission. Finally, Convict Criminology needs to work more on teasing out a theory that is meaningful to our membership and multiple audiences.

In principle, CC will still be around as long as the voices of system-contacted people continue to be marginalized and correctional facilities exist. The DCC expects to be active for many years to come. CC sincerely believes in the power of transformation. Together, we can further strive to change policy and laws dealing with incarceration.

ACKNOWLEDGEMENTS

Special thanks to the special issue editors and the anonymous reviewers of this journal for their helpful feedback.

CONFLICT OF INTEREST STATEMENT

The author did not receive support from any organization for the submitted work, nor do they have any relevant financial or non-financial interests to disclose.

ENDNOTES

[1] There are also arguments for calling Convict Criminology a theory (Richards, 2013). This is an interesting debate, but not essential to the points that I am reviewing in this paper.

[2] Ross and Tietjen (2022) expand on the differences between the older generation of Convict Criminologists and the newer ones.

[3] This includes a series of articles (e.g. Tietjen, 2019; Ross, 2020) and chapters in edited books (e.g. Jones, Ross, Richards, & Murphy, 2009).

[4] Surveys of the membership might be an option. However, there are numerous people who for one reason or another are not members of the official division, and they too may have useful opinions.

[5] A multi-authored chapter, "Convict Criminology: Prisoner Re-entry Policy Recommendations" (Richards, Ross, Newbold, Lenza, Jones, Murphy, & Grigsby, 2011) makes some policy recommendations, but they are not specifically directed toward the field of CC.

[6] I do not believe that it is necessary to go into a detailed analysis of why most of these criticisms are unfounded. These can be found elsewhere (e.g. Ross, Jones, Lenza & Richards, 2016).

[7] See https://asc41.com/divisions/division-account-balances-membership-figures.

[8] For example, a phantom CC website now exists.

[9] On a related note, in 2012, Richards edited a special issue of *Euro Vista: Probation and Community Justice*. Most of the contributors were ex-cons.

REFERENCES

Aresti, Andreas & Sacha Darke (2016) "Practicing Convict Criminology: Lessons Learned from British Academic Activism", *Critical Criminology*, 24(4): 533-547.

Aresti, Andreas, Sacha Darke & David Manlow (2016) "Bridging the Gap: Giving Public Voice to Prisoners and Former Prisoners through Research Activism", *Prison Service Journal*, 224: 3-13.

Belknap, Joanne (2015) "Activist Criminology: Criminologists' Responsibility to Advocate for Social and Legal Justice, The 2014 American Society of Criminology Presidential Address", *Criminology*, 53(1): 1-22.

Carey, Lukas, Andreas Aresti & Sacha Darke (2022) "What Are the Barriers to the Development of Convict Criminology in Australia?", *Journal of Prisoners on Prison*, 30(1): 77-96.

Custer, Bradley D., Michelle Malkin & Gina Castillo (2020) "Criminal Justice System-Impacted Faculty: Motivations, Barriers, and Successes on the Academic Job Market", *Journal of Education Human Resources*, 38(3): 336-364.

Darke, Sacha & Andreas Aresti (2016) "Connecting Prisons and Universities through Higher Education", *Prison Service Journal*, 225: 26-32.

Earle, Rod (2018) "Convict Criminology in England: Developments and Dilemmas", *British Journal of Criminology*, 58(6): 1499-1516.

Earle, Rod (2016) *Convict Criminology: Inside and Out*, Bristol: Policy Press.

Gramlich, John (2021) "America's incarceration rate falls to lowest level since 1995", *Pew Research Center* – August 16. Retrieved from https://www.pewresearch.org/fact-tank/2021/08/16/americas-incarceration-rate-lowest-since-1995/

Jones, Richard S., Jeffrey Ian Ross, Stephen C. Richards & Daniel S. Murphy (2009) "The First Dime: A Decade of Convict Criminology", *The Prison Journal*, 89(2): 151-171.

Kalica, Elton (2018) "Convict Criminology and Abolitionism: Looking Towards a Horizon Without Prisons", *Journal of Prisoners in Prison*, 27(2): 91-107.

Larsen, Mike & Justin Piché (2012) "A Challenge From and Challenge to Convict Criminology", *Journal of Prisoners on Prison*, 21(1&2): 199-202.

Newbold, Greg (2017) "Convict Criminology", in Antje Deckert & Rick Sarre (eds.), *The Palgrave Handbook of Australian and New Zealand Criminology, Crime and Justice*, London, Palgrave Macmillan, pp. 603-615.

Newbold, Greg & Jeffrey Ian Ross (2013) "Convict Criminology at the Crossroads", *The Prison Journal*, 93(1): 3-10.

Newbold, Greg, Jeffrey Ian Ross & Stephen C. Richards (2010) "The Emerging Field of Convict Criminology", in Francis T. Cullen & Pamela K. Wilcox (eds.), *Encyclopedia of Criminological Theory*, Thousand Oaks: Sage, pp. 2010-2012.

Nichols, Tom (2018) *The Death of Expertise: The Campaign Against Established Knowledge and Why It Matters*, New York: Oxford University Press.

Richards, Stephen C. (2013) "The New School of Convict Criminology Thrives and Matures", *Critical Criminology: An International Journal*, 21(3): 375-387.

Richards, Stephen C., Jeffrey Ian Ross, Greg Newbold, Michael Lenza, Richard S. Jones, Daniel Murphy & Robert S. Grigsby (2011) "Convict Criminology: Prisoner

Re-entry Policy Recommendations", in Ikponwosa O. Ekunwe & Richard S. Jones (eds.), *Global Perspectives on Re-entry*, Tampere: University of Tampere Press, pp. 198-222.

Richards, Stephen C. & Jeffrey Ian Ross (2005) "Convict Criminology", in Mary Bosworth (ed.), *Encyclopedia of Prisons and Correctional Facilities*, Thousand Oaks: Sage Publications, pp. 169-175.

Richards, Stephen C. & Jeffrey Ian Ross (2003) "Conclusion: An Invitation to the Criminology/Criminal Justice Community", in Jeffrey Ian Ross & Stephen C. Richards (eds.), *Convict Criminology*, Belmont (CA): Wadsworth Publishers, pp. 347-353.

Richards, Stephen C., Greg Newbold & Jeffrey Ian Ross (2009) Convict Criminology, in J. Mitchell Miller (ed.), *21st Century Criminology: A Reference Handbook*, Thousand Oaks: Sage, pp. 356-363.

Richards, Stephen C., Jeffrey Ian Ross & Richard S. Jones (2007) "Convict Criminology", in Gregg Barak (ed.), *Battleground Criminal Justice*, Westport: Greenwood Press, pp. 106-115.

Ross, Jeffrey Ian (2020) "Everything You Wanted to Know about Convict Criminology But Were Too Afraid to Ask", *Autonomie locali e servizi sociali*, 30(3): 615-629.

Ross, Jeffrey Ian (2021) "Context is Everything: Understanding the Scholarly, Social and Pedagogical Origins of Convict Criminology", in Jeffrey Ian Ross & Francesca Vianello (eds.), *Convict Criminology for The Future*, New York: Routledge, pp. 11-20.

Ross, Jeffrey Ian & Heith Copes (2022) "Convict Criminology from Here to There: A Content Analysis of Scholarship in a Growing Subfield", *Criminal Justice Studies*, 35(4): 442-457

Ross, Jeffrey Ian & Sacha Darke (2018) "Interpreting the Development and Growth of Convict Criminology in South America", *Journal of Prisoners on Prison*, 27(2): 108-117.

Ross, Jeffrey Ian, Sacha Darke, Andreas Aresti, Greg Newbold & Rod Earle (2014) "Developing Convict Criminology Beyond North America", *International Criminal Justice Review*, 24(2): 121-133.

Ross, Jeffrey Ian., Richard S. Jones, Michael Lenza & Stephen C. Richards (2016) "Convict Criminology and the Struggle for Inclusion", *Critical Criminology*, 24(4): 489-501.

Ross, Jeffrey Ian & Stephen C. Richards (eds.) (2003) *Convict Criminology*, Belmont (CA): Wadsworth Publishing.

Ross, Jeffrey Ian & Stephen C. Richards (2005) "Convict Criminology", in J. Mitchell Miller & Richard A. Wright (eds.), *Encyclopedia of Criminology*, New York: Routledge, pp. 232-235.

Ross, Jeffrey Ian, Stephen C. Richards, Richard S. Jones, Michael Lenza & Robert Grigsby (2012) "Convict Criminology", in Walter S. DeKeseredy & Molly Dragiewicz (eds.), *Handbook of Critical Criminology*, New York: Routledge, pp. 160-171.

Ross, Jeffrey Ian & Grant Tietjen (this issue) "Every Picture Tells a Story: Framing and Understanding the Activism of Convict Criminology", *Journal of Prisoners on Prison*, 33(1).

Ross, Jeffrey Ian & Grant Tietjen (2022) "From Fledgling Network to the Creation of an Official Division of the American Society of Criminology: The Growth of Convict Criminology 2.0", *Social Justice*, 48(4): 85-103.

Ross, Jeffrey Ian & Francesca Vianello (eds.) (2021a) *Convict Criminology for the Future*, New York: Routledge Publishers.

Ross, Jeffrey Ian & Francesca Vianello (2021b) *Criminologia dos Condenados e o Futuro*, São Paulo: Tirant Lo Blanch.

Tietjen, Grant (2019) "Convict Criminology: Learning from the Past, Confronting the Present, Expanding for the Future", *Critical Criminology*, 27(1): 101-114.

Vegh Weiss, Valeria (2021) "It's Time! Towards a Southern Convict Criminology", in Jeffrey Ian Ross & Francesca Vianello (eds.), *Convict Criminology for the Future*, New York: Routledge, pp. 112-126.

Vianello, Francesca & Jeffrey Ian Ross (2021) "What Have We Learned, and What Does the Future Hold for Convict Criminology?", in Jeffrey Ian Ross & Francesca Vianello (eds.), *Convict Criminology for the Future*, New York: Routledge, pp. 211-217.

ABOUT THE AUTHOR

Jeffrey Ian Ross, PhD is a Professor in the School of Criminal Justice, College of Public Affairs, and a Research Fellow in the Center for International and Comparative Law, and the Schaefer Center for Public Policy at the University of Baltimore. He has been a Visiting Professor at Ruhr-Universität Bochum in Germany and the University of Padua in Italy. Professor Ross has researched, written, and lectured primarily on corrections, policing, political crime, state crime, crimes of the powerful, violence, street culture, as well as crime and justice in American Indian communities for over two decades. His work has appeared in many academic journals and books, including most recently the *Routledge Handbook of Street Culture* (2021) and *Convict Criminology for the Future* (2021). Ross is a respected subject matter expert for local, regional, national and international news media. He has made live appearances on CNN, CNBC, Fox News Network, MSNBC, and NBC. Additionally, Ross has written op-eds for *The (Baltimore) Sun*, the *Baltimore Examiner*, *The (Maryland) Daily Record*, *The Gazette*, *The Hill*, *Inside Higher Ed*, and *The Tampa Tribune*. Professor Ross is the co-founder of Convict Criminology, and the former co-chair/chair of the Division of Critical Criminology and Social Justice (2014-2017) of the American Society of Criminology. In 2018, Ross was given the Hans W. Mattick Award, "for an individual who has made a distinguished contribution to the field of Criminology & Criminal Justice practice", from the University of Illinois at Chicago. In 2020, he received the John Howard Award from the Academy of Criminal Justice Sciences' Division of Corrections. The award is the ACJS Corrections Section's most prestigious award, and was given because of his "outstanding research and service to the field of corrections". In 2020, he was honored with the John Keith Irwin Distinguished Professor Award from the ASC Division of Convict Criminology. During the early 1980s, Jeff worked for almost four years in a correctional institution.

The Future of Convict Criminology
Jennifer M. Ortiz

B oth the content and authorship in this special edition provide us with a glimpse of a new era of Convict Criminology, what I refer to as Convict Criminology 3.0. In its infancy, Convict Criminology reflected the exclusionary practices that are endemic in academia. This early era reflects what I consider Convict Criminology 1.0 (1997-2008). Early membership was comprised largely of white men who had access to higher education, which reflected academia's status as a predominately white male institution. While the informal Convict Criminology that emerged in the 1990s sought to amplify the voices and lived experiences of formerly incarcerated persons (Ross & Vianello, 2021), the membership did not reflect the reality that incarceration disproportionately impacts lower-income individuals from communities of color. Moreover, the female voice was nearly non-existent within the subfield's existing literature (Cox & Malkin, 2023). After 'the first dime' (Jones et al., 2009), Convict Criminology expanded internationally and increased its presence within criminology, culminating in the establishment of a formal American Society of Criminology (ASC) division. I refer to this era as Convict Criminology 2.0 (2009 to 2019). The first 25 years of Convict Criminology was an era of reflection and growth. Today, Convict Criminology has entered a period of rebirth.

This special edition marks a departure from the historical exclusivity that existed within the first 25 years of Convict Criminology. While the narratives of men who served prison sentences dominated the first 25 years, the next 25 years have the opportunity to provide a more intersectional and progressive view of life experiences within the criminal injustice system. Most notably, this special edition does not merely include one or two articles by women, the voices of system-impacted women dominate this edition. Moreover, the authors include people with direct experience and familial experiences with incarceration, which offers a more complex view of the impact of the criminal injustice system. The articles in this special edition also offer a wide range of topics, provide both theoretical and empirical arguments and utilize both qualitative and quantitative methods. This special edition should be viewed as the first step towards a Convict Criminology for the future.

The progress reflected in this special edition is indicative of larger shifts within Convict Criminology. The formal Division of Convict Criminology (DCC) is comprised of scholars from diverse backgrounds, experiences, genders, ages, and races. Our membership consists of individuals who served time in prison *and* jail, individuals with criminal records who have never served time, individuals with incarcerated family members, and allies determined to fight back against an unjust system. Convict Criminology also continues to expand its international reach, which has helped highlight the lived experiences of system-impacted persons around the world. This diversity of perspectives is reflected in the recently published edited volume *Convict Criminology for the Future* (Ross & Vianello, 2021). Moreover, Convict Criminology has begun making great strides towards increasing our presence within the field, implementing more inclusive practices and moving towards a more activism-centered focus. In 2022, the DCC launched an Early Career Travel Scholarship and a Mentorship Program, both aimed at uplifting the voices of system-impacted scholars within the historically conservative field of criminology and criminal justice. We have come a long way and we have much further to go.

My vision for a Convict Criminology 3.0 centers on increasing our presence to create a more inclusive space for convict and system-impacted scholars. We owe it to every person currently sitting in a cell or courtroom to advocate for change within the historically racist, sexist, classist institutions in which we exist, including the American Society of Criminology and the broader academic community. The DCC must be unapologetic in its demands for equity, including the elimination of financial barriers to inclusion at conferences and universities. The DCC must engage in activism that challenges academia and the broader society's ongoing role in the oppression of scholars like us (see Ortiz, this issue). As we continue to grow in membership, we must begin to harness our collective power for change.

The most important way we can utilize our power is to work to uplift early career scholars who are formerly incarcerated, have records, and who have family members affected by the criminal injustice system. Our scholarship and mentorship programs are the first step towards that goal. Our membership will continue to work collectively to ensure that our scholars are admitted to programs, hired at universities, are published, and obtain tenure. We know that these efforts will be difficult and I have no illusions regarding how much we can accomplish, but Convict Criminology is more powerful than anyone gives us credit for. Through our use of collective activism, we will continue to use our voices to fight for all of the men, women, and gender non-conforming individuals who remain trapped within the clutches of an unjust system.

The current special edition helps move this vision forward. However, it cannot be the only step we take. We must continue to strive to move our research from the margins of a field determined to ignore us, to center stage where scholars must engage with us. The voices of those directly impacted by the criminal injustice system are vital to dismantling the oppressive and dehumanizing aspects of our field. By continuing to develop spaces to highlight our work, expanding our scope to include a theoretical foundation for Convict Criminology, and by uplifting the voices of system-impacted individuals, we can move the proverbial needle forward. Creating a dramatic shift within the field will be difficult as criminal justice researchers are often dependent on the system for funding (Ortiz, 2021). However, we must continue to call them to task for their complicity in the oppression of marginalized people, even if it upsets some people.

As the first woman and person of color to lead the Division of Convict Criminology, I recognize the need to continue our efforts to increase diversity, equity, and inclusion. As such, in my first letter to the division (see https://concrim.org/newsletter/), I outlined my vision for the future into three main points:

1. Further diversify the opinions and perspectives that exist within our leadership;
2. Develop and expand international collaboration between the DCC and convict scholars around the world; and
3. Continue supporting system-impacted undergraduate and graduate scholars.

The Convict Criminology 3.0 I envision is one of unity, unapologetic activism, and uplifting all people who have been victimized by the criminal injustice system. While many mainstream scholars have historically dismissed or outright ignored our presence and work, they can no longer continue to do so. A day of reckoning is coming. Our presence at the 2022 American Society of Criminology conference made people take notice and our presence at this year's conference will be greater. I hope this special edition illustrates to academics across the field that Convict Criminology will no longer be ignored. We are here and we are not going anywhere.

¡Pa'lante!
– Jennifer Ortiz

REFERENCES

Cox, Alison & Michelle L. Malkin (2023) "Feminist Convict Criminology for the Future", *Critical Criminology*, 1-21.

Ortiz, Jennifer (this issue) "Beyond the Ivory Tower: The Need for Collective Activism in Convict Criminology", *Journal of Prisoners on Prisons*, 33(1).

Ortiz, Jennifer (2021) "Doxa is Dangerous: How Academic Doxa Inhibits Prison Gang Research", in David C. Brotherton & Rafael J. Gude (eds.), *International Handbook of Critical Gang Studies*, New York: Routledge, pp. 624-632.

Ross, Jeffrey Ian & Francesca Vianello (eds.) (2021) *Convict Criminology for the Future*, New York: Routledge.

ABOUT THE AUTHOR

Jennifer Ortiz, PhD is an Associate Professor of Criminology at The College of New Jersey. She earned her doctorate in Criminal Justice from John Jay College of Criminal Justice in New York City. Her research interests center on structural violence within the criminal justice system with a focus on reentry post-incarceration and gangs. Dr. Ortiz is currently the Division Chair for the American Society of Criminology's Division of Convict Criminology and Book Review Editor for *Critical Criminology*. She previously served as President of the New Albany, Indiana Human Rights Commission and as an executive board member for Mission Behind Bars and Beyond, a Kentucky-based non-profit reentry organization. She can be reached via email at Ortizje@tcnj.edu or by mail at the following address:

Jennifer Ortiz, PhD
The College of New Jersey
2000 Pennington Road, SSB 333
Ewing Township, NJ 08628

BOOK REVIEWS

Convict Criminology for the Future
edited by Jeffrey Ian Ross and Francesca Vianello
New York: Routledge (2021) 248 pp.
Reviewed by Shelly Clevenger

INTRODUCTION

Convict Criminology: For the Future, published by Routledge, is a volume edited by Jeffrey Ian Ross and Francesca Vianello. It is more than a book, rather it is a call for action and a source of inspiration for scholars and for the next generation of Convict Criminologists. This volume outlines the development of Convict Criminology within the academy in the United States and more globally. This volume also highlights where the discipline is headed, including different perspectives and voices than in the past.

Scholars within criminology are pushing for change to incorporate impacted voices into research and the conversation. Recently, academics have begun to advocate for *person first* language within scholarly writing in which the term "offender" is no longer utilized, but rather *person convicted of a crime* and instead of "inmate" using the term *incarcerated individual.* The fact that scholars are cognizant of the impact of language is an indicator that people are paying attention to the impact that language can have, and recognizing that words and the people we use to describe them matter. The establishment of the American Society of Criminology's Division of Convict Criminology in 2020 shows that the issues of Convict Criminology are moving into the forefront of criminology. This division has been active in promoting responsiveness of issues relating to incarcerated, formerly incarcerated individuals and justice-impacted folks.

The release of *Convict Criminology; For the Future* in 2021 is perfectly positioned to be at the forefront of the revolution to raise awareness about why Convict Criminology matters not just for the academy and scholars, but for society. It seems we are currently in a climate where people are ready to hear and accept what Convict Criminology has been fighting for. Since its beginnings, Convict Criminology has strived to grow to include people from countries across the globe. With this current volume, many of the chapters are internationally focused and provide perspectives outside of the United States. This review will illustrate the importance of this book and how the works within it contribute to helping shape the future of not just Convict Criminology, but the larger discipline of Criminology.

FROM THE PAST TO THE FUTURE:
CONVICT CRIMINOLOGY AS AN AGENT OF CHANGE

To understand why this volume, *Convict Criminology; For the Future* is important, it is essential to visit the past. Convict Criminology is subset of the larger discipline of Criminology. It is most closely related to the area of Critical Criminology. Convict Criminology has at its core activism and change. Its scholarly roots are in the late-1980s and mid-to late-1990s. In 1988, the *Journal of Prisoners on Prisons* (JPP) was established at the University of Ottawa (Gaucher, 1988). The creation of this journal was an establishment of incarcerated or formerly incarcerated individuals as knowledgeable entities on academic issues and this publication gave credibility to the experiences of those within the criminal-legal system. In the mid-1990s, during a peak time of mass incarceration as a result of the drug war and America getting 'tough on crime', scholars noticed that one of the primary people affected by the discipline of Criminology, people who are currently or formerly incarcerated for committing crime and/or justice-impacted people – individuals charged with a crime, loved ones of those who are charged, convicted and/or incarcerated – were missing from the conversation. Scholars argued that the people who are impacted should be included and consulted in the systems that affected them. This is the premise that Convict Criminology was based upon and gave way to writing and activism in that area. The first Convict Criminology academic session was in 1997 at the American Society of Criminology conference in Atlanta. This led to scholars beginning to write books and articles for publication in this area (Tietjen, 2019). In 2001, Ross and Richards (2001) published an article that introduced the area of Convict Criminology to the world. This was followed by Ross and Richard's (2003) inaugural book *Convict Criminology.* Both are foundational pieces of Convict Criminology and established this as an area all its own. Within just over two decades since the publication of the first article on the subject, Convict Criminology has grown and has sparked a great deal of interest. This may be a direct result of the fact that it brought in the voices of those impacted and provided critical feedback to help reform correctional institutions, influence policies and practices, and assist those impacted by the carceral system worldwide. Convict Criminology also included stakeholders, such as formerly incarcerated individuals who were in the process of and/ or went on to receive a PhD to assist in creation of and dissemination of the content of the area. There was also mentorship and encouragement of formerly incarcerated and/or justice-impacted folks to go onto pursue degrees to better inform Convict Criminology (Ross, 2019; Tietjen, 2019).

Convict Criminology has evolved into other areas as time has went on to include scholars, students, and practitioners working to shed light on issues and make real change in the system and the academy. This new volume by Ross and Vianello (2021), *Convict Criminology For the Future* allows the reader to understand where Convict Criminology is headed. From the perspective of this author, this book will raise consciousness, bringing more scholars and practitioners to understand, appreciate, and be part of the movement to include justice-impacted and previously incarcerated folks in the academy and decisions on issues within the system that affect them. Each chapter in the volume is informative to the reader about the area of Convict Criminology from different perspectives, including many chapters from formerly incarcerated or justice-impacted authors, but also inspiring to the reader. In this review, each chapter will be touched upon, and an overview as well as insight into why this book is so special will be presented. Each chapter will also be mentioned as to acknowledge the work and efforts of all the valuable authors in this volume.

In the introduction, the readers hear directly from one of the founders of this area and editor of this volume, Jeffrey Ian Ross. He provides an overview of the book and gives some context as to why this volume is important. This introduction is the framework for the text and is important to understand why this book was written and what this volume hopes to achieve. The second chapter, "Context is Everything; Understanding the Scholarly, Social, and Pedagogical Origins of Convict Criminology", Jeffrey Ian Ross, as well as fellow editor for this book Francesca Vianello, provide the reader with some understanding as to why we need Convict Criminology, as well as some background. Many scholars and readers may not be aware of the history and the progression to where we are today. Both editors provide some essential information. While both chapters are introductory in nature, they provide the necessary groundwork for the rest of the book and allow the reader to learn about the history of Convict Criminology.

The next three chapters provide the reader with insights into the world of those who are incarcerated as the authors provide details about their own incarceration. These three chapters are very inspirational and powerful. They are at the heart of Convict Criminology. In chapter 3, "Crossing Borders,

Pushing Boundaries and Privileging 'Marginalised' Voices", written by Sinem Safak Bozhurt, Marisa Merico, Andreas Aresti, and Sancha Darke, the issue of motherhood and female incarceration was explored in a heartfelt but also heartbreaking way. This chapter provides insight into the world of female incarceration through the stories and first-hand experiences of two of the authors Safak Bozkurt and Marisa Merico. Each tells their story in a real, accessible way that leaves the reader full of empathy for them as people and wanting to know more about their experiences. One of the main issues discussed by Safak and Marisa is how mothers who commit crime feel guilt, sadness, and like they are "bad" mothers as they have let their children or families down. This is relatable content to many readers, especially those who are mothers. The discussions of being labeled as a terrible mother or role model by family, friends and society will resonate with many. The larger discussion, which many readers will gravitate to also is that females (regardless of their status as mothers) who commit crime are "bad" or "evil" in a way that men often are not, as there is an additional stigma related to being a female who is incarcerated. Reading about the experiences of the authors in this chapter as mothers and females in prison is one of the best things that this book has to offer. These autobiographical accounts from the authors allow the reader to connect with the material in a deep way and the stories stay with you.

The next two chapters have a bit of a different focus, but still provide perspective on the lived carceral experience. In chapter 4, "Doing Time for Convict Criminology", Rod Earle provides a dual perspective from someone who had been incarcerated and conducted research in a prison. Earle describes the benefits of autoethnography and uses vignettes in Convict Criminology to assist the researcher and the student/reader/person interested in the material. Writing about oneself and sharing a story through a vignette allows for the information to be disseminated and used in a way that is more accessible to reach a greater audience. Earle provides examples in this chapter of his own experiences. They are powerful to read. Readers will also appreciate that Earle writes about his experiences in the United Kingdom within this chapter. The international inclusion within this volume makes for interesting and surprising chapter information.

In chapter 5, "Convict Counter-information to Contest Crime-press Disinformation", Elton Kalica shares their experiences of being incarcerated in Italy. Reading about the days and the life that Kalica had in an Italian prison was moving and allowed the reader to connect to the place and time.

Kalica's description as to how they were introduced to Convict Criminology and what they have subsequently achieved was inspiring. As with the other chapters, hearing the narrative in first person allows for a more sincere, deeper connection to the material. This chapter immerses the reader and they will come away with feeling inspired as to the power that writing, activism, and hope can have for individuals serving time.

Grant Tietjen and Daniel Kavish authored chapter 6, "In the Pool Without a Life Jacket; Status Fragility and Convict Criminology in the Current Criminological Era". In this chapter, the authors provide the reader with details about a perspective known as *status fragility*. This concept should be integrated into *all* Criminology curriculum from undergraduate to PhD level courses. The authors walk the reader through why this matters and how detrimental a felony conviction can be for a person, especially someone who is in a faculty role within the field of criminal justice. The authors do a beautiful job of illustrating for the reader the ways in which this status is very fragile, and how any power differential can be detrimental to their livelihood and careers. The discussion that Tietjen and Kavish offer as to placing value and worth into the lived experiences of individuals with felony convictions is essential for individuals within and outside the academy to understand. The academic institution needs to evolve into something different, and understand and appreciate that there is knowledge that lies outside of higher education that can still be valuable. Tietjen and Kavish perfectly exemplify how Convict Criminology is the future of academia and how this can also be the answer to increasing diversity of all kinds within universities and the academy. This chapter has the power to transform the readers' thoughts on what is knowledge and how higher education can adjust by the inclusion of more Convict Criminology principles.

In chapter 7, "A Convict Criminology Approach to Prisoner Families", Alison Cox provides material that is much needed and valuable for the reader. She had a graceful presentation of why it is important to remember, respect, and include the family members of those who are incarcerated or who are justice impacted. She framed this within the larger context of Convict Criminology and gave examples that allows the reader to see why this is an essential part of the future of academia. Her discussion of the future of Convict Criminology by involving prisoners' families was well thought out and particularly impactful to read. This chapter is one that readers will latch onto and think about often. This chapter is also one that should serve as part of the plan for Convict Criminology as the area advances into its next phase in the future.

As we move into additional chapters, we hear more about Convict Criminology internationally, and it is beneficial to the reader to hear different perspectives. Chapter 8, "Developing Convict Criminology: Notes from Italy", written by Francesca Vianello, and chapter 9, "It's time; Towards a Southern Convict Criminology", written by Valeria Vegh Weis, both provide an international perspective. Francesca Vianello provides the history and context for the development of Convict Criminology within Italy, as well as an overview about the relationships between universities and prisons. This chapter provided thorough examples of how Convict Criminology is functioning in Italy. It is interesting to read from an American perspective to see how things differ in Italy. Valeria Vegh Weis focuses on the issue and obstacles that may arise implementing Convict Criminology in Latin America. Currently, most of the movement of Convict Criminology has been rooted in the global North, and part of the issue with the global South has been a language barrier (lack of Spanish speaking) and the fact that academics cannot make a living as a professor teaching full-time at a university. Weis provides a case study and a great discussion of why there has been a lull in the expansions of Convict Criminology and why this may continue if there is a lack of change. The best part of the chapter is where Weis offers potential solutions or suggestions as to how to expand Convict Criminology into the global South. This chapter is eye opening for readers to consider the issues faced in other countries and parts of the world where Convict Criminology is expanding.

The next two chapters focus on university courses within carceral institutions and provide results from original research. Chapter 10, "University education in Prison and Convict Criminology: Reflections from a Field Research Study", written by Andrea Borghini and Gerardo Pastore, presents results from research with individuals from the Prison University Campus (PUC), providing quotes from interviews with incarcerated people at the PUC in Tuscany. Borghini and Pastore intermix the quotes with issues directly related to Convict Criminology and teaching university level courses in prison. This is particularly powerful for the reader. Reading the words of the principal stakeholders (i.e. the incarcerated students) makes this chapter a valuable contribution not only to this volume, but to the literature. Bogrhini and Pastore also explore the notion of who is a Convict Criminologist in this chapter, which has been an issue within the area as to who can call themselves a "Convict Criminologist." The section within the chapter is informative for the reader and well written. In chapter 11, *The*

Convict University Project and the Autoethnography of the Biographical Changeover, Vincenza Pellegrino, Veronica Valenti, and Claudio Conte also present results of original research. The authors explore the Penitentiary University Campus of Parma (PUP) as a case study. This chapter provides additional understanding for readers as to what prison university campuses are like more generally and there are some insightful quotes from students in the PUP. The section on restorative community justice was powerful and gives the reader insight, but also encouragement for what lies ahead. While this chapter focuses on PUP, the lessons revealed from this research could be implanted globally. This chapter will be very useful to those wanting to conduct similar research or take part in education initiatives within a prison.

Chapters 12 and 13 are pieces which provide much needed suggestions for the future of Convict Criminology by charting for the reader where and how things need to change to improve the discipline and life within the institution for incarcerated individuals. Chapter 12, "Can the "Psychiatric Prisoner" Speak? Notes from Convict Criminology and Disability Studies" written by Luca Sterchele, provides direction for the future. Sterchele presents information about how disabled persons and prisoners suffering from psychiatric conditions are often excluded from prison programs, including education opportunities offered by universities and Convict Criminology initiatives. While the author focuses solely on Italy within this chapter, this same issue can be seen on a global scale. Sterchele presents research to help the reader understand the nature of prison cultures and why marginalized folks are left out of programs. This chapter is essential to the understanding of how Convict Criminology needs to grow in the future, as all incarcerated folks need to be part of this movement. Chapter 13, "Radicalization and Experiences in Detention", written by Alvise Sbraccia, focuses on changing the way that Convict Criminologists and other scholars research and conceptualize life within a carceral institution. Sbraccia presents the readers with the concept of radicalization and radicalism, and how this has been applied and how it can be going forward.

Chapter 14 and 15 examine working with an institution, as well as the ethics that are involved with doing work or teaching in a carceral setting. In chapter 14, "The Reaction of the Italian Prison Administration: In the Face of a Convict Criminologist", written by Giovanni Torrente, provides detailed information in the form of a case study about an individual within an Italian prison, "A.T.". Readers will enjoy reading about A.T. and what his journey was in terms of Convict Criminology and being incarcerated. Like other chapters in this volume, the individual case studies, quotes, and information allow for a connection with the material in a more profound way. Chapter 15, "Rethinking Punishment: Prison Research and the (Un) intended Challenges of Institution Research Ethics Review", written by James Gacek and Rosemary Ricciardelli, explores an essential part of Convict Criminology related to conducting research or education within a carceral facility, the Institutional Review Board, or ethics board at a university. This chapter provides an in-depth review of the literature. The authors provide examples and solutions for issues that past researchers have faced, with good illustrations from Canada. This chapter provides context for the reader regarding a Convict Criminology approach.

The final chapter, written by the book editors Jeffrey Ian Ross and Franscesca Vianello, provide reflections on what has been learned within the area of Convict Criminology and what they believe the future has in store. They provide nine principal questions that this current book answers. This volume does answer those principal questions, but the information in this book goes beyond that. This book provides an understanding of a larger picture of the systematic issues within the United States and elsewhere, while serving as a call to action. However, in the *Conclusion*, Ross and Vianello give the reader five activities that Convict Criminologists should consider for the future. It is admirable that the editors provide the readers with such specific direction, rather than more abstract ideals without a direction. The readers of this volume who reach the final chapter will be ready to act and the editors provided concrete ways that they can.

DISCUSSION

Overall, this book is a complete joy to read. While the subject matter is heavy, it is evident in reading each chapter that the authors who contributed to this volume care deeply about the subject matter and, in many cases, the authors were directly impacted by incarceration. While there were many different authors from all over the globe, the tone of this book was consistent. Each of the authors had the same message that Convict Criminology matters and we as scholars and as humans should care about it because this area of study impacts so many people in such a profound way. Because of the tone and the importance of this subject, *Convict Criminology for the Future*, edited by Jeffery Ian Ross and Francesca Vianello, is a volume should be on the must-read list for any criminologist. The chapters are detailed with information pertaining to Convict Criminology and each provide something unique for the reader. This is a book that can easily be used in class, and can also be used by researchers and scholars to further their understanding of this area within the discipline. While the book focuses on where Convict Criminology is headed, the nod to the past is strong and beneficial for people who may be discovering this for the first time. The authors of this volume also provide innovative and different information that even those well versed in Convict Criminology can learn something new. This may be attributed to the international chapters which give the reader rich examples, as well the inclusion of direct quotes from incarcerated individuals within some chapters.

It is my opinion that this is one of the best volumes within the area of criminology to be released within some time. The collection of chapters was well balanced. If there is one criticism that I could make, it would be that there could have been more inclusion of other countries within the book. There was a strong focus on Italy, which was very well done and thoroughly presented, as well as inclusion of Argentina and the United Kingdom which was very informative. A chapter from Australia, or an Asian or African country too could have rounded out the book. However, I applaud the editors for including so many international perspectives as it did give the readers a lot of new ideas and perspectives.

Whether people or criminologists consider themselves Convict Criminologists or see the value in Convict Criminology, we all are impacted by the carceral system. The United States currently has the highest incarceration rate in the world with 664 per 100,000 people (Prison Policy Initiative, 2021a). There are 2.3 million people currently under some form of confinement (e.g. jail, prison, youth detention) and 4.5 million under some form of supervision (e.g. confinement in institutions, probation, parole) (Prison Policy Initiative, 2020). There are over 650,000 individuals released from prison annually. Most individuals who are incarcerated are eventually released (United States Department of Justice, 2021). Returning citizens are part of our community, and in many cases our family. Everyone who is incarcerated leaves behind people, often children. A nationally representative study found that 45% of the population within the Unites States (113 million adults) had a family member who was incarcerated at least one night in jail or prison (Elderbroom et al., 2018). Understanding the experiences of those people who are incarcerated or system-involved is important to so many people and their families who are impacted. Mass incarceration is not ending quickly. That is why it is my sincere belief that this volume of *Convict Criminology for the Future*, edited by Jeffery Ian Ross and Francesca Vianello, is a valuable edition to the discipline of Criminology and society more generally. Hopefully, the writings in this book will inspire future scholars to continue the fight to change the system and implement Convict Criminology in new ways and expand its reach.

REFERENCES

Elderbroom, Brian, Laura Bennett, Shanna Gong, Felicity Rose & Zoë Towns (2018) "Every second: The impact of the incarceration crisis on America's families", *FWD. us*. Retrieved from https://everysecond.fwd.us/downloads/everysecond.fwd.us.pdf

Prison Policy Initiative (2021) *Global Reports*. Retrieved from https://www.prisonpolicy.org/global/2021.html

Prison Policy Initiative (2020) *Mass Incarceration: The Whole Pie 2020*, New York: Prison Policy Initiative. Retrieved from https://www.prisonpolicy.org/reports/pie2020.html

Richards, Stephen C. & Jeffrey Ian Ross (2001) "Introducing the New School of Convict Criminology", *Social Justice,* 28(1): 177–190.

Ross, Jeffrey Ian & Stephen C. Richards (2003) *Convict Criminology*, Belmont (CA): Wadsworth Publishing.

Tietjen, Grant (2019) "Convict Criminology: Learning from the Past, Confronting the Present, Expanding for the Future", *Critical Criminology,* 27(10): 101-114.

United States Department of Justice (2021) "Reentry", Washington (DC): Office of Justice Programs. Retrieved from https://www.justice.gov/archive/fbci/progmenu_reentry.html

ABOUT THE REVIEWER

Dr. Shelly Clevenger is Department Chair and Associate Professor in the Victim Studies Department at Sam Houston State University. She has authored peer-reviewed journal publications, book chapters and books on the connection between sexual assault, intimate partner abuse and cybervictimization. She also had the honor to present her research on cybervictimizations at the *United Nations Women* in New York City and a U.S. Congressional Briefing in Washington, DC. Dr. Clevenger is the recipient of national awards for her teaching, activism, and research, including the American Society of

Criminology's Division of Victimology Bob Jerin *Book of the Year Award* and *Faculty Teacher of the Year*. She also received the American Society of Criminology Division of Feminist Criminology *Distinguished Scholar Award* and *Inconvenient Woman of the Year Award* for her activism, as well as Feminist Criminology's *Article of the Year Award* for her sole-authored article regarding mothers of sexual assault survivors. Sam Houston State University has also recognized her for her teaching with the Faculty of the Year Award and the Community Engagement Award.

The Marion Experiment:
Long-term Solitary Confinement
and the Supermax Movement
edited by Stephen C. Richards
Carbondale (IL): Southern Illinois University Press
(2015) 336 pp.
Reviewed by David P.

The Marion Experiment edited by Stephen C. Richards provides a history and explains the increasing use of long-term solitary confinement to control problem prison populations. It explores the creation and explosion of Supermax institutions, primarily in the United States, but also includes other jurisdictions around the world. Through personal accounts of prisoners and academic research, it attempts to explain the potential and real psychological harm caused by extended periods of isolation.

The first portion of the book is particularly helpful to the reader. Whether the individual is an academic whom has never set foot in a correctional institution or a seasoned prisoner, the stories presented are enlightening, extremely personal and, at times, horrific. Although I have spent a 'decent' amount of time in CSC custody, I really have no experience when it comes to segregation. I have spent half my time in medium security, and half in minimum. I have never been to "the hole". My only experience is a shared one, forced quarantines during the COVID-19 pandemic. However, that is not the same as the abuse and lack of stimulus that prisoners describe in the book.

The use of these stories is incredibly important to understanding the underlying issues presented further into the book. In their stories, prisoners describe the reasons for their "enhanced" punishment, the conditions they faced while segregated and the despair that most felt as the days, months, and sometimes years passed by. Simply relying on academic studies can lessen the impact on the reader without encountering these first-hand accounts.

The next section of the book deals with the effects of solitary confinement on prisoners. It takes us on a journey through what incarcerated women have to endure, what young people behind bars deal with, and what the mentally ill are subjected to. Women reported experiencing above-average levels of sexual and emotional abuse while segregated, while youth reported physical, verbal, and occasional sexual violence by staff, alongside increased rates of self-harm while in segregation. The mentally ill seemed to be singled out by staff, being segregated to control their behaviour, rather than addressing root causes. The book goes on to explain that there is an extreme lack of support for mental health interventions in institutions, especially to those segregated from the general population. The book covers a wide range of prisoner populations, exploring their unique issues and experiences. It is critical to the book's success, as it encompasses a wide range of correctional environments, rather than focusing on one population set.

The final section of the book takes the reader outside of North America and deals with the solitary "system" in the United Kingdom, France, and Israel. This is the one area of the book that could have been improved. The authors, for one reason or another, decided to include the experience of a prisoner in the United Kingdom. At first, this sounds reasonable. However, the gentleman's account has absolutely nothing to do with solitary confinement. His personal account of doing time in the 1980s is interesting, but it is out of place when compared to the rest of the book's contents. The authors could have instead chosen an individual who had spent actual segregation time while incarcerated in the United Kingdom.

Overall, the authors try to flush out all of the reasons prisoners end up in segregation and why administrators turn to use these methods of control. Segregation appears to mainly be used as a tool by prison authorities to rid units of problematic prisoners. Rather than dealing with the underlying issues, authorities sweep the troubles away. While it does have a place to protect prisoners from those engaging in predation, it is overused to solve problems that could be addressed by conventional means (e.g. talking issues out, therapy, peer support and mentors, etc.) and has been used to inappropriately silence prisoners who engage in legal action or whom publicly embarrass the prison leadership. It goes into great detail on the multitudes of harm that segregated prisoners are subjected to and presents alternative solutions to the problem of the overuse of segregation.

I would recommend this book to anyone. It should be mandatory reading for all prison administrators, especially those running segregation units and Supermax institutions. It is also important for anyone pursuing a post-secondary education in the areas of justice and law enforcement. The book's strongest point is presenting personal experiences and accounts, which most academic papers gloss over. Aside from those students who ended up in prison, they lack the understanding of what these individuals have to cope with on a daily basis.

One could argue that any prosecutor, judge, legislator or parliamentarian should also be required to read this volume. The laws they enforce or craft can either have a positive or negative effect on those incarcerated. Too often public officials are pressured into a "tough on crime" agenda without fully realizing how their decisions are ultimately impacting the lives of those incarcerated and the safety of communities to which most will eventually return.

The book's editor and authors did an extremely good job at covering a wide range of issues in relation to both long-term solitary confinement and the Supermax movement. The pieces were very well researched and provide the reader with interesting, sometimes heartbreaking, examples of the harms caused under the guise of rehabilitation and public safety. It should inspire people to speak out and spark rage at how we are treating fellow human beings that, for the most part, will rejoin society sooner rather than later.

ABOUT THE REVIEWER

David P. is a 40-year-old man who has served five years in prison in two different Canadian prisons. He is eligible for statutory release in another nine years. David's interests include economics, the justice system, virology/immunology, information technology and current events.

Silent Cells:
The Secret Drugging of Captive America
by Anthony Ryan Hatch
Minneapolis: University of Minnesota Press (2019) 172 pp.
Reviewed by Lucas Ridgeway

A nthony Ryan Hatch is an Associate Professor in the Science in Society Program at Wesleyan University in Atlanta. *Silent Cells* is his second publication through the University of Minnesota Press, with his first being *Blood Sugar: Racial Pharmacology and Food Justice in Black America* from 2016. He dedicates *Silent Cells: The Secret Drugging of Captive America* to:

> …the millions of people the world over who experience bondage of mind and body and to those who yearn for their immediate, unconditional, and permanent liberation". In this book, the author aims "to the fullest extent permissible by available evidence, to dislodge the dominant and partial narrative of psychotropics as agents of healing in favor of a more nuanced view that recognizes these drugs' great potential as instruments of human suffering (Hatch, 2019, p. 135).

He furthermore submits that it is the carceral institutions themselves that have a drug addiction problem and therefore need to be treated in the same way that we would treat any other addict moving forward. Not only does he expand on this idea of corporate personhood, but he also uses this platform to enlarge the definition of total institutions (Goffman, 1961). In short, and relevant to the main hypothesis put forward in this short but concise treatise, prisons, asylums, active-duty military personnel, foster care systems, elder care institutions, unaccompanied immigrant children, assisted care facilities, and undeclared POWs should all be considered active components of a captive state.

The primary focus of *Silent Cells* is on the American prison-industrial complex though the same arguments extend to the above-mentioned tentacles of total institutions. Hatch calls this broader system of confinement, Captive America. Throughout this provocative text, the author employs "historical and comparative analyses of archival, scientific, and policy documents to chronicle meaning making in the social, medical, and ethical dimensions of psychotropics" (Hatch, 2019, p. 19). He proposes that a collective psychic death is taking place alongside the untold story about how America has achieved its mass incarceration inside their liberal democratic state. Hatch attempts to prove his hypothesis predominantly with statistics, although he is often forced to take on an alternative *ad hoc* approach due to incongruent national reporting standards. However, he did manage to effectively use the numerous case studies and regional data sets to successfully argue "that psychotropics have become central not only to mass incarceration in prisons but also to other kinds of mass captivity within the US carceral state" (Hatch, 2019, p. 10). Crucial to this argument is his rationale that states, "Psychotropic drugs manufacture two kinds of silent cells: one at the level of the bodies and brains of captive people and the other at the level of knowledge about the material effects of those drugs on people" (ibid). These two interlocking concepts of silent cells permeate this book.

The problem at hand is undeniably the most prominent in the United States, as over 5 million people are already serving time in prisons (US DOJ, 2022) or on probation and parole (US DOJ, 2021). Additionally, their laws grant institutions the power to administer psychotropic drugs to any detainee (citizen or otherwise), even when an individual may not need or want the drugs. Noticeable to the astute incarcerated reader will be the numerous examples of government-produced ignorance, non-knowledge, medical incompetence, and bureaucratic malfeasance in the weaponizing of medicine for the purposes of carrying out state violence and repression. One shocking case study that demonstrates these unjust policy choices and social inequalities is of a Black woman, Kamilah Brock, who worked as a banker in New York City and was arrested because she did not have her hands on the steering wheel while she was stopped at a red light. Her BMW was impounded as she was forcibly detained without any charges ever being filed. Returning the next day to retrieve her vehicle, the officers called the Harlem Hospital, labelling her, 'an emotionally disturbed person'. She was handcuffed to a gurney, at which point lorazepam and lithium were injected under duress. On her release from the hospital, 10 days later, she was issued a bill for $13,637, all for challenging "the bedrock assumptions that uphold white supremacist capital patriarchy" (Hatch, 2019, p. 92). Meanwhile, a report in June 2018 from the *Minneapolis Star Tribune* told the story that emergency medical services had injected criminal suspects with the powerful tranquiller Ketamine at the behest of the Minneapolis police a total of 62 times (Mannix, 2018).

Apart from anecdotal evidence, Hatch effectively explains exactly why silence is central to the meaning and practices of subordination. He uses Michel Foucault's (1976) framework of biopower and social theorist Achille Mbembe's (2003) concept of necropower to position his biopolitical arguments to demonstrate the coercive ways in which psychotropics serve to manufacture prisoners' silence. This orientation asks us to interrogate the ways in which racism, sexism, and class inequality work together as complementary, rather than competing explanations, for mass captivity. He also cites legal scholar Patricia Williams (1987) who defines this 'spirit-murder' as "disregard for others who lives qualitatively depend on our regard" (p. 151). Achille Mbembe (2003) detailed, "Governments target particular human social groups for death, define those groups as enemies, herd them into isolated territories with no viable social infrastructure, and use overwhelming technological force to kill them" (p. 14). Thus, the socially sequestered have been socially abandoned in Captive America. Anthony Ryan Hatch surmises that the question should not be whether these practices are legitimate or illegitimate, but rather how social power functions to obliterate any meaningful distinction between normal medicine and abnormal killing in our so-called free society.

Towards the end of this book there is an excellent case study on George Zimmerman, the exonerated killer of Trayvon Martin and the role that psychotropics potentially played in enabling his violent conduct. Similarly, this topic has taken on a new global significance in the context of the ongoing epidemic of gun violence and mass shootings, as these tragedies are always followed by new debates about access to mental health care and the role that psychotropics played in pushing perpetrators into violent behaviours. However, prosecutors in the United States cannot currently argue that psychotropic drug use is a contributing factor when attempting to convict murderers, as it is not possible to prove that the consumption of a psychotropic drug caused a specific individual to commit violence independent of the other factors that shaped the violent event itself.

The idea of utilizing 'chemical strait jackets' or 'chemical restraints' is explored significantly in this study since over 73% of maximum-security prisoners in the US are on some form of psychotropic drug such as an antipsychotic, antianxiety, antidepressant, or mood stabilizer compared with 70% of active-duty military members (Beck and Maruschak, 2000). In both cases, they are not only used to manage mental illnesses, but also to help people cope with exposure to stressful institutional environments, like prison or warfare. Furthermore, the author postulates, "What if the new plan for governing and controlling the millions of people forced to live in Captive America is to move them into new locations inside their own brain cells, into mental prisons that perform the same work as the old physical prisons or barracks or hospital rooms, but with new technologies of pacification?" (Hatch, 2019, p. 9). As a precursor to this claim, he shows how psychotropics themselves first arrived in prisons in the 1950s. Hatch shows that between 1962 and 1975 virtually all of the human research subjects used in safety and bioavailability studies were American prisoners despite the post WWII Nuremberg Code. The Nuremberg Code is an ethical framework agreed upon by both the American Medical Association and the World Medical Association, which states explicitly that it is unethical for prisoners to participate in medical experiments.

Throughout *Silent Cells* Anthony Ryan Hatch is not afraid to state his conclusions and he efficaciously shows the reader just how such blatant violations have continued to occur without intervention. I found this short book to be both an excellent read for the seasoned academic and a siren song to the uninitiated. For me, *Silent Cells* has established a baseline for opening up many of the conversations that we need to be having surrounding these issues. This study offers us a critical perspective on the key carceral debates of our time and provides some concrete linguistic terms that will aid all parties to arrive on, at very least, an initial consensus for productive discussions moving forward. I commend the author and his publisher on a seminal work that conveys such an immediate call to action to bring this tragedy to light.

REFERENCES

Beck, Allan J. & Laura M. Maruschak (2001) "Mental Health Treatment in State Prisons, 2000", *Bureau of Justice Statistics* – July. Retrieved from https://bjs.ojp.gov/library/publications/mental-health-treatment-state-prisons-2000

Foucault, Michel (1976) *Histoire de la sexualité (volume 1) : La volonté de savoir*, Paris: Tel Gallimard.

Goffman, Erving (1961) *Asylums: Essays on the Social Situation of Mental Patients and Other Inmates*, New York: Anchor Books.

Hatch, Anthony Ryan (2019) *Silent Cells: The Secret Drugging of Captive America*, Minneapolis: University of Minnesota Press.

Mannix, Andy (2018) "At urging of Minneapolis Police, Hennepin EMS workers subdued dozens with a powerful sedative", *Star Tribune* – June 15.

Mbembe, Achille (2003) "Necropolitics", *Public Culture*, 15(1): 11-40.

United States Department of Justice (2022) "Prisoners in 2021 – Statistical Tables", *Bureau of Statistics* – December. Retrieved from https://bjs.ojp.gov/sites/g/files/xyckuh236/files/media/document/p21st_sumB.pdf

United States Department of Justice (2021) "Probation and Parole in the United States 2020", *Bureau of Statistics* – December. Retrieved from https://bjs.ojp.gov/content/pub/pdf/ppus20.pdf

Williams, Patricia (1987) "Spirit-Murdering the Messenger: The Discourse of Fingerpointing as the Law's Response to Racism", *University of Miami Law Review*, 42(1): 127-157.

ABOUT THE REVIEWER

Lucas Ridgeway is a Canadian federal prisoner at Bath Institution. He is the Book Clubs for Inmates Ambassador, Protestant Representative, and Alcoholic Anonymous Chairperson. He produces a weekly radio service called *Spiritual Connection* on 101.3 FM (CJAI FM in Kingston, ON). Podcasts can be downloaded at www.cjai.ca/podcast-main/SpiritualConnection/index.php. He would like to be reached by mail at the following address:

Lucas Ridgeway
P.O. Box 1500
Bath, ON
K0H 1G0

AVAILABLE TITLES AND CALL FOR BOOK REVIEWS

Journal of Prisoners on Prisons

The *Journal of Prisoners on Prisons* (*JPP*) welcomes book review submissions. Book reviews range from 800 to 1,200 words. Interested reviewers should contact the *JPP* with a request for one of the available titles (listed below). Should the book still be available, it will be mailed immediately.

For publishers: If you would like to have your new titles reviewed in the *JPP*, please send to the address below for consideration.

Book Reviews – Journal of Prisoners on Prisons
c/o Department of Criminology
University of Ottawa
120 University Private – Room 13020
Ottawa, Ontario, Canada
K1N 6N5

AVAILABLE TITLES

Bourgeois, Louis (ed.) (2022) *Mississippi Prison Writing*, Oxford (MS): Vox Press, 267 pages.

Boyd, Susan (2022) *Heroin: An Illustrated History*, Halifax: Fernwood, 256 pages.

Correia, David and Tyler Wall (2021) *Violent Order: Essays on the Nature of Police*, Chicago: Haymarket Books, 222 pages.

Davis, Angela Y. (2022) *Angela Davis: An Autobiography*, Chicago: Haymarket Books, 420 pages.

Hill, Marc Lamont (2020) *We Still Here: Pandemic, Policing, Protest, and Possibility*, Chicago: Haymarket Books, 128 pages.

House, Jordan and Asaf Rashid (2022) *Solidarity Beyond Bars: Unionizing Prison Labour*, Halifax: Fernwood, 180 pages.

Jones, El (2022) *Abolitionist Intimacies*, Halifax: Fernwood, 192 pages.

Meissner, Caits (2022) *The Sentences That Create Us: Crafting A Writer's Life in Prison*, Chicago: Haymarket Books, 339 pages.

Milward, David (2022) *Reconciliation and Indigenous Justice: A Search for Ways Forward*, Halifax: Fernwood, 240 pages.

Paynter, Martha (2022) *Abortion to Abolition: Reproductive Health and Justice in Canada*, Halifax: Fernwood, 176 pages.

Reinisch, Deiter (2022) *Learning Behind Bars: How IRA Prisoners Shaped the Peace Process in Ireland*, Toronto: University of Toronto Press, 240 pages.

Wilkerson, George T. and Robert Johnson (2022) *Bone Orchard: Reflections on Life Under Sentence of Death,* Honeoye Falls (NY): Bleak House Books, 138 pages.

UPCOMING SPECIAL ISSUE – CALLS FOR PAPERS

Profiling and the Canadian Carceral State | Les profilages et l'État carcéral canadien
Justin Piché and Sandra Lehalle /
Observatoire des profilages

SPECIAL ISSUE EDITORS | DIRECTION DE L'ÉDITION SPÉCIALE

Justin Piché, PhD
Associate Professor | Professeur agrégé
Department of Criminology | Département de criminology
University of Ottawa | Université d'Ottawa

Sandra Lehalle, PhD
Associate Professor | Professeur agrégé
Department of Criminology | Département de criminology
University of Ottawa | Université d'Ottawa

Observatoire des profilages
www.observatoiredesprofilages.ca

SPECIAL ISSUE THEME | THÉMATIQUE DE L'ÉDITION SPÉCIALE

The Canadian Carceral State routinely engages in profiling of people pushed to the margins by colonialism, racism and white supremacy, capitalism and classism, patriarchy and heteronormativity, ableism, and other violent structures. This is evident in who is targeted, harmed, and killed by policing, imprisonment, immigration, child apprehension, health, social services and assistance, and other carceral institutions. The *Journal of Prisoners on Prisons* invites contributions by current and former prisoners, their loved ones, and grassroots community organizations that document, critique, and propose alternatives to profiling evident in carceral practices and experiences. Prospective contributors can also submit pieces examining resistance efforts behind and beyond bars to build decarceral futures.

Les profilages des personnes marginalisées par le colonialisme, le racisme et la suprématie blanche, le capitalisme et le classisme, le patriarcat et l'hétéronormativité, le capacitisme et d'autres structures violentes est une pratique récurrente chez l'État carcéral canadien. Cela est évident lorsqu'on observe qui est ciblé, blessé et tué par les services de police, l'emprisonnement, l'immigration, l'appréhension d'enfants, de santé, ainsi que d'autres institutions carcérales. Le *Journal of Prisoners on Prisons* invite des contributions de prisonniers actuels and anciens, de leurs proches et d'organisations communautaires qui documentent, critiquent et proposent des alternatives au profilage évident dans les pratiques et expériences carcérales dont ils/elles ont vécu. Les contributeurs potentiels peuvent également soumettre des contributions portant sur les efforts de résistance derrière et au-delà des barreaux qui ont pour but de bâtir un avenir décarcéral.

CONTRIBUTION – FORMATS – CONTRIBUTIONS

This special issue welcomes contributions from a wide range of scholarly work including:

- Auto-ethnographic accounts that examine experiences of imprisonment to illuminate broader issues faced by incarcerated people;
- Theoretical, critical and analytical essays;
- Scholarly research articles based on quantitative, qualitative, arts-based and/or mixed- methods research;
- Book reviews;
- Artistic content – photo or graphic essays, digital art, poetry, etc.;
- Interviews or discussions transcribed from recordings; or
- Commentaries.

Ce numéro spécial accueille les contributions d'un large éventail de travaux universitaires, notamment:

- Récits auto-ethnographiques qui examinent les expériences d'emprisonnement pour éclairer les problèmes plus larges rencontrés par les personnes incarcérées ;

- Essais théoriques, critiques et analytiques ;
- Articles de recherche scientifique basés sur des recherches quantitatives, qualitatives, basées sur les arts et/ou utilisant des méthodes mixtes ;
- Revues de livres ;
- Contenu artistique – essais photographiques ou graphiques, art numérique, poésie, etc. ;
- Entrevues ou discussions retranscrites à partir d'enregistrements ; ou
- Commentaires.

SUBMISSION GUIDELINES | DIRECTIVES DE SOUMISSION

At the *JPP,* we support incarcerated people's right to exercise freedom of expression pursuant to section 2 of the *Canadian Charter of Rights and Freedoms* and embedded in national constitutions elsewhere across the world. We believe that publishing the writing of incarcerated people is a necessary tool to facilitate transparency in carceral settings. We welcome submissions from all current and former prisoners, and are eager to hear your input on the above-mentioned issues. Please share this notice with anyone who may be interested in contributing to our journal. We ask that those who choose to submit include a short biographical statement and let us know if you would like to be published anonymously. We look forward to reviewing your submissions that follow the journal's guidelines below and hope to hear from you soon.

- The Journal will not publish any subject matter that advocates hatred, sexism, racism, violence or that supports the death penalty.
- The Journal does not publish material that usually focuses on the writer's own legal case, although the use of the writer's personal experiences as an illustration of a broader topic is encouraged.
- The Journal does not usually publish fiction and does not generally publish poetry. Illustrations, drawings and paintings may be submitted as potential cover art.
- Articles should be no longer than 20 pages typed and double-spaced or legibly handwritten. Electronic submissions are gratefully received.

- Writers may elect to write anonymously or under a pseudonym.
- For references cited in an article, writers should attempt to provide the necessary bibliographic information. Refer to the references cited in past issues for examples.
- Editors look for developed pieces that address topics substantially. Manuscripts go through a preliminary reading and then are sent to review by the Editorial Board. Those that are of suitable interest are returned to the author with comments or suggestions. Editors work with writers on composition and form, and where necessary may help the author with referencing and bibliographic information, not readily available in prisons. Selected articles are returned to authors for their approval before publication. Papers not selected are returned with comments from the editor. Revised papers may be resubmitted.
- Please submit biographical and contact information, to be published alongside articles unless otherwise indicated.

Au *JPP*, nous soutenons le droit des personnes incarcérées à exercer leur liberté d'expression conformément à l'article 2 de la *Charte canadienne des droits et libertés* et enchâssé dans les constitutions nationales ailleurs dans le monde. Nous croyons que la publication des écrits des personnes incarcérées est un outil nécessaire pour faciliter la transparence en milieu carcéral. Nous accueillons les soumissions de tous les prisonniers actuels et anciens, et sommes impatients d'entendre vos commentaires sur les questions mentionnées ci-dessus. Veuillez partager cet avis avec toute personne qui pourrait être intéressée à contribuer à notre revue. Nous demandons à ceux et celles qui choisissent de soumettre une courte notice biographique et de nous faire savoir si vous souhaitez être publié de manière anonyme. Nous sommes impatients d'examiner vos soumissions qui suivent les directives de la revue ci-dessous et espérons avoir de vos nouvelles bientôt.

- Le Journal ne publiera aucun sujet faisant l'apologie de la haine, du sexisme, du racisme, de la violence ou soutenant la peine de mort.
- Le Journal ne publie pas de matériel qui se concentre généralement sur le cas juridique de l'auteur, bien que l'utilisation des expériences

personnelles de l'auteur comme illustration d'un sujet plus large soit encouragée.

- Le Journal ne publie généralement pas de fiction et ne publie généralement pas de poésie. Des illustrations, des dessins et des peintures peuvent être soumis comme couvertures potentielles.
- Les articles ne doivent pas dépasser 20 pages dactylographiées et en double interligne ou lisibles à la main. Les soumissions électroniques sont les bienvenues.
- Les auteurs peuvent choisir d'écrire de manière anonyme ou sous un pseudonyme.
- Pour les références citées dans un article, les auteurs doivent s'efforcer de fournir les informations bibliographiques nécessaires. Reportez-vous aux références citées dans les numéros précédents pour des exemples.
- Les éditeurs recherchent des articles développés qui abordent des sujets de manière substantielle. Les manuscrits font l'objet d'une lecture préliminaire, puis sont envoyés pour examen par le comité de rédaction. Ceux qui présentent un intérêt approprié sont renvoyés à l'auteur avec des commentaires ou des suggestions. Les éditeurs travaillent avec les auteurs sur la composition et la forme et, si nécessaire, peuvent aider l'auteur avec des références et des informations bibliographiques, qui ne sont pas facilement disponibles dans les prisons. Les articles sélectionnés sont retournés aux auteurs pour approbation avant publication. Les articles non sélectionnés sont retournés avec les commentaires de l'éditeur. Les articles révisés peuvent être resoumis.
- Veuillez soumettre des informations biographiques et de contact, à publier avec les articles, sauf indication contraire.

IMPORTANT – DATES – IMPORTANTES

Submissions by authors: 1 May |
soumissions par auteurs :   mai 2024

Editorial decision and reviewer comments to authors: 1 July |
décision éditoriale et commentaires aux auteurs :   juillet 2024

Revised manuscripts:	15 October |
manuscripts révisés :	octobre 2024
Final editorial decision to authors:	15 December |
décision éditoriale finale aux auteurs :	décembre 2024
Publication date:	2025
Publication date :	2025

SUBMISSIONS | SOUMISSIONS

Via email to jpp@uottawa.ca or by mail to the address below:

Journal of Prisoners on Prisons
c/o Department of Criminology
University of Ottawa
120 University Private – Room 14049
Ottawa, Ontario, Canada
K1N 6N5

———————

Par email to jpp@uottawa.ca ou par la poste à l'adresse suivante :

Journal of Prisoners on Prisons
c/o Départment de criminologie
University d'Ottawa
120 Université – Salle 14049
Ottawa, Ontario, Canada
K1N 6N5

COVER ART

"Breaking Out" (front cover)
Serge Tkachenko
2015

Serge Tkachenko was imprisoned in the Ojibway Correctional Facility located in Marenisco, Michigan when he produced this acrylic piece for the Prison Creative Arts Project's 20th annual exhibition.

"Intersection" (back cover)
Oliger Merko
2016

Oliger Merko was imprisoned at the Ionia Correctional Facility located in Ionia, Michigan when he produced this acrylic piece for the Prison Creative Arts Project's 21st annual exhibition.